JOHNNY RINGO

JOHNNY RINGO

Steve Gatto

Protar

House

P.O. Box 14007
Lansing, Michigan 48901

ISBN # 0-9720910-0-9 (Hardcover)
ISBN # 0-9720910-1-7 (Softcover)

Library of Congress Control Number: 2002107134

First Edition: July 2002

Protar House
P.O. Box 14007
Lansing, Michigan 48901

CONTENTS

Acknowledgments vii

1. The Discovery 1
2 Gone to Texas 5
3 Hoodoo War 15
4 Serious Threats 31
5 A Notorious Man 39
6. San Simon Cowboys 53
7. Election Scandal 69
8. Border Raids 75
9. A Game of Draw 87
10. Earp-Clanton Feud 95
11. Champion of the Cowboys 107
12. Ringo and the Cowboy War 115
13. Arrest Warrants and Border Patrols 123
14. The Posse 135
15. Last Ride From Tombstone 145
16. Legend of Johnny Ringo 171

Appendix 183
Notes and Sources 193
Bibliography 229
Index 235

Acknowledgments

I would like to thank the many institutions throughout the country for their continuing work in preserving a wealth of documents that enable researchers to find details about Old West characters and incidents. The collections housed in the Arizona Historical Society Library and the University of Arizona Library are valuable resources to anyone researching John Ringo. In addition, the Arizona State Archives in Phoenix, Arizona, and the Texas State Archives in Austin, Texas, provided much material for review.

No research could be done without the various county courthouses and court clerk's offices that have maintained records. Among these I would like to thank the staffs of the Cochise County Clerk's Office, Bisbee, Arizona; Pima County Clerk's Office, Tucson, Arizona; Mason County Clerk's Office, Mason, Texas; Burnet County Clerk's Office, Burnet, Texas; Lampasas County Clerk's Office, Lampasas, Texas; Llano County Court Clerk's Office, Llano, Texas; El Paso County Clerk's Office, El Paso, Texas; and the Grant County Court Clerk's Office, Silver City, New Mexico.

Over the years many individuals have aided me in researching the Old West. I would like to thank Neil Carmony, editor of John Clum's *Apache Days and Tombstone Nights* (1997), for his thoughts on the Old West. Thanks also to Dave Johnson, author of *John Ringo* (1996), who has freely exchanged information about Ringo with this researcher over the years. I would also like to thank Ben T. Traywick, Tombstone's official town historian, for his assistance over the years. The documents he has reproduced in his own books have been important sources of information. I would also like to thank Chris Petersen and Ted Liliensteins for their work on the cover illustration for this book.

Bob Pugh of *Trail to Yesterday Books* in Tucson, book collector "Mickey V," and Kevin Mulkins, a dedicated collector of Tombstone books and documents, deserve acknowledgment for their moral support and encouragement. Finally, a special thanks goes out to John Ringo. His life and deeds remain a fascinating topic to Old West enthusiasts, and his death is one of the most debated deaths in Old West history.

1

THE DISCOVERY

On a hot July afternoon in 1882, John Yoast, a wood hauler employed by Sorgum Smith, was driving a wagon team on a dirt road next to Turkey Creek in the Chiricahua Mountains. Known as the ancestral home of the fierce Chiricahua Apache tribe, it was an isolated area that was sparsely populated with ranches, but that also maintained steady traffic along the trail, which led to a mill. As the horses slowly pulled the lumber wagon along the thoroughfare and at a point about 20 yards north from a road leading to Morse's mill, Yoast "noticed a man in the midst of a clump of trees, apparently asleep."[1] Since the tree was reportedly a favorite spot for teamsters who took their noon break at the location, Yoast paid little attention to the man. With no apparent need for further inquiry, the wood hauler passed the location, "but on looking back, saw his dog smelling of the man's face and snorting."[2] The dog's reaction to the man at the tree aroused Yoast's curiosity. He halted his team, got down from the wagon and went to investigate the situation.

Upon arriving at the clump of oak trees, which sprang "from the same stem" and diverged outward, "leaving an open space in the center," he found a lifeless body, dressed in a blue shirt and vest, sitting on a large rock facing west, with the head inclined to the right and the back resting against the tree.[3] The body had been lying in the hot sun for about twenty-four hours and had already begun to turn black. On closer inspection, Yoast noticed a gunshot wound with "a hole large enough to admit two fingers about half way between the right eye and ear, and a hole correspondingly large on top of his head."[4] A pistol containing five cartridges was firmly clenched in the man's right hand and a Winchester rifle fully loaded rested against the tree. Around his waist were two cartridge belts. One belt was for rifle cartridges. The other, which was buckled on upside down, was for pistol cartridges. Other than the gunshot wound, the only mark of possible violence on the body was part of the forehead and scalp, including part of the hair, which looked as if someone had cut it with a knife. Strangely, the man wore no boots but had strips of an undershirt wrapped around his feet as if they were meant to be some kind of makeshift moccasins. John Yoast instantly recognized the dead man, having known him for years in both Arizona and Texas. Immediately, Yoast announced loudly his discovery, and within a few minutes, several men arrived at the location of the dead body. After conducting an informal inquest at the death scene, they buried the body at the spot it was found.[5]

The name of the dead man at the tree that day in 1882 was John Ringo, sometimes called John Ringgold, notorious cowboy, Texas feudist, suspected outlaw and rustler, and more recently, a reputed cowboy gang leader.[6] At the time of his death, Ringo was well known in Arizona. He was at the peak of his notoriety in the territory and was perceived throughout Arizona as the leader of a band of desperadoes. "There was few men in Cochise County, or southeastern Arizona better known. He was recognized by friends and foes as a recklessly brave man, who would go any distance, or undergo any hardship to serve a friend or punish an enemy," wrote the *Tombstone Epitaph* on July 18, 1882. Another newspaper, the *Arizona Daily Star*, alluding to the public's perception that Ringo was the leader of a cowboy gang, remarked, "He was known in this section as 'King of the Cowboys,' and was fearless in the extreme."[7] Seven months earlier, John Ringo had thrust himself into the forefront of the Earp-Clanton feud, emerging as the chief antagonist of Wyatt Earp. Ringo became the so-called champion of the cowboys, and in late March 1882, he rode for ten days in Cochise County Sheriff John Behan's posse that was on Wyatt Earp's trail when the rogue lawman left the territory.[8]

Perhaps foreboding future disputes over the cowboy's death, the *Epitaph* remarked, "Many people who were intimately acquainted with him in life, have serious doubts that he took his own life, while an equally large number say that he frequently threatened suicide, and the event was expected at any time."[9] It was presumed that Ringo's death was from suicide, but rumor and innuendo spread throughout the territory that someone may have killed the notorious cowboy. Several years later, Buckskin Frank Leslie, another infamous Tombstone character, took credit for killing Ringo.[10] Around 1920, one account even alleged that Wyatt Earp had dispatched the reputed cowboy leader on his way out of Arizona.[11] For more than a century, mystery and controversy have circulated about the details of Ringo's demise, making his death one of the most hotly debated deaths in Old West history.

With the passing of John Ringo in July 1882, essentially came the end of a turbulent period in Arizona territorial history - an era of outlawry and border depredations, personal animosities and feuds that gained exposure in the press and critical attention at the highest levels of government.[12] Less than a year before, on October 26, 1881, the Earp brothers and Doc Holliday had squared off with the Clantons and McLaurys, in Tombstone, leaving Billy Clanton and Tom and Frank McLaury dead in the street.[13] Thus started the Earp-Clanton feud, in which Ringo quickly became involved on the side of the Clantons. Before it was over, unknown assassins seriously injured Virgil Earp, and Morgan Earp was killed. Wyatt Earp then went on a personal vendetta, killing Frank Stilwell and Florentino Cruz, and he later claimed to have killed Curly Bill Brocius, Arizona's most famous outlaw at the time, in a shotgun duel at Iron Springs in the Whetstone Mountains.[14] Easily on a par with the Earp-Clanton feud in notoriety were the border conflicts during 1881, which almost started an international incident and received a great deal of coverage in the newspapers.[15] These hostilities pitted American cowboys in Arizona against Mexican citizens and soldiers in Sonora, with vengeance the order of the day, and both sides extracting a toll in blood. John Ringo was reputed to be a leader of the cowboys and suspected, though there is little evidence to identify who was involved in the criminal activity, as a participant in the depredations committed by cowboys in the territory. The situation reached such significance with government officials that in May 1882, President Chester Arthur threatened to declare martial law if the cowboys committing crimes in Arizona did not disperse.[16]

Although his life culminated with his death in Arizona, the cowboy also had a notorious past in Texas, leaving behind an indelible reputation as a desperado with his participation in the Hoodoo War seven years earlier.[17] Nonetheless, John Ringo's death did more than signal the consummation of the life of a notorious and dangerous man that had attained infamy throughout parts of the Southwest. It strangely began the cowboy's after-death journey into becoming a legendary cowboy whom writers romanticized to the point that he was considered one of the deadliest gunfighters of the Old West. Half a century after his death, writers transformed the real John Ringo into the legendary Johnny Ringo - deadly gunfighter, gentleman outlaw - "the fastest gun in all the West, the quickest ever known."[18]

This is the story of the real Johnny Ringo.

2

GONE TO TEXAS

Seven years earlier, on Christmas Day in 1874, John Ringo was in the Texas town of Burnet, where for some reason the cowboy decided to celebrate the Yuletide spirit by shooting his pistol into the air in the public square. While the revelry was relatively innocent, the indiscriminate shooting and rowdy behavior created a disturbance in the Texas town that would not be soon forgotten. A few months later, the Burnet County grand jury, based upon the Christmas Day incident, indicted Ringo on a charge of disturbing the peace for unlawfully discharging "a pistol in and around a public square."[1]

This was the first known criminal act involving a pistol (or anything else) for John Ringo, who at twenty-four, for these times was not considered a young man. Nevertheless, the shooting was far from being a desperate encounter since nobody was injured or killed, and the incident provided him with little notoriety. But by the following year, rumors of far more serious crimes in nearby Mason County provided Ringo with a reputation in the area of being a notorious and dangerous man.

Over the next few years John Ringo exhibited a tendency for using his pistol, or at least threatening to use it, and, consequently, on a number of occasions he was arrested for this propensity. He gained notoriety by participating in the Hoodoo War, which earned him an infamous reputation in Texas, before moving on to Arizona in 1879, where he received more recognition before his death. Over half a century later, Ringo was romanticized by writers to the point that he became a legendary cowboy who was considered one of the deadliest gunfighters of the Old West.

"Ringo was and is to western writers the classic cowboy-gunfighter," declared one biographer.[2]

Unlike other Old West figures such as Wyatt Earp, John Wesley Hardin, or even Ben Thompson, John Ringo left no writings describing his activities throughout his life. Consequently, many of the stories that have evolved over the years are from old-timer reminiscences, which are often not completely reliable or not supported by any contemporary evidence.

Some later accounts insist, categorically and without corroboration, that Ringo was from Texas or possibly Missouri, his family was respectfully connected, and that he was the black sheep son of a wealthy family.[3] "Many believed, though it is improbable, that he had a college education," wrote Walter Noble Burns in 1927.[4] In contrast, William Breakenridge, who had personally known Ringo in Arizona, outright declared that he "had a college education."[5] A few accounts contend that his real name was, in fact, John Ringgold, as if the claimants had some real knowledge concerning his true background, and that he simply shortened his name to hide his identity or to protect his family from his bad reputation.[6] He was rumored to be a second cousin of the notorious Younger brothers, who rode with the James boys, the most famous outlaw gang in Western history.[7] Some accounts have even alleged that Ringo rode with Quantrill and participated in dastardly deeds like the sacking of Lawrence, Kansas, during the Civil War.[8] Other stories assert that he started his reckless predilection with a pistol in Texas when he killed three men to avenge the murder of his brother.[9] One old-timer, in an anonymous reminiscence, later commented that the notorious cowboy had been involved in a Texas feud called the "Ringo War" and that he had killed twenty-two men.[10] The above accounts and rumors that were used and re-used by Western writers were, for the most part, a considerable distance from the truth.

John Ringo had no part in spreading the folklore that evolved during the twentieth century when writers, who often relied solely on old-timer claims, began to publish books about

Western figures and Old West incidents. Nonetheless, Ringo probably made little effort to correct the garbled accounts of his past or half-truth rumors that were told during his life by people that had limited knowledge of the facts.

John Peters Ringo was born on May 3, 1850, in the town of Washington (Clay Township), Wayne County, Indiana.[11] The town's name was later changed to Green's Fork. Martin Ringo, his father, was born in Kentucky but his family moved when he was young to Indiana. His mother, Mary Peters, was born and raised in Liberty, Missouri. Martin Ringo had family connections in Liberty and had met Mary Peters while serving in the Army during the Mexican War. After being discharged from the Army, Martin Ringo married Mary Peters on September 4, 1848, in Liberty.[12] Shortly after their marriage the newlyweds moved to Indiana, where in May 1850, John was born. Four years later, Mary gave birth to her second son, Martin Albert Ringo.[13]

During the summer of 1856, the family moved to Missouri, staying in Liberty for a short time. The Ringos eventually settled in the town of Gallatin, a short distance from Mary's family and her hometown of Liberty.[14] In Missouri, Mary Ringo gave birth to three daughters: Fanny Fern, Mary Enna, and Mattie Bell.[15] While not the wealthy family that folklore would have us believe, the Ringos were certainly middle-class and they did have family relations throughout the area that made them respectfully connected. Martin was a "part owner of Clendenen & Ringo, dealers in groceries and general merchandise," and a solid member of Gallatin's business community.[16]

The family maintained a farm a short distance from the town. Mary was a religious woman, having studied the subject in school, and both of her parents' families were well respected members of Liberty's community. There is little doubt that John received from his mother daily instruction of the mores of society and the value of education. Presumably, John, like most kids his age during this time, was required to perform chores around the family farm, and he may have at times frequented his father's store. Throughout his childhood in Missouri he attended school, probably receiving his instructions from New York born school teacher E. W. Thompson.[17]

Some later accounts claim that Ringo attended William & Jewel College in nearby Liberty, Missouri, but no evidence exists that he ever attended that institution or any other college. Yet, it is probable that his early schooling in the fundamentals of reading and writing may have caused some people in the frontier territories to believe that he had more education than most and that he might even have graduated from college.

As the Civil War raged in 1864, Martin Ringo, who suffered from tuberculosis that he had contracted during the Mexican War, decided to move his family to California.[18] It is likely that the Ringos hoped that the move west would improve Martin's health, but the problems associated with the ongoing Civil War probably provided another good incentive to relocate. On May 18, 1864, the Ringos, with one wagon pulled by mules and another pulled by oxen, and all the belongings they could carry in the wagons, left Liberty, Missouri, with a large wagon train. Mary kept a diary of the journey and she made the following comments about the first day of her trip:

> Left my family and started on my long trip across the plains, went 10 miles, had some trouble with the oxen and camped for the night and here I took my first lesson in camp life, cooked my supper and went to bed but couldn't sleep until after the chickens crowed for day and after a short nap I awoke.[19]

Mary's journal dispels the myth that young Johnny Ringo was riding with Quantrill during the Civil War. Instead, at fourteen years old, Johnny's task was to drive the family's oxen wagon along the trail as they headed west. When the Ringos reached the more densely populated city of Leavenworth, Martin Ringo helped

Mary Ringo

young Johnny with the oxen team while going through the town. As the group traveled west, they experienced the usual difficulties that occurred on long wagon trips during this period. The weather changed from time to time and the different landscapes provided new challenges. In June, Johnny "got his foot hurt quite badly by wheels running over it."[20] He slowly recovered from the accident. However, another boy was not so fortunate as he was "run over by a wagon and killed" on the same day.[21]

More trouble occurred later that day when a wagon master shot and killed one of his teamsters. The reason for the dispute is not known, but it may have resulted over the death of the boy earlier in the day. The shooting was, quite possibly, Johnny's first observation of a sudden and violent death. When the wagon train was not on the move, the men took the opportunity to fish and hunt. On one such hunting expedition that resulted in the party killing a buffalo, Johnny went along, despite his sore foot, and he "saw a great many Elk and Antelopes."[22]

As the wagon train went further into the frontier, they began to see fewer homesteads and ranches with each passing mile, and, instead, began more frequently to encounter Indians or signs of their presence. At first, the Ringos' wagon train met friendly Indians who simply offered to trade items like "buffalo robes and antelope skins" for other goods.[23] But on July 15, at a telegraph office in Wyoming, the wagon train was warned of Indian raids and atrocities on other emigrants. Despite the ominous warnings, the group continued on the trail for two more miles, when two of their wagons, which had temporarily become separated from the larger group and were in the process of rejoining it, were attacked by hostile Indians. Luckily, firing from the larger group forced the Indians to abandon their attack and flee across a river, where later that day the Indians killed a man from another wagon train. The Ringos' party returned to the telegraph office, where they were joined by more wagons heading west. The next day the group, still uneasy and tense from the encounter the day before, traveled ten miles and again saw Indians. On two separate occasions the party circled the wagons in a defensive corral, fearing an attack from Indians was imminent. During one of these maneuvers, some members of the group began firing at the Indians, who, in actuality, turned out to be friendly Indians. Fortunately, none of the Indians were injured in the mistaken attack by the wagon party. Nevertheless, the Indians rode to Fort Laramie and informed the U.S. Army of the incident. Consequently, the Ringos' wagon train was temporarily detained by the Army at Fort Laramie and forced to make peace with the Indians by giving them "flour, bacon, sugar, and coffee."[24]

On July 21, the party finally left Fort Laramie. Soon afterwards, they again began to hear stories of Indian atrocities on other wagon trains. Some emigrants came to the Ringos' camp on July 25 and told them that one of their men had been killed by Indians the night before. "We find posted on a tree a notice that the Indians have killed six men near here. We hear they had a fight ahead of us," a tense Mary noted.[25] More reports of Indian atrocities reached the party on July 28, when a report was received that "three miles from their camp a raiding party killed some men and took the women prisoner."[26] The next day the wagons passed "the corpse of a man lying by the side of the road, scalped."[27] Later that night a man named Davis was shot in the arm by Indians. The Indian problem had created a tense feeling in the wagon party. At this point in the long and arduous trip, on July 30, 1864, a fatal accident occurred while the Ringos were crossing through Wyoming. Martin Ringo accidentally shot himself with his own shotgun. This horrible tragedy was later reported by the *Liberty Tribune*:

> Death of Martin Ringo, Esq.
>
> We regret to announce the death of Martin Ringo, formerly of this city, but more recently from Gallatin, Mo. He was killed by the accidental discharge of his gun, between Ft. Laramie and Salt Lake, on his way to California. The load entered his eye and came out the top of his head, scattering his brains in all directions. – Mr. Ringo was esteemed by his acquaintances as one of the best of men, and his sad fate will be deeply regretted. His family continued their journey to California.[28]

The initial report of the death of Martin Ringo lacked details. However, a week later another story appeared in the *Liberty Tribune* concerning the tragedy based on a letter written by William Davenport to Robert Miller of Liberty, Missouri, the publisher of the local newspaper and Mary Ringo's brother-in-law:

> Just after daylight on the morning of the 30th July Mr. Ringo stepped outside of the wagons, as I suppose for the purpose of looking around to see if Indians were in sight, and his shotgun went off accidentally in his own hands, the load entering his right eye and coming out the top of his head. At the report of his gun I saw his hat blown up twenty feet in the air, and his brains were scattered in all directions. I never saw a more heart-rendering sight; and to see the distress and agony of his wife and children was painful in the extreme. . . . He was buried near the place he was shot in as decent a manner as was possible with the facilities on the plains.[29]

Despite the sudden tragedy and the painful loss of her husband, Mary found the strength to continue the journey due in large part to the need to provide for her children. The grieving family pushed on with the wagon party, making their way to Salt Lake City, and then to Austin, Nevada, before eventually arriving in San Jose, California. For about a year they stayed on the ranch of Colonel Coleman Younger, a respected man in San Jose.[30] Younger was an uncle to the famous outlaws, the Younger Brothers, who rode with Frank and Jesse James. During John Ringo's life, rumors spread that he was a second cousin to the famous Younger brothers. In actuality, Ringo was not a blood relative of the Younger brothers. His aunt simply had married their uncle. Ringo had a similar connection to the James boys. Benjamin Simms, Mary Ringo's uncle, had married Frank and Jesse James' mother, Zerelda, before the Civil War. In another interesting twist, Ringo had family connections to the Dalton Brothers, another infamous outlaw gang. In California, Martin Ringo's estate, valued at $1,600 was probated in November 1865, and the money was left to the five Ringo children. Since they were all minors, Mary Ringo was appointed their guardian and supervised their inheritance of the estate.[31]

The young Johnny Ringo grew up to be large in stature, measuring between six feet two and six feet four, depending on which account is used. One contemporary newspaper later referred to him as "Ringo, alias 'Long John'," clearly implying that he was a rather tall man.[32] In an age where men were considerably smaller than they are now, Ringo easily stood out in a crowd. It is likely that his size contributed to his imposing presence that some contemporaries would later recall.

At San Jose, John quit school and began working to help support his family. By 1870, Martin had joined his brother in the workforce, quitting school and taking a job as a printer's assistant with the *San Jose Mercury* newspaper. Mary Ringo began operating a boarding house for additional income to support her family. At nearly twenty-one years old, an age at which many young men of this era had already left home or even been married, the time had come for Ringo to head out on his own.

A later account claimed, without any documentation, that Ringo had become a teenage alcoholic and delinquent, and that he had left his family "in the lurch" sometime in 1869.[33] However, John was working as a farmer in the area as late as July 25, 1870.[34] "He did not leave San Jose on account of any crime, he went to southern California with a harvesting outfit," recalled his sisters years later.[35] In actuality, there is no evidence whatsoever that Ringo was a teenage alcoholic or delinquent in San Jose, and when he left home it appears that his family was financially secure and not in a difficult situation.

Sometime in late 1870 or early 1871, Ringo left California heading east, probably to visit his family in Missouri or Indiana. At some point, he headed south, possibly stopping in Little Rock, Arkansas, to visit family there before continuing on to Texas. He likely visited relatives in Hopkins County and San Saba County before eventually settling in the Burnet County area. Little is known about Ringo's activities in Texas before his Christmas Day shooting spree. One account claims, without corroboration, that Ringo left Texas for a short time, going to Lincoln, New Mexico, with the Horrel family, where he participated in the "Horrel War," before returning to Texas in 1874.[36] But no evidence supporting this assertion has been found. The first provable record of him in Texas is the incident on Christmas Day 1874. On April 5, 1875, the Burnet County Grand Jury indicted Ringo on the charge of disturbing the peace:

> John Ringo . . . on 25th day of December A.D. 1874, did then and there unlawfully discharge a pistol in and around the public square and . . . on a public street in the town of Burnet . . . did then and there unlawfully . . . disturb the peace.[37]

Nine days later, on April 14, 1875, Burnet authorities issued an arrest warrant for Ringo on the charge of disturbing the peace.[38] Nearly three months later the rowdy cowboy was arrested on July 9, 1875.[39] Nevertheless, Ringo was immediately released by the sheriff of Burnet upon "taking bond for his appearance at the next term" of the court.[40] The sureties for his $200 bond were M. B. Thomas and John Calvert. A few months later a bitter feud in Mason County, Texas, was being waged between cowboys in the area and German settlers in Mason. By October 1875, it was public knowledge that Ringo was believed to have murdered James Cheyney in Mason during September 1875, though he had not yet been formally charged with the crime, and that he was a known participant in the bloody Hoodoo War that began in nearby Mason County.

3

HOODOO WAR

The 1870s proved to be turbulent years for Texas, which had always had problems with mob violence and vigilante justice. But the "terrible seventies," as historian C. L. Sonnichsen wrote, was made even more intense due to the sheer number of violent feuds that erupted throughout the state during the period.[1] Texas feuds often were bloody vendettas that included shootings, murders, assassinations, ambushes, and lynchings. Perhaps, the most bitter of these feuds was the Hoodoo War, also known as the Mason County War, which raged in central Texas and peaked in violence during 1875. Into this feud was drawn a seemingly unknown John Ringo, whose only known previous brush with the law was for disturbing the peace.

The Hoodoo War began as a conflict ostensibly over cattle ownership between German settlers in the Mason County area and American born men who lived in neighboring counties. An underlying ethnic prejudice helped to fuel the antagonism between the factions. The Germans made continuous allegations that the Americans were stealing their cattle. In response, the Americans maintained that they were the proper owners of the livestock and that they had the right to gather their own stock. After a series of confrontations, which were based largely on confusion over stock laws, the mob violence and vigilante justice that commonly was used to settle disputes in other Texas communities erupted in Mason County, and quickly the situation escalated into a bloody feud that spread to neighboring counties.[2]

While the Mason conflict peaked in 1875, one of the causes of the problem occurred the previous year. M. B. Thomas, a respected cattleman from Burnet County, hired ten men (one may have been

Ringo) to gather his stock that was grazing near Mason County. When Sheriff John Clark of Mason was informed that the Thomas party was gathering cattle near the town, he quickly formed a posse to intercept them. Clark's party rode into nearby Llano County, raiding the Thomas herd, returning the livestock to the Mason area and scattering them into the hills. Thomas' party was taken to Mason and thrown into the county jail. The *Burnet Bulletin* published an account of the incident:

> Thomas and his men surrendered without resistance. . . . The cattle were not recaptured, but were turned loose. . . . Thomas and his men were carried to Fort Mason, and all of them eleven in number, were thrown into a foul dungeon, which was reeking with filth and stench, where they sweltered four days and nights, with nothing to eat but bread and water . . . Several of the men fainted from the terrible heat and snffocation [sic: suffocation] in the close hot naucious jail . . . .[3]

Upon hearing of the arrest of Thomas and his men, around forty men from the surrounding area headed to Mason to attempt a rescue. Seeing the large group heading toward Mason and fearing that they intended to free the prisoners or start trouble in Mason, Ernst Jordan, a settler near Mason, took a different route to town, gathering men, mostly German, on the way. In Mason, the two opposing groups met, but the confrontation resulted in no violence.[4] After a hearing, the Thomas party was released on a sizable bond and escorted out of the county by members of Clark's posse. Upset over their treatment in Mason County, Thomas and his men filed charges against Clark and his party in Llano County for robbery and false imprisonment. The complaints resulted in Clark and twenty-seven other men being indicted by the Llano County Grand Jury.[5] Meanwhile, Thomas' Mason County case was eventually heard and he was fined $2500 for driving cattle that he did not own. Nonetheless, the evidence showed that only two cows in the entire heard were not owned by the Thomas party.[6] Maintaining that he and his men had been gathering their own stock worth several thousands of dollars, not rustling cattle, Thomas asserted that they had every right to claim the cattle. George Gladden, possibly one of the men arrested by the sheriff's posse, later had a fistfight with Dan Hoerster, the Mason County Brand Inspector and a member of Clark's posse, in Ben Stewart's store in Mason.[7] This incident helped to intensify the feelings of everyone involved, and antagonism in the area continued to grow.

On February 13, 1875, Sheriff Clark arrested nine men driving cattle in McCulloch County and brought them to Mason to face the charge of illegally driving cattle.[8] The men made bond and were released. Four of the men decided to leave town. The remaining five men were arrested a second time after the brands of the stock were inspected.[9] While the men were being held in the Mason jail, a lynch mob formed on the evening of February 18. Lieutenant Dan Roberts of the Texas Rangers, who was in Mason getting supplies for his men, later recalled what occurred that night:

> James Trainer and myself went with Sheriff Clark to the jail and when we got within twenty steps of the mob, who were assembled at the jail door, we were ordered to halt, and in tones that meant business. They told the Sheriff that they would not hurt us, provided we kept our distance. We backed off to the court house, say thirty steps from the jail and the Sheriff ran up the stairs to a south room, put his rifle through the window and told the mob that the first d—d man that touched that jail door, he would kill him. Seeing that they might have to kill all three of us, about ten men came right in by Trainer and myself, didn't even say "good evening" and went upstairs to talk to Clark. They told the Sheriff that they meant no harm to him or the county, but they were going to have those men, even if they had to hurt him in doing so. There were about forty men of the mob, Clark saw he was "up against it". The Sheriff came down and told Trainer

> and myself to get off a little distance and watch them until he could go for help.[10]

According to Roberts, the mob used battering rams to break down the jail door and headed south of the jail with the prisoners. The sheriff returned with five or six men and then, with Roberts and Trainer, went in pursuit of the mob. Nevertheless, the mob succeeded in hanging Elijah and Pete Backus, and Tom Turley. Although nearly dead, Turley was cut down in time to save his life. Abe Wiggins was found "with his brains shot out."[11] He was shot in the head by the lynch mob when they realized they would not be able to hang him before the arrival of Clark and the others. In all the confusion, Charley Johnson, a 15-year-old boy escaped.

"This was the first, though unfortunately not the last, appearance of the 'Hoodoos' who gave the Mason County war its odd name. They were members of a vigilance committee which attempted, by ambushes and midnight hangings, to get rid of the thieves and outlaws who had been holding a carnival of lawlessness in Mason County, as in other parts of Texas," Sonnichsen noted.[12] Tom Gamel, a Mason resident and former posse member, later claimed that Sheriff Clark had suggested to him that the posse should simply lynch the rustlers, rather than taking them to Mason to face charges.[13] Gamel wanted no part of any lynching and refused to go along with it. After the Backus men were removed from the jail and killed, Gamel claimed his life was threatened. Knowing that there was a great deal of hostility toward Clark by outside groups, he aligned himself with these men. In March 1875, he gathered a group of thirty men, primarily from outside Mason County, to stop any attempt to murder him. Clark made a call to his friends, mostly Germans, and they gathered in Mason. The two opposing factions were prepared to fight. However, bloodshed was prevented when the two sides came to terms on a peace agreement.[14] John Ringo likely was one of the men aiding Gamel. With the situation temporarily cooled, the group returned to the surrounding counties. Nevertheless, the peace did not last long.

Deputy John Wohrle led Tim Williamson into an ambush and shot the cattleman's horse to prevent him from fleeing.

A short time later, in May 1875, an American named Tim Williamson was arrested by Deputy John Wohrle on an old charge of cattle theft.[15] While Williamson was being brought to Mason, Wohrle deliberately led him into an ambush. When Williamson realized that a mob was about to murder him, he reportedly begged Wohrle to let him ride for safety. Instead of aiding the man, Wohrle shot Williamson's horse to prevent him from attempting to flee. A group of men then descended upon Williamson, and he was finally killed by a man named Peter Bader.[16]

The news of Williamson's murder spread quickly throughout the area. In a short time it reached Scott Cooley, a close friend of Williamson. Some accounts claim that Cooley was Williamson's adopted son, having brought Cooley back to Texas with him while he was on a cattle drive to Kansas.[17] However, it is more likely that Cooley's strong bond and friendship for Williamson developed when he worked for Williamson on two separate cattle drives to Kansas, possibly in 1872 and 1873.[18]

Scott Cooley, a twenty year old former Texas Ranger, took Williamson's death very hard. He openly declared that he would seek revenge. His threat was later reported by the *San Antonio Herald* on August 30, 1875: "The day the news of Williamson's murder came to the Ranger camp, to which force Cooley at one time belonged, he sat down and cried for grief for the loss of one who he said was his best friend in the world and declared then that he would have revenge." The killing of Williamson by the mob proved to be a huge mistake. Cooley had no cattle or business interests in the area. He was not concerned with the Germans' complaints that men were stealing their cattle. Scott Cooley only wanted justice, or more realistically revenge, for the murder of his friend, Tim Williamson. If the law was not going to act, Cooley would take matters into his own hands.

Having grown up on the Texas frontier, Cooley was no stranger to conflict or vengeance. In 1872, Texas newspapers reported at least two encounters in which the "Cooley brothers" helped to chase down and kill raiding Indians.[19] Two years earlier, Cooley's father, Matthias Cooley, had been killed by a man named Horton during a

Scott Cooley openly declared that he would revenge the death of Tim Williamson.

dispute. The next day, the Cooley brothers killed Horton in revenge.[20] The *Austin Statesman* noted the following about Cooley's actions while serving with the Texas Rangers during a fight with Indians: "The boys brought some fresh scalps with them, and they report that Scott Cooley, who was fired at and run into camp, not only cut a wounded Indian's throat, but stripped a large piece of skin from his back, saying that he would make a quirt [riding whip] out of it."[21] Starting in September 1875, Ringo and Cooley, for nine months, would be constant and close companions. Scott Cooley personified the tough frontier Texas cowboy. Cooley's mannerisms, including his reckless behavior and vindictive attitude, likely were major influences on Ringo.[22]

By July 1875, the Mason County Grand Jury had still not issued any indictments for the killing of Tim Williamson. "No effort whatever so far as is known was made by the authorities to endeavor to discover the perpetrators of this outrage further then [sic] to hold a coroner's inquest over the remains," noted one newspaper.[23] Following the failure of Mason authorities to file any indictments regarding Williamson's murder, Cooley rode into the town of Mason and discretely attempted to discover the names of the men who were responsible for the murder of Williamson. Cooley's first act of vengeance was to kill former Deputy Sheriff John Wohrle, the man that had arrested Williamson and led him to his death. The *San Antonio Daily Herald*, on August 16, 1875, ran a reference to the killing: "We hear of a white man killing and scalping another white man recently, at Mason, but were unable to get the particulars." Two days later, on August 18, 1875, the *San Antonio Daily Herald* published a more complete account of the killing of John Wohrle:

> Horrible murder at Mason.- From the Freie Press of the 17th inst., we translate the following:
> On the 10th of August, during the afternoon, Mr. John Wohrly [sic], a quiet respectable citizen and former Deputy Sheriff, was assisting a man by the name of Haruett in digging a well, when a young man of about twenty-four years of age, rode up and began

> conversating with Wohrly in the most friendly manner. stating among other things that he was looking for a piece of leather with which to fasten his gun to his saddle, which request was complied with. While the villain was apparently fixing the leather to the saddle, Wohrly and another man who was present, began hauling Haruett up from the bottom of the well. While they were thus engaged the stranger took advantage of this opportunity to shoot Wohrly through the back of the head, the ball coming out near his nose. Wohrly fell dead, his companion being without arms fled, and Haruett fell to the bottom of the well, a distance of forty feet, where he remained senseless. The murderer then fired six shots into the dead body of Wohrly, stabbed it in four places with his knife, and finally took his scalp; whereupon the fiend mounted his horse and rode off. It is probable that the murderer will evade all earthly punishment as he is evidently the paid assassin of men who will back him up.

The newspaper naturally assumed the Wohrle was killed as a result of the continuing problems in Mason County, and implied that some of the American cowboys had hired an assassin to murder him. But Cooley's motivation was neither money nor a concern over which side legally owned the livestock in the area. "It seemed that Cooley's only motive was to find the man or men responsible for Williamson's death - he did not take sides with either element," recalled Tom Gamel.[24]

The next man killed on Cooley's vengeance ride was Karl "Charley" Bader, Peter Bader's brother. Apparently, Cooley was looking for Peter Bader and mistakenly killed his brother Karl on August 19, 1875.[25] Nevertheless, because there were no real facts known at the time about the killing of Karl Bader, some conflicting accounts have developed. Some claims state that Scott Cooley did the killing alone. Other accounts allege that Scott Cooley, George

Gladden, and the Baird brothers were responsible.[26] Claims have also been made that Cooley and Ringo killed Bader.[27] One newspaper later stated that the killing was supposed to have been done by Moses Baird and George Gladden.[28] Considering Scott Cooley's vow of vengeance and that he had killed John Wohrle nine days earlier, it is likely that he was the person who was responsible for Karl Bader's death.

The killing of Williamson by the German mob turned out to be a mistake in that it had unexpectedly unleashed an avenging angel upon Mason County in the form of a ruthless Scott Cooley intent on seeking personal vengeance and retribution. Nonetheless, the Germans' next act was an even bigger mistake and caused the situation to escalate into a full scale feud. On September 7, 1875, John Ringo's close friends, Moses Baird and George Gladden, were contacted by James Cheyney, a well known gambler in the area, who apparently told the two men they were wanted for some reason in Mason. Baird and Gladden quickly mounted their horses and began to ride toward Mason. The two men rode straight into a waiting ambush party led by Sheriff John Clark of Mason. Moses Baird was killed, and George Gladden was shot several times but lived.[29] The San Antonio *Herald* published the following account on September 14, 1875:

> KILLING AT FREDERICKSBURG. A letter from Fredericksburg, dated Sept. 8th, has been received in this city, and conveys the following startling news: "H-ll has broke loose up here. Mose Beard [sic] was killed yesterday; Geo. Gladden is badly wounded, but there is some hope of his getting well. He is shot through the arm, and in the face. . . . We fear this is but the beginning of a bloody solution of the difficulties about stock, that have become so serious of late.

George Gladden exhibited a great deal of courage under fire. After being critically wounded, Gladden helped Baird onto his horse and jumped up behind him in an attempt to escape. However,

Gladden's injuries were too severe, and both men eventually fell from the horse after riding a short distance. Peter Bader rode up to Baird, who was badly wounded, and shot him while he lay on the ground. Bader added insult to Baird's death by cutting one of Baird's fingers off to take a ring. Charlie Keller, a member of the ambush party, protected Gladden from being killed by the mob, and he was taken to Loyal Valley in critical condition.[30] Sheriff Clark defended the posse's action by claiming self-defense. Clark tried to convince the public that Gladden and Baird had ridden up to his fifty men and had opened fire.[31] The reason for the ambush is unclear. Yet, it is possible that Clark and the others mistakenly believed that Moses Baird and George Gladden had killed Karl Bader.

The killing of Moses Baird is generally considered to be the event that triggered the feudal character of the Hoodoo War. He was a very popular man in the area and many people were upset over his death. Henry Holmes, an attorney in Mason, wrote a letter to Governor Richard Coke describing the events that had taken place around Mason County. "Mr. Beard [sic] is a man of large connextions [sic] in Burnet County and if something is not done a civil war will be inaugurated."[32] Unfortunately, Clark and the rest of the Germans who comprised his posse did not realize the extent of the family connections of the American cowboys in the area. Many of the cowboys were related or connected in some manner, and the situation quickly became a blood feud. Jeff Ake, who knew the cowboys in the area later stated: "Keeping out of a fight where nigh everybody in a county was either a relative or a friend of one side or another was mighty close to impossible, and your life would be hell if you did."[33] Men from all over the area were now prepared to fight. One of these men was John Ringo.

Another problem that the killing of Moses Baird produced was that Scott Cooley, realizing that he now had allies in the area, quickly aligned himself with the Baird-Gladden faction. According to Tom Gamel, two days after Moses Baird and George Gladden were ambushed he went to Loyal Valley, where he found John Baird, Scott Cooley, John Ringo, and a man named Williams at Gladden's house.[34]

Eight men of the Gladden-Baird party rode boldly into Mason on September 25, 1875. Ringo and Williams broke from the pack and rode over to James Cheyney's house. It was rumored that Cheyney had received 50 dollars for his part in setting up Moses Baird and George Gladden to be ambushed.[35] Tom Gamel later recalled, "Chaney [sic] asked Ringoe [sic] and Williams down and they stepped upon the porch and washed their faces. Chaney washed and was drying his face and while he had his face covered with a towel, Ringo and Williams shot him down and rode back to where their friends were awaiting them."[36]

After killing Cheyney, Ringo and Williams rode over to Dave Doole's store and yelled for him to come out. However, Doole had been warned by Gamel a few days earlier that if some men were to ride up and holler for him to be wary, and he came out with a gun in his hand. "Come in or ride on," Doole yelled out.[37] Since Doole had obviously been forewarned, Ringo and Williams rode over to Bridge's hotel to join their friends. A reference to the killing of Cheyney was reported by the *San Antonio Herald* on September 29, 1875: "The last mail from Mason brought the news that Mr. Cheyney and two others had been killed, and the sheriff found it difficult to avoid being murdered." Major Jones of the Texas Rangers in a letter to the Adjutant General implicated John Ringo in Cheyney's murder:

> About a week before Hoester [sic] was killed John Ringgold and another man of the Gladden-Cooley party killed Cheyney in the presence of his family while he was arranging breakfast for them, then Gladden, Cooley, Ringold and others of the party rode into town and ate their breakfast at the hotel and boasted publically at the table of what they had done, telling those present that they had made beef of Cheyney and if someone did not bury him he would stink. They remained in town some time and one of them, Gladden, had an interview with Justice Hey during the time. The fact of their having done the killing is of public

> notoriety, and yet no warrants was or has yet been issued for their arrest. I asked the Justice why no warrants had been issued for their arrest, his reply was, no complaint had been made against them, though he held the inquest.[38]

It was public knowledge that Ringo and Williams had killed James Cheyney and that Ringo was now riding with the Cooley party. Contrary to folklore, Ringo had not entered the Hoodoo War seeking vengeance for the death of his brother, who, in actuality, died of tuberculosis two years earlier in San Jose.[39] Instead, Ringo's entry into the bloody feud, while not as romantic as some writers have imagined, was based on the brutal murder of a close friend and the near death of another friend. But, in central Texas, that was how feuds often began.

Concern over the situation in Mason caused William Steele, the Adjutant General of Texas, to order the Texas Rangers to immediately head to Mason. In a letter to Steele, Major John B. Jones described what he encountered:

> In passing Kellors, on the Llano en route for Mason, I was surprised to see fifteen or twenty men, armed with winchester carbines and six-shooters, rise up behind a stone fence, in a fighting attitude. Halting to ascertain the meaning of this demonstration, I was informed that a report had reached them that the Gladden party of Cold Springs and the Beard party from Burnett, some thirty men in all, were at Cold Springs and intended coming up today or tonight to burn out the Dutch [the Germans] consequently they had assembled to defend themselves and their property.[40]

Four days after the killing of Cheyney, the Cooley gang, as they were now being called, struck again. On September 29, 1875, Dan Hoerster, who was thought to have been involved in the ambush of Moses Baird and George Gladden, was killed in Mason. Waiting in ambush, Cooley and Baird opened fire on Hoerster, Peter Jordan, and Henry Plueneke as they rode down the street. Hoerster was hit four times in the neck by Baird's gun and was instantly killed. Jordan and Plueneke dismounted and ran into a store before returning fire.[41]

There is no record of Ringo participating in the shooting or that he was even present. However, since Hoerster was killed only four days after Cheyney, it is possible that Ringo was present when Hoerster was killed, but was not mentioned in later accounts. Following the killing of Hoerster, Baird, Cooley, and Gladden made their way to Gamel's saloon where Baird said, "Let's all have a drink - - I never felt so happy in all my life."[42] The men then went outside, over to the Southern Hotel, and a second gunfight commenced. As they were leaving Gamel's saloon, the men forcibly recruited Bill Coke, who worked on John Gamel's ranch, and made him participate in the ensuing fight. When the second gun battle started, Coke immediately fled town, losing his gun as he rode to Gamel's ranch.[43]

After the Cooley party left the town of Mason, the Germans formed a posse and went after them. The posse arrived at John Gamel's ranch and discovered that Bill Coke was at the ranch. The men arrested Coke, and six men began to escort him back to Mason. However, the prisoner never arrived in Mason and was never seen alive again. The six men who were escorting Coke claimed that he had escaped from their custody.[44] Major Jones' Rangers arrived in Mason only hours after Hoerster was killed, and in a letter he commented about the current state of affairs in Mason County:

> I have three parties out after them (the Cooley gang) now and will have the county thoroughly searched for them but have very little hope of catching them at present as they are well mounted, know the country well and have many friends in this, and adjoining

> counties. The National prejudice is so very bitter here. American against German and vice versa, that I find it impossible to get a consistent or reliable account of the troubles and am sorry to have to report that very few of the Americans whom I have met yet manifest any disposition to assist in the rearrest of the perpetrators of yesterdays deed, or any particular desire to have them arrested. . . .[45]

The presence of the Rangers in Mason cooled the situation for a while. It was so quiet that the *San Antonio Daily Herald* wrote: "There has not been any mortuary report from Mason for a week or so. What's the matter?"[46] The silence only lasted two weeks. "The Fredericksburg correspondent of the Freie Press mentions the killing of a Mr. Mueller in Mason. So it seems the war is not over yet."[47]

Occupied by more pressing difficulties, Ringo did not appear before the Burnet County Court on August 5, and the district attorney moved for forfeiture of the bond. The court then ordered the sureties "to show cause if any they have or can why this Judgement . . . should not be made final. . . ."[48] Though existing court papers do not indicate the outcome, it is likely that Ringo's bond was eventually forfeited. Believing that he was currently in nearby Llano County, the court issued another warrant on August 17 for his arrest. Sheriff W. P. Hoskins of Llano County returned the warrant not served, noting that "John Ringo is not to be found in my County."[49] The Burnet County Court issued another arrest warrant for Ringo in October 1875. This warrant stated that the sheriff of Burnet County was ordered to bring John Ringo before the court in January 1876.[50] On November 25, rumors began to circulate that the Texas Rangers had captured Cooley and Ringo. "At last the Rangers appeared to be in earnest, as we hear that on last Saturday they came up on Scott Cooley and John Ringgold. Cooley is reported to be wounded and Ringgold a prisoner."[51] The reports that Cooley and Ringo were captured by the Rangers, were, of course, greatly exaggerated. Nonetheless, a month later both men would be in custody.

Dan Hoerster was killed in Mason four days after Ringo and Williams shot James Cheyney.

George Gladden continued to fight in the Hoodoo War after he recovered from the wounds he received during the ambush by Sheriff John Clark's party.

4

SERIOUS THREATS

John Ringo and Scott Cooley had a strong following in Burnet County and they felt reasonably safe using the area for shelter. It was public knowledge that both men were involved in the bloody feud in nearby Mason County and that each man was suspected there of murder. Yet, Mason officials had officially charged neither Ringo nor Cooley for any crime whatsoever, and no arrest warrants had been issued from that county for the two men. They presumably thought that as long as they maintained a strong following around them, the Mason mob would not dare to touch them in Burnet County. Nevertheless, they quickly learned that even in Burnet County they were not immune from arrest. Sheriff John Clymer of Burnet County arrested John Ringo, most likely in early December, on a "disturbing the peace" warrant that was still in effect.[1] But he again released Ringo after "taking a bond" of $150 on December 6, 1875.[2] Ringo's sureties were John Baird and George Gladden, active participants in the Hoodoo War in Mason County.

After his release from the jail, Ringo remained in the Burnet area with Scott Cooley, who was publicly believed to be the leader of the Mason County desperadoes. Three weeks later, on December 27, 1875, both John Ringo and Scott Cooley were arrested by Burnet officials for "seriously threatening to take the life" of Sheriff Clymer and Deputy J. J. Strickland.[3] The reason for the threats remains unknown, but Ringo's earlier arrest on the disturbing the peace warrant may have created some animosity between the Mason County desperadoes and the Burnet law officers. Friends of the arrested men immediately took steps to get them released from the jail. "Gladden and Baird tried to get Clymer to take them as security for Ringo and

Cooley," recalled Deputy J. J Strickland.[4] However, this time Clymer would not approve the two Mason County feudists as security for the bonds. Meanwhile, J. C. Carson, a brother-in-law of John Baird, brought whiskey and provisions on a couple occasions to the jail for Ringo and Cooley.[5] Nevertheless, Sheriff Clymer was not taking unnecessary risks with his noted prisoners. According to Strickland, "Sheriff [Clymer] did not allow anyone to talk to the prisoners without someone being present."[6] Soon a large number of men began threatening to break open the jail to liberate the prisoners. In response, Sheriff Clymer added dozens of men for security to prevent an assault on the jail. The *Austin Statesman*, on January 2, 1876, published an article concerning the serious situation occurring in Burnet:

> War in Burnet. – Ex-Policeman Johnson returned from Burnet Friday, where he had been to conduct a prisoner, and reports a horrible state of affairs in that town. The notorious desperado Cooley and one of his companions had been arrested and placed in the Burnet jail, and when Mr. Johnson arrived there about twenty men were dashing about the town threatening to break open the jail, which was being guarded by fifty or more men, and liberating the prisoners. There was so much excitement in the place in the morning that the sheriff would not receive the prisoner taken up by Mr. Johnson, so he was in constant expectation of an attack. Later in the day, however, the prisoner was received, and Mr. Johnson started home, meeting many armed men along the road. A feeling of dread and insecurity for life seemed to pervade the entire community, and strangers were anxious to get out of those parts.

Realizing the difficulty in maintaining a strong presence at the jail for a lengthy time, Sheriff Clymer decided to move the prisoners under heavy guard to the Travis County jail in Austin, a distance of sixty miles, for safekeeping until the next term of the Burnet County Court. Deputy Strickland and about twelve men brought Ringo and Cooley to Austin. The *Austin Statesmen* published the following article about the prisoners' arrival in the town:

> Cooley and Ringgold – On Sunday morning the Statesman announced that Scott Cooley and John Ringgold, two of the Mason county desperadoes, had been arrested and placed in the Burnet jail, which was under heavy guard to prevent the release of the prisoners by an armed body of men that were dashing about the town. On Sunday morning deputy sheriff Strickland, accompanied by ten or twelve men, brought the prisoners to this city for safe keeping until the meeting of the Burnet district court on the fourth Monday in this month. Arriving in the city the whole party stopped at Salge's snack house for lunch, and people gathered to see the two men who had been "on a rampage" in the counties of Mason and Burnet. The prisoners were apparently cool and reserved, and chatted freely as any of the guard, and each recognized a person in the crowd, Cooley who is said to have been a very quiet man until about a year ago, is a short solid man about twenty eight years old, and looks like he may have some Cherokee blood in him. He is charged with having killed deputy John A. Whorlie, [sic] of Mason county, and it is said that after killing him he also took off his scalp. Ringgold, who is taller and perhaps older than Cooley, is said to have taken an active part in the Mason county war, and he and Cooley are charged with having threatened the lives of Sheriff Clymer, of Mason, and his deputy Strickland. The prisoners are now in the Travis county jail, and the guard left for home yesterday.[7]

News that John Ringo and Scott Cooley had finally been arrested quickly spread throughout Texas. Two hundred miles to the north, the *Dallas Herald*, on January 8, 1876, commented, "Scott Cooley and John Ringgold, two Mason county desperadoes, had to be brought from the Burnet jail under strong guard to Travis county and are safely incarcerated. . . ."

For some reason, John Ringo's name began to be reported publicly as Ringgold or Ringold. These articles helped to create confusion over his true identity throughout his life, and the confusion continues to this day. Why his name was reported as Ringgold is still not known, but it is possible that the mistake was due to the way German newspapers, like the *Fredericksburg Freie Press*, translated Ringo's name. Since court records in the area consistently used the name Ringo, including his first known indictment for disturbing the peace in Burnet on December 25, 1874, it is doubtful that he purposefully used the name as an alias.

Despite the arrest of Cooley and Ringo in Burnet, the people of Mason County quickly learned that the Hoodoo War was far from over. While John Ringo and Scott Cooley were in the Travis County jail at Austin, John Baird and George Gladden shot and killed Peter Bader, the man who killed Tim Williamson and started Scott Cooley's rampage.[8]

In late January 1876, ten men escorted John Ringo and Scott Cooley from Austin to Burnet to appear before the grand jury. The *Austin Stateman* noted the return of two of the men to Austin:

> DEPUTY SHERIFFS Henry Stokes and Fred Peck arrived yesterday morning from Burnet, where they had been with the posse of ten men that conveyed Scott Cooley to Burnet from the jail in this city. They report that they saw no signs of resistance or of any attempt being made to release the prisoner on the road. . . .[9]

The people of Burnet now considered that their lives were in danger because of their determination to enforce law and order. Consequently, they purchased an extensive supply of firearms and quickly formed a minuteman company.[10] On February 1, 1876, the Burnet County grand jury indicted John Ringo and Scott Cooley on two counts of "Seriously threatening to take the life of a human being."[11] The following day, Ringo went before the court on the disturbing the peace charge on which he had failed to appear in court on August 5, 1875. Court documents signed by Swift Ogle, foreman of the jury, indicate the results of John Ringo's first known criminal indictment: "We the jury find the Deft guilty and assess the fine at Seventy Five Dollars."[12]

John Ringo and Scott Cooley made an application for a change of venue on February 3, 1876.[13] After pleading not guilty to the charges against them, the court granted their application for a change of venue, and the court transferred the cases to Lampasas County.[14] The court set bond at $500 for each defendant on each of the two counts. Nonetheless, the two men remained in custody unable to make bond.[15] In March 1876, a heavily armed guard brought Ringo and Cooley to Lampasas from Burnet to appear before the district court. The newspapers in Lampasas and Dallas announced their arrival in the town.

> Quite an excitement was raised among our citizens last Sunday by the arrival in town of the notorious Mason county outlaws Scott Cooley and John Ringgold, who were brought here from Burnet under heavy guard. These are the same men who killed and scalped the Deputy Sheriff of Mason county a few months ago.[16]

It is likely that Ringo had no part in the killing and scalping of John Worhle, but most people probably accepted the assertion as the truth. John Ringo received notoriety from the rumors and innuendos of his participation in the Hoodoo War, and the newspaper articles about his activities made him a widely known man in Texas. Indeed, two hundred and sixty miles away the *Galveston Daily News* commented: "Deputy J. J. Strickland has acquired some notoriety for his courageous conduct in arresting the celebrated desperadoes, Scott Cooley and one Ringo, alias 'Long John,' both of whom are now in jail at this place."[17] In March 1876, a Lampasas County jury convicted both men on two counts of "seriously threatening to take the life of a human being."[18] The details of the sentence Ringo and Cooley received are unknown. Friends of Ringo and Cooley soon began to take steps to free them from the Lampasas jail. News of an attempted release of Scott Cooley and John Ringo from the Lampasas jail was published in newspapers throught the area:

> DISAGREEABLE.- Between midnight and daylight on Sunday last [April 30], four disguised men suddenly sprang upon the jail guard at Lampasas, seized and tied him to a picket fence, his face towards the foe and his back towards the fence. They with pistols presented towards him, commanded him to be silent or die. He didn't die. Two of the four proceeded to the jail, and after handing Scott Cooley a file, they began boring and chiseling to make a hole where by the prisoners (Cooley and John Ringo) might escape. But they were compelled to raise the siege without obtaining their object. The near approach of daylight is supposed to have caused them to abandon their enterprise. The guard was carried about two miles on the San Saba road and turned loose upon the range. He returned to his old feeding place about daylight, and, after calmly surveying the premises and making himself sure that his late companions were all gone, and conscientiously believing his obligation of silence and secrecy were removed, he dared to speak, and speaking he said he was thankful it was as well with him as it was. Burnet Buletin [sic].[19]

Four days later, several men forcibly "busted out" John Ringo and Scott Cooley from the Lampasas jail.[20] There would be no more wasted time trying to bore a hole in the jail's wall. On the night of May 4, a mob of men went to Sheriff Albert Sweet's home and bluntly told him to surrender the keys to the jail, or they would kill him and his family and take the keys anyway. Sheriff Sweet quickly complied with the request. Deputy J. T. Walker later described the events that had occurred that night at the jail: "I was walking up with one of the guards near Stanifer's store when I saw a party of men coming up. Some 13 or 15 in no. [number]. They told us not to shout that they had the keys & that if we hurt any of them that they would burn up the town with every one in it."[21] Walker immediately realized the uselessness of trying to put up a fight with the mob, who he could not identify because "the party were disguised, some had their faces blackened with lard [and] handkerchiefs tied over their faces."[22] Ringo and Cooley, who had spent the past four months in three different county jails, were free from custody. "Their hobbles was laid over a log and cut in two with an axe which was near the jail door."[23]

The two fugitives headed toward Llano County, crossing the Llano River on a ferry owned by Solomon "Hoss" Maxwell. According to Maxwell, who jokingly referred to Scott Cooley several times as "Sonny," the two men were riding on the ferry with a load of hogs, which became frightened for some unknown reason and rushed to one side of the ferry. Consequently, the ferry tipped over and everyone on board fell into the river. Ringo and Cooley, wearing full-length coats, quickly started to swim to shore. Maxwell thought the whole incident was funny until the posse that was following the fugitives arrived and informed him who he had called "Sonny."[24]

Over a year later, the *Austin Statesman*, on July 15, 1877, announced the arrest of the men that were accused of releasing John Ringo and Scott Cooley from the Lampasas jail:

> The Lampasas Dispatch tells us that Sheriff Strickland, of Burnet county, is waking up the evil-doers in lively style. He has arrested several of the crowed who

> broke open the Lampasas jail in May, 1876, and released Scott Cooley and John Ringo. The parties arrested are Champ Farris, Bud Farris, Jim Mason, Andrew Murkeson, Ed Brown, Bill Cavin and John Carson. Cavin turned State's evidence and was released.

Ed Cavin later testified that John Carson had told him that "Ringo ought never to forget Joe Olney. That he had ridden day and night to get him out."[25] It appears that Olney had assembled together the men who broke open the Lampasas jail, freeing Ringo and Cooley.

5

A NOTORIOUS MAN

Following their release from the Lampasas jail, Ringo and Cooley quickly headed toward Joe Olney's ranch in Llano County. Around eight o'clock in the morning on May 5, A. R. Johnson, who was riding from Llano to Mabry's store, saw "some men in the Llano River swimming and two standing on the bank with guns."[1] It is likely that Ringo and Cooley were part of the group. Later that morning several men converged on the Olney ranch but their arrival was staggered throughout the day. "They did not come there together. Joe Olney came for his breakfast and I think Mr. Ringo came next & alone," recalled James Randall.[2] Next came Jack Carson and Jim Mason, who arrived at the ranch "about the middle of the morning."[3] According to Randall, "Cooley came in after Mason & Carson."[4] Also at the ranch were Audie Murchinson, Bud Farris, Bill Wills, Charlie Furguson, Ed Cavin and a few others.[5] Later that evening, Llano Sheriff W. P. Hoskins, who had official business with Joe Olney, also arrived at the ranch. The sheriff later described the situation he observed:

> I went to see Joe Olney on official business & got within 25 yards of the house before they saw me. There appeared to be considerable excitement among them when they saw me. Some got on their horses and others picked up their guns. I continued to ride up to them and spoke to Joe Olney and he asked me to get down. When I got down Scott Cooley threw a cartridge in his gun &

> steped [sic] behind his horse. I then turned & walked off he having lowered the muzzle of his gun. I remained there about twenty minutes. I did not see J.C. Carsons [sic] until after I went into the house & came out; when I walked out of the door he was sitting against the back of the house one or two others were sitting near him & Jno. Ringo got up from near him & spoke to me . . . Ringo shook hands with me & I asked him what he was doing there & he made some foolish remark, I then left.[6]

Later that night John Ringo, Scott Cooley, Ed Cavin, Charlie Furguson and Jim Mason left the Olney ranch together and went in the direction of the town of Llano. The following morning Sheriff Hoskins encountered J. C. Carson at Mabry's store. After shaking hands with the sheriff, Carson commented, "That was rather a rough crowd you rod [sic] up on yesterday evening."[7] Hoskins responded, "I think it was."[8] Three days later, Ringo and Cooley made their first appearance as free men in Mason County since their arrest in Burnet over four months earlier. "Scott Cooley and crowd here. – No one knows what they are after," remarked Lucinda Holmes in her diary.[9] News of their escape and return to Mason County spread quickly throughout Texas:

> A Gentleman, recently arrived from Loyal valley, tells us that Scott Cooley and Ringgold were recently released from the jail at Lampasas by several armed men, who intimidated the jailer. They went to the hotel at Loyal Valley, in broad daylight, armed to the teeth, and eat [sic] dinner with perfect composure, and rode off unmolested. We simply mention the circumstances to show how completely awed the peace officers are on the frontier.[10]

John Ringo and Scott Cooley camped in Llano County for several weeks. On June 9, 1876, the *Austin Statesman* published a letter from a man who described what was occurring in the area: "A Gentleman from the frontier says that Scott Cooley, Ringgold and others, who were recently taken out of the Lampasas jail, have gone into camp, and that they defy the law and authorities, and that there is no protection for life or property in many place upcountry. . . ."

Around this time, Scott Cooley, the man who had started the bloody vendetta of the Hoodoo War, reportedly decided it was time to quit the feud.[11] But before he could leave the area and start a new life, it was reported in June 1876, that Scott Cooley had died suddenly from brain congestion near Fredericksburg.[12] Two months later the *Austin Statesman* confirmed that the notorious Mason County desperado, Scott Cooley, was dead:

> The Blanco stage driver says the report published some time ago in this paper that Scott Cooley was dead, is correct. He died of disease, which is not generally the case for desperadoes. Those who kill invariably are killed themselves.[13]

Some claims have been made that Cooley was murdered by a woman who slipped poison into his drink at Fredericksburg.[14] Whether Scott Cooley died a natural death or was murdered, one of the main instigators in the Hoodoo War was dead. Nonetheless, for a short time his name was still included in news reports about events occurring in the area: "The deputy sheriff of Burnet county has summoned a posse of men and gone into Mason county to arrest Cooley, Ringgold and associates. The clan numbers many and a fight is expected."[15]

The Hoodoo War was essentially over and the German mob disbanded, but antagonism would continue for several years. With Scott Cooley's death, John Ringo emerged as the leading feudist in the Mason County area. In the next few months, rumor and innuendo about Ringo's activities often would be published in the newspapers. On June 24, 1876, Burnet County charged Ringo with "aiding a prisoner to escape from the custody of a lawful officer."[16] A few weeks later the *Burnet Bulletin* published a report in which Ringo was accused of trying to free men from custody:

> Deputy Leverett, of Llano County, who has just returned from carrying Reddin to Austin for safekeeping, reports that thirteen of Reddin's friends were seen ambushed in the cedar brake side of Austin, waiting for them to pass, so as to liberate the prisoners and kill the guard. But, luckily, Leverette and Sheriff Strickland went by Round Rock, and thereby avoided the attack. It is reported that someone of the waylaying party remarked that they would never have as good an opportunity to kill Strickland and Leverette. The notorious Ringo, who seems to have been the leader, is certainly a very desperate and daring man. All but three of the party finally dispersed, leaving them to waylay Leverette on his return. But the news reached him, and, with the aid of the Sheriff of Travis County and about thirty men, he made a search for but failed to find them.[17]

The newspaper stories during this period indicate that Ringo's reputation in the area was rapidly growing. Within a month, the *Burnet Bulletin*, on July 25, 1876, announced another event in which it claimed Ringo was involved: "[T]he sheriff [of Mason], with twenty-five men, started to Kimble County to capture a party of cattle thieves, it is thought that there will be much trouble and probably bloodshed, Ringo is in charge of the stolen cattle. . . ."

On August 9, 1876, John Ringo, Scott Cooley, who had died two months earlier, and John Baird had charges in the Burnet County District Court transferred to the Justice Court. The crime that the men were charged with is unknown.[18] Information concerning Ringo continued to spread throughout Texas as the *Galveston News,* on August 18, 1876, reported on the troubles in Mason County:

> TROUBLE IN MASON
> (Special Telegram to the Galveston News.)
> Fredericksburg, Aug. 17, 1876
> Trouble has started again in Mason county, John Ringo and Bill Randall have been driving cattle off from Gooch, Hogan, Neighbors, and others. Citizens are after them, and a call has been made on Gillespie county for the Mounted Rifles to help capture them.

The news stories from the Burnet area declaring that Ringo was a notorious outlaw began to be circulated and republished throughout the state. On September 1, 1876, the *Austin Daily Statesman* republished the special telegram that was reported by the *Galveston News* and proclaimed Ringo to be a cattle thief. This following account was published by the *Burnet Bulletin* on September 1, 1876:

> Mr. A. T. Taylor, just from Llano County informs us that rumors are prevalent that a fight had taken place between the party having charge of stolen cattle in Kimble County and the pursuers. Several were killed and wounded, R.E. Tucker, who once lived here, was found to have charge of the cattle and was killed in the fight. Mr. Taylor is certain that it is a mistake about John Ringo being connected with the cattle stealing.

Whether Ringo had actually stolen the cattle or not, with the constant stories being published in the newspapers, some people likely now considered him to be a rustler. A few days later, John Ringo was in the Mason area near Bluff Creek, where he encountered Hal Holmes, an attorney and prosecutor in Mason. Ringo threatened Holmes, who quickly returned home. Upon his arrival he told his wife, Lucinda, of his brush with the Mason County desperado. "Hal started to Bluff Creek and came back on account of Ringold being out there. . . . Heard that Ringold had threatened Hal so Hal got his arms ready if he should come to the house -- I feeling fearfully worried and could not sleep much tonight," a worried Lucinda Holmes wrote.[19] Sheriff Strickland of Burnet, considered the conditions in the area to be dangerous and made a call for help:

> Sheriff Strickland, of Burnet county, reports a bad state of affairs in Llano county, and it is probable that the Governor will order Major Jones up there with a squad of men to make arrests and enforce law and order. It is charged that a number of desperadoes and roughs have organized, and that they are defying all law and order, and that they have threatened the lives of two men named Roundtree and Oatman. . . .[20]

The Rangers were sent to the county to restore order and capture the desperadoes that were causing the problems in the area. On October 16, J. C. Sparks told "Sergeant Robinson to proceed to Loyal Valley in Mason county to ascertain, if possible, the whereabouts" of Ringo, Gladden, and others for whom he held arrest warrants.[21] Sparks learned that Ringo and Gladden were at Mosley's ranch in Loyal Valley. Ringo and Gladden were later arrested on the Llano River near Castell by the Texas Rangers and a posse led by the Sheriff Bozarth of Llano County on October 31, 1876.[22] Both men were placed in the Llano County jail.

Four days after the two desperadoes were placed in the Llano jail, the Rangers were ordered to return immediately to Austin. Fearing that the two prisoners would be liberated from the jail by friends once the detachment was gone, the Rangers brought Ringo and Gladden to Austin and placed them in the Travis County jail on November 7, 1876, to await their court proceedings.[23] News of their capture was reported by the newspapers in the area. The *Austin Weekly Statesman*, on November 9, 1876, published the following article:

> **JOHN RINGO, GEORGE GLADDEN AND NEAL KANE ARE IN THE TRAVIS COUNTY JAIL.**
>
> On Sunday, three desperadoes, men who have been a terror in the counties of Mason, Llano, Burnet, Lampasas, etc, were brought to Austin and lodged in the new jail . . . John Ringo is the party taken from the Lampasas jail last May by about forty men. He has been convicted of threatening the life of Sheriff J. J. Strickland, of Burnet, and was regarded as one of the most desperate men in the frontier counties. Gladden has been indicted in Llano county for the murder of Peter Bader, and five capiases [sic], charging him with theft, have also been issued for his arrest. These men were arrested last Tuesday at Mosley's ranch, in the Western portion of Llano county, by Sergeant Robinson, commanding a detachment of seven men of Company C, Texas Rangers, assisted by Sheriff Bosarth [Bozarth], of Llano, and six men. The rangers and the sheriff and his party left camp Monday night, rode to within a short distance of Mosley's ranch and put up for the night. In the morning they surrounded the house and closed in

> on it, but did not find their men. They then retired a few hundred yards and put out pickets. Later in the morning Gladden and Ringo arrived and were arrested. . . .

Over the next few days, Ringo's and Gladden's capture and transportation to Austin were mentioned in the newspapers throughout the state. About the celebrated desperadoes' arrest, the *Burnet Bulletin,* on December 8, 1876, published a letter from Llano. The author was disturbed that the sheriff of Llano had not received a better share of the glory for capturing Ringo and Gladden. The writer exclaimed that "the whole thing was planned and carried out by their sheriff." It appears that the capture of the two desperadoes was considered somewhat of a prize. Indeed, John Ringo's notoriety in Texas had grown considerably since the Christmas Day shooting in Burnet in 1874. Now regarded as a notorious and desperate man, who had participated in the bloody Hoodoo War, Ringo was considered by the public to be a dangerous man.

With Ringo and Gladden in jail, the people of Mason probably felt it was safe to begin to indict the participants of the war. The Mason County grand jury, in November 1876, indicted John Ringo and George Gladden for Cheyney's murder.[24] Following their indictment for murder in November 1876, it is likely that Ringo and Gladden were taken to Mason from Austin to answer the murder charge, and that they pled not guilty. Although Gladden apparently did not participate in the shooting of Cheyney, the Mason County grand jury indicted him anyway. Meanwhile, on December 7, 1876, Gladden was convicted of the murder of Peter Bader and sentenced to life in prison.[25] George Gladden appealed his conviction on a technicality; however, the appeal was denied.[26] He would remain in prison for several years before eventually receiving a pardon from the Governor on December 30, 1884.[27]

Ringo was brought back to Austin and held in the more heavily secured Travis County jail. He was under the indictment of murder in Mason and the conviction from Lampasas for threatening the life of a deputy. At this time there were a large number of Texas outlaws in the Travis County jail. This is where Ringo met and became friends with John Wesley Hardin, the most notorious gunman in Western history. Hardin later recalled meeting Ringo: "In that jail I met some noted men. Bill Taylor, George Gladden, John Ringo, Manning Clements, Pipes and Herndon of the Bass gang, John Collins, Jeff Ake, and Brown Bowan."[28]

Ringo's motion for appeal on his conviction was finally heard by the appellate court in March 1877. At first, his conviction was affirmed by the appellate court. However, John Ringo's counsel asked for a rehearing due to an error in the trial judge's statement to the jury for their instructions.[29] On July 27, 1877, the court held that the jury should have been instructed that the alternative to a prison sentence for this type of crime was a fine. Therefore, since there was an error in the jury instructions, the conviction was reversed and the case remanded for a new trial.[30] A fire at the Mason courthouse during January 1877 destroyed many records, including Ringo's murder indictment.[31] On May 18, 1877, a substitute indictment was filed charging him with the murder of James Cheyney. The substitute indictment listed the witnesses as Hespert Nicholas, S.F. Bridges, and Martin Monan:

> The State of Texas
> vs
> John Ringo, Geo. Gladden, }Murder
> and others.
> On the names and by the authority of the State of Texas the Grand Jurors of Mason County in said State at the November Term A.D. 1876 . . . . on their oaths in said court present that John Ringo, George Gladden and others with force and arms

> in the county of Mason and state of Texas did heretofore to wit on 25th day of September A.D. 1875 then and there willfully feloniously and of their malice aforethought in and upon the body of James Chaney [sic] . . . make an assault and that they the said Ringo, Gladden and others with certain guns and pistols then and there charged with gunpowder and leaden balls and then and there in their hands . . . shoot off and discharge . . . into the body of said Chaney . . . strike penetrate and wound . . . in the right side giving to him the said Chaney one mortal wound . . . the said Ringo, Gladden and others . . . the said James Chaney did kill and murder against the peace and dignity of the state.[32]

John Ringo was still in jail waiting for his new trial on the charge of threatening the life of the Burnet sheriff and his deputy. On September 26, 1877, his case was continued by the court because the prosecutor lost all the papers concerning the crime.[33] While the Lampasas District Attorney was attempting to find or replace the papers in John Ringo's threat against Clymer and Strickland, Mason County issued an arrest warrant dated October 29, 1877.[34] The sheriff of Mason County went to Austin and took charge of Ringo on November 2 and brought him to Mason to answer the indictment of murder.[35]

Ringo was held in the Mason County jail until November 12, when he was arraigned. On that day the court ordered fifty men to be present on November 15 at 9:00 a.m. for jury selection.[36] The district attorney requested that the case be continued on November 15, apparently because he was having difficulty finding someone to testify.[37] Ringo was held in the Mason jail until November 19, when seven Texas Rangers transported him back to the Travis County jail.[38] Toward the end of November 1877, Ringo and Gladden were taken to Llano County. The *Austin Statesman* on December 4, 1877, reported his arrival in Austin:

> Distinguished Arrivals. - . . . George Gladden, recently committed to the State prison for life, will be confined to a felons cell here-to-day. John Ringo, charged with all manner of crimes, will cross the bridge this morning with Gladden. The pretty pair will rest for a time in the jail of this city. Sheriff Bozarth, of Llano, had these terrible fellows in charge. The people will be curious to see these two men, famous for the devilish deeds they have done.[39]

It is possible that Ringo and Gladden were taken to Llano because they faced potential charges in that county. Unfortunately, the Llano courthouse was destroyed in 1886 and it is impossible to verify if the two men had been charged with a crime in that county. In December 1878, Ringo's attorney filed a writ of habeas corpus and demanded that a bond be set for his client.[40] On December 20, 1877, John Ringo was brought by Texas Rangers back to Mason.[41] "The rangers, under Corporal Warren, arrived in Mason a few days before Christmas with John Ringo, who was tried by virtue of a writ of habeas corpus and the bond fixed at $2500. The bond was filed and Ringo set at liberty," the *Galveston Daily News* noted.[42] William Gamel put up 480 acres of land, worth $1200 dollars. The remainder was secured by promissory notes from R. K. Mosely, C. W. Wingfield, A. Foley, and George Antal. Ringo was released on bond and ordered to appear on March 10, 1878, to stand trial for the murder of James Cheyney.[43]

Although he had spent over a year in custody, once freed on bond it did not take Ringo long to get into more trouble. On February 4, 1878, John Ringo and Robert McIvers were arrested by five Texas Rangers in Junction City, Kimble County, for disturbing the peace. Nevertheless, the sheriff of Kimble County quickly released the men after taking a bond.[44] A little over a month later, on March 10th, the Mason court rescheduled to a later date the James Cheyney murder case.[45] The following month, Ringo personally appeared in Mason to swear out a written statement, claiming that several men were necessary witnesses that must be brought before the court and allowed to testify in order for him to have a fair trial:

> Before one Wilson Hey clerk of the county court and for said county personally appeared John Ringo who was after being duly sworn deposes and says that his case cannot safely go to trial without the testimony of Bud Faris, Audies Murchinson, Wm. Olney who reside in county of Llano, State of Texas and Carl Akard who resides in Badera Co.. Mark Hopkins who resides in Gillespie. Westly Johnson, Sam Monroe who reside in Kimble county. All of which reside in State of Texas and whose testimony is material for the defense. He therefore prays that attachments do issue to the sheriffs of the counties above named returnable to the District Court of Mason County on the 13th day of May A.D. 1877 [sic] that they may then and there testify in behalf of defendant.
>
> Signed John Ringo[46]

On May 13, 1878, the district attorney was apparently ready to have a murder trial for John Ringo, and he motioned the court for forty men to be brought in for jury selection. The court granted the motion and ordered the men to appear on the 15th of May.[47] Two days later, on May 15, rather than start jury selection in the case of the "State of Texas v. John Ringo," the district attorney requested that the case be dismissed because he could not procure testimony to make out the case.[48] With no witness either available or willing to testify against him, John Ringo's indictment for the murder of James Cheyney was dismissed. News of the dismissal was quickly reported throughout the state. The *Galveston News* exclaimed: "The case of John Ringo, charged with the murder of James Cheney, was, on motion of the district attorney, dismissed."[49] Nevertheless, Ringo was still awaiting his re-trial for threatening the life of Burnet Sheriff Clymer and Deputy Strickland in December 1875. He had been convicted, but the verdict was reversed and remanded on appeal. The case was continued until November 11, 1879, when it was finally dropped on the suggestion of the deaths of Ringo and Cooley.[50]

John J. Strickland, the former Burnet law officer who continuously pursued Ringo and Cooley, was himself sought by the law by 1881. Strickland had been convicted of a felony and placed in the penitentiary. On July 5, 1881, the *Burnet Bulletin* commented about the former sheriff of Burnet County:

> We learn that the notorious J. J. Strickland, once Sheriff of Burnet county; has escaped from the Penitentiary, and that Sheriff Tucker of Williamson has made three ineffectual attempts to arrest him. He is armed to the teeth.

Six months after his Mason County murder charge was dismissed, John Ringo, put his name in or was nominated to run for constable in Precinct #4 - Loyal Valley, Mason County. In November 1878, Ringo won the election by "capturing about two thirds of the votes cast."[51] With the Hoodoo War more or less over and many of his friends dead, in jail, or out of the state, Ringo began to settle down in Loyal Valley. After winning the election, on November 22, 1878, Ringo registered his brand in Mason County - a V on the left side.[52]

With everything seemingly going his way, John Ringo inexplicably left Texas. How long he worked as a constable and when he left Texas are not known for sure. Family of Joe Olney would later claim that John Ringo went west looking for Joe Olney to tell him that his brothers were under arrest in Llano, Texas.[53]

According to the account, Ringo located Olney, who was using the name Hill, either in Mexico or New Mexico, and both men returned to Texas to bust the Olney brothers from the jail. Once the men were freed, they all left Texas but split up near Ysleta, Texas.[54]

At Ysleta, John Ringo and Joe Olney headed across New Mexico for Arizona. It was a considerable distance to Arizona and danger from Indian attacks was a real possibility. Therefore, it appears that Ringo may have joined a wagon party that was heading west. One account places Ringo at Ysleta around November 1879, where he joined Jennie Parks Ringgold's father's wagon train that was heading for Silver City, New Mexico:

> By November, father and Price Cooper decided that it was safe for them to leave Ysleta. Just as they were ready to start, two men on horseback road up and asked to join the party. Both of the strangers were heavily armed, each carrying a Winchester, two revolvers, and two gun belts of cartridges. One of the horsemen was John Ringo . . . .[55]

During the journey the wagon train encountered Indian problems. At first, the men did not feel that they could make it back to Ysleta before they would be overrun by the Indians. Therefore, they circled the wagons and started to prepare for an attack. The women, however, feared that they would all be killed if they stayed, and they pleaded for the men to make a run for Ysleta for the children's sake. The men agreed and the party raced back to Ysleta without being attacked. After a short stay at the town, the wagon train proceeded to Silver City, New Mexico, arriving in mid-November 1879.

6

SAN SIMON COWBOYS

After leaving Texas, John Ringo drifted to the frontier territory of Arizona, which by 1879 was already experiencing depredations along the border with Mexico. Reports of border raids were common items in the local newspapers and complaints concerning the criminal activity were also sent to government officials. "Bands have been formed in Arizona which cross the Mexican frontier, in the district of El Setar. They steal horses in Arizona which they come to sell in Mexico, where they also steal cattle which they drive off to sell in Arizona. They commit all sorts of crimes," protested a Mexican official in December 1878.[1] Though the perpetrators of these crimes often were not identified, and Mexican bandits and Indians also committed their share of criminal acts, the cowboys, as they were called, received the lion's share of blame for the depredations committed in the area.

Yet, the term "cowboy" was used indiscriminately by newspapers and the public as a means of labeling the often unidentified outlaws committing crimes in Arizona and Mexico. "'Cow-boys' is a generic designation, originally applied to Cow drivers and herders in Western Texas, but the name has been corrupted in the Territories of New Mexico and Arizona and its local significance includes the lawless element that exists upon the border, who subsist by rapine plunder and highway robbery, and whose amusements are drunken orgies, and murder," noted E. B. Pomroy, the United States Attorney for Arizona.[2]

Ringo settled in the San Simon Valley, an area that stretched between Arizona and New Mexico and was home to a thriving community of outlaws and desperadoes. The area was also perfect for ranching, providing easy access to the markets for livestock in both Arizona and New Mexico, and a short distance to towns in Mexico. In addition, a railroad depot was established at the town of San Simon during 1880, which brought with it another possible outlet for the distribution of livestock.[3] Nonetheless, while the San Simon Valley was ideal for ranching and distribution of livestock, other individuals, who arrived before Ringo, had already discovered that the remote location was particularly suited for criminal activity. Bandits used the Mexican border to their advantage, raiding on one side, finding safe haven on the other.

The men who inhabited the San Simon Valley were a mixture of honest ranchers, cowboys, miners, hard cases that had unsavory resumes that included participation in Texas feuds and the Lincoln County War, stagecoach bandits, and rustlers. It was often difficult to differentiate between the law abiding settlers and the men committing crimes in the region. But occasionally the names of suspected desperadoes did surface in government correspondence or in territorial newspapers. One of the suspected outlaws was identified as Robert Martin and he was accused of being the leader of a party of outlaws that was committing crimes in both Arizona and Mexico.[4] When allegations of cowboy offenses in Arizona and Mexico reached Governor John C. Fremont, he was greatly surprised to hear that "bands of robbers" were organized in Arizona. At the time, Fremont was under the impression that Mexican bandits like Brigido Reyes, were mainly responsible for the problems occurring in the area.[5] However, by January 1881, the Governor finally accepted the apparent existence of Robert Martin's band of outlaws, which he estimated numbered from 100 to 120.[6] Although, it is likely that Fremont's estimation was greatly exaggerated.

Robert "Bob" Martin, alias Dutch Martin, was a notorious outlaw known during the 1870s for his outlawry throughout the Southwest in jurisdictions such as the state of Texas, the territories of New Mexico and Arizona, and the country of Mexico.[7] Yet,

Bob Martin's activities are rarely discussed by historians or writers, and little is known about his background. Martin was suspected of complicity in a number of crimes involving members of the Jesse Evans gang in New Mexico, active participants of the Lincoln County War, and he was considered an associate of John Kinney, "The King of the Rustlers."[8] Bob Martin may have been one of the "Silver City Rangers," a group of New Mexicans that descended upon San Elizario, Texas, during the El Paso Salt War, which resulted in the revenge killings of several Mexicans.[9] Four months later, in May 1878, Bob Martin and William Bresnaham, another possible El Paso Salt War veteran, who was later known in Arizona as "Curly Bill Brocius," were arrested in El Paso Del Norte, Mexico, for an attempted robbery that occurred across the border in Texas.[10] The two outlaws were extradited by Mexican officials when U.S. Army officers paid a reward of $75.00 for their capture.[11]

In September 1878, Bob Martin and Curly Bill were convicted of attempted robbery, and sentenced to five years in prison.[12] While awaiting an appeal of their conviction, both men escaped from the custody of Texas Rangers in November 1878 and apparently quickly made their way to Arizona.[13] Bob Martin was shot in the head and killed near Stein's Pass in the San Simon Valley on November 22, 1880.[14] Ironically, Bob Martin, the man proclaimed to be the leader of 120 cowboys, was killed by a gang of four rustlers.[15] By early 1881, Curly Bill Brocius had gained notoriety for killing Tombstone Marshal Fred White on October 28, 1880.[16] After that well-publicized incident, Curly Bill was largely considered the most famous outlaw in Arizona and one of the leaders of the cowboys.

Tombstone folklore often portrays the cowboys of Arizona as one organized gang, whose mission was to wreak havoc and commit crimes in both the United States and Mexico.[17] Nevertheless, while cowboys congregated in the same places, drank and caroused in the same saloons, and even freely associated with one another at times, only rumor and innuendo suggest that these men were part of a single gang. In actuality, some bad guys would occasionally get together, decide to steal cattle or rob a stage or commit some other crime, and then go their separate ways. There were several factions of men commonly referred to as cowboys that roamed throughout the area and, as Bob Martin's death clearly illustrates, these groups had no special allegiance to any one man or gang. Some of these men, like Charles Ray, "alias Pony Deal or Diehl," were known outlaws before arriving in Arizona.[18] Pony Deal was a veteran of the Lincoln County War, a probable participant in the El Paso Salt War, and a suspected cattle thief and murderer.[19] In contrast, Sherman McMasters was a Texas Ranger before coming to Arizona. In fact, Bob Martin and Curly Bill escaped from McMasters' Ranger detachment in Ysleta, Texas, during November 1878.[20] But in the West, it was not uncommon for a man to be a law officer in one place and an outlaw in the next. Together, Deal and McMasters were accused of holding up at least one stage in Arizona. By late 1881, Sherman McMasters switched sides again, riding with rogue Deputy U.S. Marshal Wyatt Earp and his posse in the so-called "Vendetta" ride during March 1882.

Other men seem to have come to the area to work as miners before turning to a life of outlawry. Will and Milt Hicks were apparently miners in Grant County, New Mexico, for a time.[21] However, the brothers, later reported as members of Curly Bill's gang, both were charged in 1881 with cattle theft, before leaving Arizona to avoid arrest.[22] Arthur Boucher, alias William Grounds, alias "Billy the Kid," also started out in the New Mexico town of Shakespeare working as a miner in 1880, but he too soon changed vocations.[23] Grounds later was suspected of criminal activity and indicted for cattle theft in November 1881, along with Curly Bill Brocius, F. C. "Led" Moore, and Zwing Hunt, another transplanted Texan.[24] William Tettenbaum, alias Russian Bill, a thirty year-old immigrant from Russia, likewise started out in the Shakespeare district as a miner in 1880.[25] A little over a year later, during November 1881, Russian Bill and another would-be cowboy hard case, Sandy King, were lynched by vigilantes in the mining town of Shakespeare.[26]

Men like William Stark and Al George initially intended to pass through Arizona while traveling to California but, upon reaching the San Simon Valley, decided to stay and start a ranch.[27] Both men were later charged with cattle theft and indicted for larceny.[28] Still, some cowboys like Dick Lloyd, though somewhat rowdy and reckless while drinking whiskey, came to Arizona driving cattle and stayed in the area working on ranches, presumably as honest cowboys.[29] John Ringo, once in Arizona, blended in quickly with the often rowdy and violent rural cowboy element. On December 9, 1879, Ringo shot Louis Hancock in a Safford saloon for refusing to drink whiskey with him. The following article about the incident was published by the *Arizona Daily Star*:

> More of it.
>
> Last Tuesday night a shooting took place at Safford in which Louis Hancock was shot by John Ringo. It appears Ringo wanted Hancock to take a drink of whiskey, and he refused saying he would prefer beer. Ringo struck him over the head with his pistol and then fired, the ball taking effect in the lower end of the left ear, and passed through the fleshy part of the neck, half inch more in the neck, would have killed him. Ringo is under arrest.[30]

"Moral - when you drink with a man that is on a shoot, and he says whiskey, don't you say beer," warned the *Arizona Daily Star*.[31] Louis Hancock, a 31 year-old Texas-born laborer living in Safford with his brother-in-law, James Hayes, learned this lesson the hard way.[32] After recovering from the shooting, which likely left a nasty scar as a reminder of his encounter with Ringo, Hancock continued to live in Safford for several years. Nevertheless, writers have repeatedly claimed that Hancock was killed by Ringo and, in most instances, the encounter is portrayed as occurring in Tombstone.[33]

Ringo was arrested but was released on bond. His case was scheduled to be presented to the Pima County Grand Jury in Tucson during March 1880. When Ringo's court date was about a week away, the cowboy decided that he could not appear before the grand jury on the scheduled date. Instead, on March 3, 1880, he wrote a letter to Sheriff Charles Shibell of Tucson to explained why he could not appear:

> Dear Sir, being under Bond for my appearance before the Grand jury of Pima Co., I write to let you know why I can not appear - I got shot through the foot and it is impossible for me to travel for awhile. If you get any papers for me, and will let me know, I will attend to them at once. As I wish to live here I do not wish to put you to any unnecessary trouble, nor do I wish to bring extra trouble on myself. Please let the Dist Atty know why I do not appear, for I am very anxious that there is no forfeiture taken on the Bond.[34]

Hugh Farley, District Attorney for Pima County, clearly was not satisfied with Ringo's non-appearance before the grand jury. On March 11, 1880, the District Attorney for Pima County requested the court to forfeit Ringo's bond since he failed to appear before the grand jury and asked that a bench warrant be issued for his arrest. "On motion of Hugh Farley, Esq. Dist. Atty. it was ordered that as Deft. had failed to appear during the session of the Grand Jury that his Bond be, and this same hereby declared forfeited, and that a Bench Warrant be issued for the arrest of said Deft.," noted the court's docket entry.[35] The court granted the prosecutor's motion and a capias warrant was issued for Ringo. How the case was settled is not known.

Some writers, based upon the "Ringo letter," have mistakenly claimed that John Ringo had shot himself in the foot. However, the letter provides no explanation concerning how Ringo was shot or whether the wound was self-inflicted. What the letter does state is Ringo's wish to live in Arizona, presumably as a more or less law-abiding citizen, rather than a wanted man. Still, his presence in the San Simon area, along with later allegations that he was a leader of a cowboy gang, have caused many writers and historians to conclude that he was involved in the cowboy depredations occurring in the area. Ringo's actions during the year of 1880, however, provide little evidence that he was the leader of a gang of cowboys raiding across the Mexican border.

Shortly after his failure to appear before the Pima County Grand Jury, Ringo surfaced on April 2, 1880, in Shakespeare, New Mexico, where he and a man named M. C. Blakely sold for $1000, "an undivided two thirds 2/3 interest in the Blakely Mining Claim situated in the San Simon Mining district" to John E. Price, of Shakespeare, New Mexico.[36] Five days later, on April 7, 1880, Ringo was again in Shakespeare, where he executed a power of attorney to James B. Price of Jefferson City, Missouri. According to county records, the power of attorney provided that Price had six months to sell the "Sydney Johnson Mine," located in the San Simon mining district, for not less than $2000, and that Price could personally keep any money paid for the mining claim over that amount.[37]

Less than a month later, on May 4, 1880, William Grounds wrote a letter to his mother in Texas, in which he discussed buying a horse from John Ringo. "Ma I got 2 horses. I bought one the other day and paid $65.00 for him. I got him from John Ringo the man that was with Scott Cooley that time up at Scald Springs," noted Grounds.[38] The young Texan no doubt was aware of John Ringo's Texas reputation.

Around July 12, 1880, John Ringo, Joe Hill, Ike Clanton, and George Turner drove some cattle worth $2000 dollars to the San Carlos Indian Reservation from New Mexico. Upon reaching the reservation, the contractor temporarily refused to purchase the livestock because he claimed that no duty had been paid on the cattle. Nonetheless, Newton, the contractor, eventually did buy the cattle but likely used the cowboys' failure to pay duty on the cattle as a means to obtain the livestock at a lower price.[39] After selling some stock at the Indian reservation, the men went to the nearby town of Safford to blow off some steam. A letter written by J. B. Collins to Barton Jacobs of Tucson, describes their activities:

> I write to ask you to use your influence in getting the parties who tried to wreck your property this week, and who insulted and endangered the lives of your employees at the mill at Safford. I will now fire you a sketch of their doings as I learn them partly from your brother and others. Joe Hill, who they call their King Pin, Dutch Gingo [Ringo] and Ike Clanton carried about $1500.00 or $2000.00 worth of cattle to San Carlos. It seems that the contractor found out that these cattle came into San Simon without paying duty, and he caused them much trouble as he would not purchase until he heard from Gov officer at Silver City who has jurisdiction over that section. I expect Newton made a point on this and got the cattle low of them, which angered them very much. They got here about the 12th, and after shooting in Detrys house a few times, they paid me a visit and shot a couple of times. I took Clanton's pistol away from him & told him and his Dutch friend if they make any more brakes I would use my shotgun on them. So they concluded that Safford was a better field for their operations. They reached there in due time and commenced operation by shooting the lamps in John Harrison's saloon and shooting through Mr. Bill Kirkland's house. Then they opened up in Franklin's store. Shot at everything they fancied, made your brother pour out drinks which they would stir with the muzzles of their pistol. Tried to compel Wickersham to dance for them by pulling a pistol on

> him, but it was left for them to have their jolliest time by shooting fifty shots into your mill & make one of your employees furnish the cartridges. They made Katz shut off water and then compelled him to get up in a corner with a lot of Mexicans and not leave on the pain of being shot, and they wanted to know of Joe Cottrall which one of the party he wished them to kill. Hill the King Pin and Clanton left for Soloman's where they were said to have another jollification, and they have Turner under arrest waiting for the return of the J.P.. Now there are but 4 all told and it is too bad that they cannot get put through, and I think you have the cause & power to do it. I could not get a single man here to help me arrest them, but I am good for all four of them here. I trust you will see fit after due enquiry to get the Sheriff to send & bring the gang into Tucson and have them put through. It will be Gods blessing for this Valley to get rid of them. You must excuse this long letter, I feel like if young Katz was my brother I would not let up on them while the law would reach them.[40]

A. M. Franklin, the manager of the store that was the scene of the cowboys' Safford shooting spree, later recalled fondly several of his encounters with John Ringo. In one account, Franklin was driving some cattle near Galeyville and lost part of his herd in a bad storm. When he had difficulty locating the herd he went to the nearby town of Galeyville, where he saw John Ringo and told him about the lost cattle.

> On a trail drive through a canyon towards Galleyville. Went into Galleyville. I saw John Ringo, Curly Bill and 1/2 dozen others watching me. I espied John Ringo, I spoke to him - he and I were old friends. In Fact he once saved my life. "Hello,

> kid", he answered, "what are you doing here"? I told him I lost some cattle and come to see if I could get help finding them . . . well, I'll tell you what you do. you give me a hundred dollars of your money and I will try and get those steers rounded up. . .". Three days later John Ringo and his men came riding into camp at - with all but nine of the cattle.[41]

According to Franklin, Ringo and the other cowboys apparently did not have too much trouble finding the cattle. Of course, Franklin surmised that Ringo and the others had probably taken the cattle in the first place. Another Franklin recollection provides the only known description of John Ringo's shooting ability:

> I knew Ringo well. He was about 6 ft. 2 in., light but not a blond with the most pathetic blue eyes I ever saw. A cheerful good looking fellow with a half eyes cynical smile, and a powerful mind. When he said a thing, he meant it and every one knew it. In that was his strength. Of course, he had his pistols too. He could put two beer bottles, mouth towards him, let his pistols hang from his fingers, then with a dexterous jerk, I don't know just how, He would have them in position and break both bottles at once. His main stunt however, was shooting from his hip.[42]

In one article, Franklin added that Ringo "made a bet that he would send the bullets into the open necks of the bottles twice out of five, at 50 feet. He won many of a bet of this kind."[43] A. M. Franklin seemed to take delight in recalling Ringo's shooting abilities, but he took special pride in telling accounts of how the notorious cowboy had, in Franklin's words, "saved my life several times."[44] Franklin commented:

> Once I remember a fellow had it in for me and when I went in a saloon he began to cuss me out. He tried in every way he could to make me answer back. Of course, he was armed and all he wanted was an excuse. About that time Ringo came in. He heard enough to catch the drift then sauntered to the bar, slapped down his money and announced, "All of Franklin & my friends have a drink." Everyone drank the obnoxious fellow included.
>
> At another time a crowd was trying to start something in the store, Ringo took in the situation at a glance. Stepping up besides me & slamming his gun on the counter, he remarked, "If there is going to be a row I think I would like to be in on it." Every one suddenly had business elsewhere.[45]

Written before the popular books on Tombstone were published, Franklin's reminiscence can be neither proved nor refuted. There is no way to confirm Franklin's recollections of Ringo's shooting ability. Although, one New Mexico newspaper shortly after Ringo's death remarked how the cowboy had put on fine shooting exhibitions while in Shakespeare, New Mexico.[46] Another old-timer claimed that John Ringo "was admittedly the best pistol shot in the country."[47] Breakenridge simply commented that Ringo was a good shot.[48] Many old-timers later recalled John Ringo's imposing presence, so it's understandable that men might think twice before engaging in a row with Ringo - even more so if they knew of Ringo's encounter with Louis Hancock, who refused to drink Whiskey with the cowboy and ended up shot.

Ike Clanton, who along with Ringo had participated in the "treeing" (tormenting for fun) of Maxey and Safford, a few weeks later came to the growing boom town of Tombstone. Like Ringo, Clanton only visited Tombstone occasionally. One of his visits inspired the following item in the *Daily Epitaph* of August 6, 1880:

> FROM NEW MEXICO
>
> From Mr. I. Clanton, who arrived in Tombstone yesterday from New Mexico, we learn that emigrants from Colorado, Texas and Kansas are rapidly coming into the Territory. The mines in the Victorio District are looking exceedingly well. A short time since a new camp, known as San Simon, was opened, and from present indications, will soon eclipse any other in the Territory. The leads are large, averaging 125 ounces to the ton. The camp is located about eighty miles east of Tombstone. While at Fort Bowie, Mr. Clanton was informed, on what he considered reliable authority, that a portion of Victorio's band had returned to New Mexico and were at present in the Black Range. He brought with him fifty head of beef cattle for the Tombstone market, being five days on the road from San Simon.

Joseph Isaac "Ike" Clanton, together with his brothers Phineas ("Phin") and William ("Billy") and his father Newman H. Clanton, arrived in southeastern Arizona from California in 1873. The clan settled first in the Gila Valley, where they farmed and raised cattle and where Newman Clanton tried without success to promote a new town called "Clantonville."[49] By 1878 the Clantons had moved to a ranch in the San Pedro Valley. Their place was about four miles south of Charleston. During 1880, Ike began spending time at San Simon and its vicinity. It appears that both John Ringo and Ike Clanton had aspirations for the San Simon area, and the news report of the growing camp may have been designed to help further that goal.

Tombstone's origins date back to 1877 when Ed Schieffelin discovered a rich silver lode in southeastern Arizona. He named his first claim "Tombstone." The ore lay beneath a high, rolling, mostly treeless desert. In 1878, after hearing of Schieffelin's silver discoveries, hopeful prospectors trekked to the Tombstone district. First a haphazard collection of tents, the camp grew rapidly, and more substantial buildings were constructed. The Pima County Board of Supervisors incorporated Tombstone as a "village" in November 1879.

About December 1, 1879, former Dodge City lawman Wyatt Earp and his common-law wife, Celia Ann "Mattie" Blaylock, slowly drove their wagon into Tombstone.[50] In two other wagons rode Wyatt's older brothers, Virgil and James, and their wives, Allie and Bessie. Morgan Earp and his wife, Louisa, would come to town a few months later. Contrary to popular legend, Wyatt did not have a big reputation stemming from his Dodge City days when he first came to Arizona, and his name was unknown to the average citizen in southern Arizona. Before leaving Prescott, the territorial capital, Virgil Earp was appointed deputy United States marshal by U.S. Marshal Crawley Dake.[51]

Doc Holliday, a dentist turned gambler, had been a friend of Wyatt Earp since their days in Dodge City.[52] Like the Earps, Doc migrated west to Arizona. In June 1880, the twenty-nine year old was living in Prescott, Arizona.[53] Also like the Earps, Doc's name was unfamiliar to southern Arizonans when he first came on the scene. Holliday suffered from tuberculosis and compounded his health problems by drinking heavily. Surly and argumentative, he often got into altercations in the saloons and gambling joints he frequented. Thin and frail, Doc was quick to pull a gun when he became involved in a confrontation.

On July 25, 1880, Wyatt Earp and his brothers Virgil and Morgan joined a group of soldiers led by Lieutenant Joseph Henry Hurst, a brevet captain, who were trailing thieves in possession of six mules taken from Camp Rucker (located in the Chiricahua Mountains forty miles east of Tombstone). Since Virgil was a deputy U.S. marshal, he had jurisdiction over cases involving theft of government property. The party followed the trail left by the stolen mules until they reached a ranch on the Babocomari River (about fifteen miles west of Tombstone). The ranch was owned by brothers Tom and Frank

McLaury, who were originally from New York. They migrated west to Fort Worth, Texas, where their older brother, William, was practicing law. The McLaurys were friends of the Clantons and later moved their ranch to the Sulphur Springs Valley. By 1881, Tom and Frank McLaury shared business interests with Ike Clanton.[54] After trailing the mules to a location near the McLaury ranch, they found Frank McLaury there, and Lieutenant Hurst had a private conversation with him. Then the lieutenant and his men went on their way.

A few days later, Hurst announced the following in the *Daily Epitaph*, "A reward of $25 will be paid for the arrest, trial and conviction of each of the thieves who stole six (6) Government mules from Camp John A. Rucker, A.T., on the night of July 21st, 1880."[55] Hurst identified the suspected thieves as Pony Diehl, A. T. Hansbrough, and Mac Demasters, who was probably Sherman McMasters. "It is known that the thieves were aided in the secretion of the stolen animals by parties known by the names of FRANK PATTERSON, FRANK M'LOWERY, JIM JOHNSON, and other parties unknown," Hurst further alleged.[56] Immediately Frank McLaury responded to Hurst's accusation:

> On the morning of July 25th, 1880, this man Hurst came to my ranch with an escort of soldiers, accompanied by several citizens, and he took me aside and told me, in substance, that he had had stolen from Camp Rucker six government mules, stated that they were stolen by Pony Deihl, A. S. Hansbrough and Mac Masters. I told him I had not seen either the men or the stock. He asked me if I did not know the men. I replied to him that I knew two of the men. He insisted that I should do what I could to see these men and have the stock returned, and to tell the men that he did not want to make any arrests. I told him I would do what I could to assist him. In the course of the next day I saw Deihl and told him exactly what Hurst had told me. Deihl replied

> that he knew nothing of the stock and had not seen it. I then saw Hurst and told him what Deihl had said to me, and I interested myself no farther about it. The next thing I heard of was the placard which I refer to wherein my name is spoken of as a thief. If J. H. Hurst was a gentleman, or if I could appeal to the courts for protection, I would proceed differently in this matter, but Hurst is irresponsible and I have but one course to pursue, and that is to publish to the world that J. H. Hurst, 1st. Lieut. 12th Inft., A.A.Q.M., is a coward, a vagabond, a rascal and a malicious liar. This base and unmanly action is the result of cowardice, for instead of hunting the stock himself he tried to get others to do it, and when they could not find it, in order to cover up for his own wrong acts, he attempted to traduce the character and reputation of honest men. My name is well known in Arizona, and thank God this is the first time in my life the name of dishonesty was ever attached to me. Perhaps when the matter is ventilated it will be found that the Hon. Lieut. Hurst has stolen those mules and sold them, for a coward! will steal, and a man who can publish the placard that bears his name is a coward. I am willing to let the people of Arizona decide who is right. Frank McLaury. Barbacomori, August 2, 1880.[57]

The mules were never recovered, no arrests were made, and the matter was quietly dropped. Wyatt later stated that the incident created bad blood between the McLaurys and the Earps.[58] It was later considered that this was the Earps' first encounter with the so-called cowboys. Shortly following the mule incident at the McLaury ranch, Wyatt Earp was appointed a deputy sheriff for Pima County.[59]

In late October 1880, William "Curly Bill" Brocius, a San Simon cowboy, killed Tombstone Marshal Fred White.[60] News reports later alleged that a group of five cowboys, who were the same men that had treed the town of San Simon a few days earlier by taking over a locomotive at the a train depot, "began firing at the moon and stars" on Allen Street.[61] The *Arizona Daily Star* remarked, "Marshal White appeared on the scene and seized one of the cow-boys, who is known as Curley, and demanded his surrender."[62] White tried to jerk the gun from the cowboy's hand, but the six-gun suddenly discharged, hitting White in the groin. Deputy Sheriff Wyatt Earp, who had also responded to the shots in the street, immediately knocked the cowboy down and arrested him. Also arrested with Curly Bill were Andrew Ames, Edward Collins, Jim Johnson, Dick Lloyd, and Frank Patterson.[63] Ames was later fined forty dollars for carrying a concealed weapon and discharging it on the street. Collins, Johnson, and Lloyd were fined ten dollars each for carrying a concealed weapon. Patterson was discharged with no fine because it appeared to the court that he had tried to prevent the disturbance.[64] Curly Bill was transported to Tucson and placed in the Pima County jail to await the disposition of his case.[65] On December 27, 1880, Curly Bill was released after Justice Peter Neugass, after hearing eyewitness testimony, concluded the shooting was an accident.[66] Wyatt Earp's testimony and evidence that Fred White made a death bed statement that the shooting had been an accident proved crucial in the Justice's decision.[67]

7

ELECTION SCANDAL

The 1880 Pima County election was scheduled to be held on November 2, and as the election day approached, Ringo turned his attention to politics. For two days at the end of August 1880, John Ringo was at Tucson for the Democratic County Convention, where he expected to be a delegate for the San Simon Cienega district.[1]

After the convention was called to order by the Chairman of the Democratic County Committee, five men were appointed to the Committee on Credentials to report the names of the men who were entitled to seats at the convention. For the San Simon Cienega district, James Speedy and John Ringo were selected to be delegates at the convention.[2] At first, an objection to Ringo's selection was entered because he had no Arizona residence, but on further "examination the Committee recommended admission."[3]

No record has been found of any allegations made at the Democratic Convention that accused Ringo of being an outlaw, rustler, or the leader of a gang of San Simon cowboys. But, then, no reference to Ringo's shooting of Louis Hancock at Safford in December 1879 was apparently made at the convention either. Ringo's recommendation as a delegate was allowed even though the Committee on Credentials included James Hayes of Safford, who was Louis Hancock's brother-in-law.[4]

Two months later, in October, the Pima County Board of Supervisors met to designate polling places and appoint inspectors and judges for each precinct. At Precinct 27, for San Simon Cienega, the polling place was to be at Joe Hill's house and election officials for the precinct included Ike Clanton, John Ringo, and A. H. Thompson.[5] Yet, concerns over residency continued to be expressed regarding the San Simon Cienega polling place and the election officials. In late October 1880, the Pima County Board made the following order: "It appearing to the Board that Joseph Hill has removed from the San Simon Cienega Dist. On motion ordered that J. C. Clanton be and hereby is appointed registering officer instead of said Hill removed from the district."[6] A few days later, the Board of Supervisors "ordered that the polling place be changed from the house of Joe Hill to that of J. Magill."[7] Moreover, since the Board still had doubts over the residency of the election officials, it revoked its previous order appointing Clanton, Ringo, and Thompson, and appointed two different men as polling officials: "On motion the former order appointing inspector and judges of elections for precinct no. 27 is hereby revoked there being some doubt whether the persons so appointed are residents of Arizona and J. Magill is hereby appointed inspector and Mr. Hughes and Mr. Hary judges of election for said precinct no. 27."[8]

A day before the county election, on November 1, 1880, Ringo and Clanton rode to Shakespeare to record a ranch claim:

> Notice
>
> Know all men by these presence that We the undersigned have this day located for grazing and farming purposes 320 three hundred and twenty acres of land lying in what is called the Animas Valley located about five miles West of the Animas Mountains about 28 Miles North of the Gaulupa Canyon at the mouth of a cienega running into the Maur Valley from the West, and shall be known as the Alfalfa Ranch or Cienega this first day of November A.D. 1880.
>
> John Ringo[9]
> J.I. Clanton
>
> Witness
> W.J. Patrick
> Fr. K. Johnson

The following day, on November 2, 1880, the Pima County election was held. The incumbent Pima County sheriff, Charles Shibell,

Ike Clanton and John Ringo formed a ranch in the Animas Valley.

a Democrat, was opposed in the election by Republican Robert Paul, a long-time employee of Wells, Fargo & Company. The preliminary count indicated that Charles Shibell had won a third term as Pima County sheriff by the narrow margin of about forty votes.[10] On November 15, 1880, the Pima County Board of Supervisors announced the final vote count for sheriff (1,726 votes for Charles Shibell, 1,684 for Bob Paul) and declared Shibell the winner of the election. He was sworn in for the third time on January 1, 1881.[11]

On December 18 Bob Paul filed an appeal with the district court in Tucson claiming fraud in San Simon and other precincts.[12] The San Simon tally was blatantly off, and Paul contended that someone had stuffed the ballot box. Since irregularities were common in elections held in territorial Arizona, his action was not viewed as frivolous. The *Tombstone Epitaph* for November 7 had noted:

> **No Intimidation**
>
> At the recent election 104 votes were cast at San Simon precinct, 103 of which were Democratic. The odd vote is said to have been cast by a Texas cowboy, who, when questioned as to why he was voting the Republican ticket said: "Well, I want to show those fellows that there wasn't any intimidation at this precinct."

On January 29, 1881, Judge Charles French threw out the entire San Simon vote (and a few ballots from other locales) and ruled that Robert Paul had won the election for Pima County sheriff, 1,684 votes to 1,628.[13] Charles Shibell appealed but to no avail. On April 12, 1881, the Arizona Supreme Court upheld the lower court's decision, and Paul assumed the office of sheriff on April 25, 1881.[14]

For a brief moment it appears that John Ringo, Ike Clanton, and Joe Hill had accomplished what clearly was their primary objective during the election of 1880: assuming local control over the San Simon area. As a result of the Pima County elections, Ike Clanton had been elected Justice of the Peace and Joe Hill was named constable for

San Simon.[15] Nonetheless, their political and legal control over the rural Arizona area was snuffed out nearly three months later when Judge Charles French threw out the entire San Simon vote. Following the election in November, not much is known about John Ringo's whereabouts for the remainder of 1880. His sisters later recalled that he had visited them "in San Jose in 1880 and was a fine upright gentleman."[16] The exact date of any visit to California is not known.

On February 1, 1881, the Arizona legislature created Cochise County by shearing off a large chunk of eastern Pima County.[17] No county election was scheduled to be held until November 1882. Any further political ambitions that John Ringo and Ike Clanton may have had for the San Simon area were promptly postponed while they were forced to wait two years for the first Cochise County election to take place.

The creation of the new county, however, apparently did unexpectedly benefit John Ringo. Judge Charles French ordered that all cases before the district court that originated in the newly organized Cochise County were to be handled by the district court of that county.[18] "All cases before the District Court which originated in the territory now embraced in Cochise County have, by order of Judge French, been transferred to the District Court for that county," the *Arizona Weekly Star* noted on March 24, 1881. Three days later, on March 27, 1881, the *Arizona Weekly Citizen* reported that the district attorney for Pima County had dismissed the following case against John Ringo: "Territory vs. John Ringo and Ben Schuster - Nolle pros entered." After the charges were dropped, the Cochise County District Court did not reinstate the case. It is likely that the complaint against Ringo and Schuster, along with other cases from this period, simply were misplaced and forgotten in the transition.[19]

Shortly after the district attorney dismissed the case against John Ringo, the notorious cowboy left Arizona, heading east toward Texas. By May 2, 1881, Ringo arrived in Austin and likely stopped to visit friends in the area. While in Austin, Ringo was arrested by city marshal Ben Thompson on May 2, 1881. The *Austin Daily Statesman*, reported the details of the incident the following day:

> Mr. John Ringo was in town early Sunday morning and was passing his time down in a house in the jungles. Along about 4 o'clock he missed his purse. and stepping out in the hall where some three or four of Austin's nice young men were seated, he came down upon them with his little pistol and commanded them to "up hands," he quietly searched the whole tea party. Not finding his purse. He smiled beamingly upon the young men, and retired to his room while they quietly slid out and reported the facts to the police. Marshal Thompson in person went down to the house, but was refused admission to the room, whereupon he cheerfully kicked open the door, and to the infinite disgust of Mr. Ringo, scooped him in. He was disarmed, and officer Chenneville, who had arrived, march him to the station, and yesterday he was fined $5 and cost for disturbing the peace, and $25 and costs for carrying a pistol. He settled with the city and left a wiser if not sadder man.[20]

While the newspaper managed to use his correct name, the court did not. The arrest report for May 2 stated, "John Ringold," was arrested at 6:00 a.m. for carrying a pistol and disturbing the peace. His occupation was listed as a stockman.[21] When Ringo left Texas is uncertain. However, it is likely that after leaving Texas, Ringo went north to visit family and friends in Missouri. By July 1881, the *Tombstone Nugget* announced that John Ringo had returned to Arizona from Liberty, Missouri, and had checked into the Grand Hotel.[22]

8

BORDER RAIDS

As early as December 1878, complaints were received by territorial officials and the U.S. government about bands of robbers committing crimes in Mexico.[1] But for over two years nothing had been done about it. A large part of the problem was that neither the federal government nor the territorial government had jurisdiction over crimes committed in another country. Additionally, little could be done to capture suspected criminals who were identified only as cowboys. When suspects were occasionally named, unless they were publicly identified as thieves in newspapers, few people even knew about the accusations. While complaints were made by Mexican officials and newspapers published articles about border raids into Mexico committed by cowboys from San Simon, not many people in Arizona or New Mexico cared.

The problems in the San Simon area concerning horse and cattle thieves, however, were not restricted solely to border raids. W. J. Crosby of Shakespeare, New Mexico, wrote a letter to the editor of the *Arizona Daily Star* on November 25, 1880, reporting on the current conditions in the San Simon area.

Horse and Cattle Thieves

From W. J. Crosby we receive the following note:

SHAKESPEARE, N.M.
Nov. 25,1880
EDITOR STAR - During the past month a number of horses and mules have been stolen at intervals from

> various sections of this county, the latest being eight head from Leiterdorf, and several head from San Simon, in Pima county, fourteen head were stolen from the Stage Company at Mason's ranch last week. A posse of San Simon ranchmen, consisting of Messrs. Turner, Marten [Martin], Colt, Raymond and a Mexican named Dominguez, started in pursuit on Monday last following the trail to near Dowling's ranch, and after a hard fight, lasting from daylight yesterday until three o'clock in the after noon, they succeeded in killing one of the thieves whose name is given as King, and seriously wounding another named Bill Smith. King was a cripple and leader of the gang, which were four in number. The posse captured 22 head of stock and returned with them. They will be well rewarded for this courageous action. They propose capturing the two remaining desperadoes and some 14 head of stock, known to have been stolen by the same gang.
>
> This may be a useful lesson to horse and cattle thieves throughout this section. Ropes and trees are very convenient in the neighborhood.

Crosby's letter turned out to be inaccurate and premature as a second dispatch from Shakespeare corrected the earlier report. "The report telegraphed to the Star Nov. 24th, from Shakespeare, of the killing of King and wounding of Bill Smith, alleged horse thieves of San Simon, which was stated to have occurred at Downing's ranch, Animas mountains, proves to have been false," the *Arizona Daily Star* reported.[2] The article commented that the fight that had occurred between the San Simon ranchmen and the horse thieves was bloodless. According to the *Star's* report, "Turner and Martin, when returning to San Simon from Shakespeare on Friday evening last, were ambushed at Granite Gap by King and his gang. Martin was killed."[3]

Bob Martin's death illustrates the complexity of the situation in the San Simon area. Martin had been identified in official complaints from Mexican officials to the U.S. government and Arizona territorial government as the leader of a gang of San Simon cowboys that were raiding across the Mexican border stealing livestock.[4] Nevertheless, contemporary newspaper articles referred to Martin and the others as "San Simon ranchers," who had organized to fight off rustlers.[5] While it's possible that Bob Martin and other cowboys in the San Simon area raided the border of Mexico to obtain livestock on occasions, most allegations were generally based on rumor and innuendo, rather than firm evidence. Still, it would have been an easy and quick way to build a herd of cattle to stock a ranch in the San Simon Valley. Once the livestock was in the United States, it would have been difficult, if not impossible, to recover the stock because alleged crimes in Mexico were not crimes in the United States.[6] In actuality, the only real recourse that Mexicans had to recover cattle or horses was to forcibly take back the stolen livestock. Of course, it was also necessary for Americans to use the same self-help methods to regain livestock stolen by Mexicans.

This appears to have been the situation along the Arizona and New Mexico border. Often gun battles would be waged before one party or the other would retreat. It also appears that there were other cowboys, perhaps less ambitious, that preferred to steal livestock from ranches in Arizona and New Mexico, rather than journey into Mexico. These individuals were not picky when it came to where the cattle originated or who currently had possession of the livestock.

Shortly after John Ringo's arrest by Ben Thompson for carrying a pistol and disturbing the peace in Texas, the border problems between the cowboys in Arizona and Mexican citizens in Sonora escalated greatly with deadly results. On May 13, 1881, Ringo's friend George Turner, Galeyille butcher Al McCallister, and two others went into Mexico to obtain cattle in order to fulfill a contract to furnish beef to the army at Fort Bowie. As the men were returning to Arizona they were attacked near Fronteras, Mexico, and killed by Mexican citizens led by Jose Juan Vasquez, who suspected that the Americans had stolen the cattle in Mexico and were attempting to drive them into Arizona. "These four men had rounded up a band of cattle and were camped for the night, when they were surrounded by the Mexicans and their surrender demanded," proclaimed a first hand report printed by the *Nugget* on June 9. When the Americans responded to the surrender demand with gunfire, their volley was "returned with such deadly effect that three of the party fell dead, the other lived long enough to kill Vasquez," according to one witness.[7]

The news of the Fronteras killings and especially McAllister's death, started rumors in Arizona that friends of McAllister might retaliate against the town of Fronteras. In early June 1881, one Army report declared that "forty or fifty Cowboys of bad character are ready for action between Los Animas and Galeyville."[8] Fearing an invasion of Mexico was imminent, Mexican federal troops led by Commandant Filipe Neri were prepared to repel the attack at the border. As tension along the border grew, newspapers in Arizona further provoked the situation by publishing unsubstantiated rumors that seventy cowboys were preparing to raid Mexico to avenge the death of the four cowboys who had been killed.[9] Whether the gossip was a hoax or not, rumors of unconfirmed attacks on Mexico began to surface even though the United States Army reported that there was no evidence of raiding parties either to or from Mexico.[10]

J. W. Evans, a deputy United States marshal in Tucson, reported one such uncorroborated rumor: "It is reported that a few days since that they [the cowboys] went into Fronteras Sonora and killed about forty mexicans in the retaliation for the killing of four of their companions by the mexicans some weeks since."[11] About a week later, on June 24, Sonoran Governor Luis Torres wrote to Deputy Evans concerning the impending invasion: "The time has come when your aid will be of great importance to me as it was in the time of Brigido Reyes and his crowd. I mean the invasion intended by the 'Cow boys' to our territory near Fronteras."[12] Governor Torres noted that Commandant Neri had troops stationed at the border to guard their border from the impending attack, but he made no reference whatsoever to forty Mexican citizens being recently killed at Fronteras.

While it appears that Americans threatened to retaliate against Fronteras for the killing of Ringo's friend, George Turner, and his party, marauding cowboys apparently never attacked the Sonoran town. Nevertheless, John Ringo, "King of the Cowboys," was not in Arizona when these events occurred, having left the territory sometime in April 1881.[13] Upon his return to Arizona from Liberty, Missouri, in mid-July 1881, it is likely that he learned the details of the past few months from friends.[14] Two weeks later, during late July 1881, another gun battle erupted over cattle ownership between cowboys and Mexicans. The *Tombstone Nugget*, on August 3, 1881, reported that a party of Mexicans had raided into the United States, but before they could return to Mexico with the livestock, a party of ranchers intercepted them:

> **Cattle Thieves Routed**
> From Bob Clark, who recently returned from New Mexico, the NUGGET learns that about the 26th of last month, a party of Mexicans from Sonora made a raid into the Animas and adjoining valleys, and rounding up several hundred animals, started with them through the Guadalupe Pass [in New Mexico near the point where New Mexico, Arizona, and Sonora converge] for Mexico. The Mexicans numbered about thirty all told. The cattlemen organized about twenty in number, and pursuing the marauders, overtook them on the plains near the Pass. A running fight ensued, which resulted in the flight of the Mexicans, and the recovery of the cattle.

One old-timer later claimed that cowboys had raided Sonora stealing the livestock and that the Mexicans were only trying to recapture the stolen herd. When the cowboys descended upon them, the two parties exchanged gunfire. Fearing that they were outnumbered, the Mexicans abandoned the herd and returned to Mexico empty-handed. The account asserts that John Ringo was involved in the ensuing gun battle with the Mexicans, which resulted in several Mexicans supposedly being killed.[15] Contemporary reports, however, failed to identify the men involved or whether anyone was killed in the ensuing fight.

A few days later, on July 27, 1881, another Mexican party was making its way north heading for Arizona. It was a large pack train that intended to buy goods in Arizona and then take them back to Mexico to sell for a big profit. Suddenly, the Mexican pack train was ambushed. The *Epitaph* published the following account of the incident on August 5, 1881:

> An Interrupted Breakfast
>
> Report comes to us of a fresh outrage perpetrated by the cow-boys in Sonora. Early last Monday morning a party of sixteen Mexicans from the interior of Sonora on their way to this Territory to purchase goods and carrying $4000.00 for that purpose, stopped in a curve in the road at Las Animas, near Fronteras, to prepare their frugal breakfast. While busily engaged preparing their tortillas they were saluted with music of twenty rifles fired by cow-boys who lay in ambush awaiting them. The Mexicans took this as an invitation to leave and did not stand on their order of their going but left all their mules and pack saddles in which they carried their money for the purchase of goods. When they stopped running they were at Fronteras and their party was four short. The missing men are supposed to have been killed. The citizens of Babispe and troops are after the cow-boys and are disposed to take summary vengeance if they overtake them.

The incident is popularly referred to as the Skeleton Canyon Massacre by many writers, even though the attack occurred a short distance from the Mexican town of Fronteras and fifty miles from Skeleton Canyon.[16] Though none of the participants in the massacre were identified at the time, John Ringo is commonly included amongst the men in the ambush. The Mexican government filed official protests with the Governor of the Arizona Territory, but little action was forthcoming. Meanwhile, the border raids continued to be reported in the newspapers. "The Arizona cowboys continue to have a high time on the Mexican border. They are represented to be in possession of large bands of cattle and horses, ready for the Texas market," the *San Francisco Evening Bulletin* commented.[17]

In mid-August 1881, more border problems erupted and four Americans, including Newman H. Clanton, the father of Phin, Ike, and Billy Clanton, were killed. Along with the elder Clanton, Dick Gray, Charles Snow, William Lang, and the wanted outlaw Jim Crane were killed. The men were ambushed near the town of Gillespie, New Mexico, in the Guadalupe Canyon area. It was estimated that a Mexican party of twenty to thirty had ambushed the men in the early morning hours while they were still asleep.[18]

The *Epitaph* reported the incident on August 16, 1881. It was noted that Jim Crane, one of the men who was wanted for the Bud Philpot killing in March 1881, had joined the men around midnight the night prior to the ambush and was there only to share the camp for the night.[19] This fact and the fact that Jim Crane was killed at their camp would later be used by modern writers to assert that the men were part of one gang. The event was discussed by mining man George Parsons, who arrived in Tombstone during February 1880 and kept a daily diary. His entry for August 17, 1881, stated that:

> Bad trouble on the border and this time looks more serious than anything yet. Dick Gray - the lame one - was killed by some Mexicans along with several others among them the notorious Crane

> and revenge seems the order of the day, a gang having started out to make trouble. This killing business by Mexicans, in my mind, was perfectly justifiable as it was in retaliation for the killing of several of them and the robbery by cow-boys recently this same Crane being one of the number. Am glad they killed him, as for the others - if not guilty of stealing cattle - they had no business to be found in such company. . . .

Considering Parsons' comments, it would seem that the people in Tombstone did believe that the attack was done by Mexicans and that their motive was to retaliate for the killings that occurred near Fronteras in late July 1881. Parsons had no sympathy for Crane, whom he considered a notorious outlaw, expressing joy over his being killed. But Parsons was not completely sure that the whole party had been actually out to steal cattle. He justified the killing of the others based on the fact that they were killed with Crane. Since no one had any compunctions about labeling Crane a bad man, it seems logical that Parsons or reporters from the local newspapers would not have shrunk from describing the 65-year-old Clanton as a shady character if his reputation so warranted. Parsons didn't mention him at all, and likely knew nothing about him.

The survivors of the massacre and the relatives of the victims were in full agreement about one fact - the shooters were Mexican soldiers. Even Mexican sources alluded to the possibility that Mexican soldiers had committed the atrocity. "Our people have been great sufferers. We have lost many citizens killed and much property stolen. We are taking active steps to protect our citizens and repel raiders," commented General Adolfo Dominquez, spokesman for General Otero, commander of the Mexican troops on the Sonoran frontier.[20] The Sacramento *Daily Record-Union*, based on the remarks of General Dominquez, wrote, "It is not improbable that the killing in Guadalupe Canyon might have been done by Mexican regulars under Captain Carrillo, as they were headed in that direction. Carrillo has about fifty men in his company."[21]

Talk of a large gang of cowboys massing in Arizona to seek vengeance for the killings, similar to the gossip that had been heard following the Turner massacre, again began to be heard. But the rumors of a raiding party were quickly quashed. "The wild rumor of the vast crowd of determined men going out to avenge the dead men is all bosh. There were eleven men in the party and the object of their trip was to bury the dead," reported the *Arizona Weekly Citizen.*[22] It appears that John Ringo was one of the cowboys who rode to the scene of the attack.

With the press declaring that the cowboy depredations along the border were at an all time high, the Governor began to slowly respond with inquiries about the situation that was occurring in Southeastern Arizona. In response, Joseph Bowyer, the manager of the Texas Consolidated Mining Company in Galeyville, sent a letter to the Governor of Arizona on September 17, 1881. It was later published by the *Tombstone Epitaph* on December 9, 1881:

> Dear Sir: In reply to your inquiry concerning the Cowboys who are reported to have been and still are raiding the line of Sonora and Arizona, I will say: The gang who are known as cowboys are engaged in stock raising in the valley of San Simon and Cloverdale in the southeastern portion of Arizona, and from good authority I learn that the cattle, horses and sheep now controlled by said cowboys have been stolen from the citizens of Sonora and Arizona and New Mexico; they are reported to have about 300 head of cattle at or near Granite Gap in New Mexico and close to the line in Arizona. It is a well known fact that they are in the habit of making raids along the border. Until recently it has been custom to steal cattle and horses in Arizona and drive them into Sonora

> and New Mexico for sale; Consequently quite a traffic was keep up. . . . About a month ago the cowboys went across the border into Sonora, and seeing a good-sized pack train in charge of mexicans, laid ambush and at word of command, made a dash and succeeded in capturing the whole outfit, consisting of about $4000.00 in Mexican silver bullion, mescal, horses and cattle. One of the cowboys in relating to me the circumstances said it was the d--st lot of truck he ever saw. . . . There was three Mexicans killed in the affray. A notorious cowboy known as John R - offers to sell all the mutton the town can consume at $1 per head. No secrecy is observed in this kind of transaction. . . .

It is obvious that Ringo was the notorious cowboy who offered to sell the town of Galeyville all the mutton it could eat for one dollar per person. Whether he had stolen the stock or not, with news reports indicating that the San Simon cowboys were all rustlers, it likely was inferred by the people that the stock had been stolen. Moreover, with news reports claiming that the San Simon cowboys had ambushed the Mexican party near Fronteras, the people of the Territory now assumed that John Ringo had been involved. The Governor relayed the information he received from Bowyer to the Secretary of State of the United States:

> At Galeyville, San Simon and other points isolated from large places the cow-boy element at times very fully predominates, and the officers of the law at times are either unable or unwilling to control this class of outlaws, sometimes being governed by fear, at other times by hope of reward. At Tombstone, the County seat of Cochise County, I conferred with the sheriff of said county upon the subject of breaking up three bands of outlaws, and

> I am sorry to say he gave me little hope of being able in his department to cope with the power of the cowboys. He represented to me that the deputy United States Marshal, resident of Tombstone, and city Marshal of same, and those who aid him (the deputy marshal) seemed unwilling to heartily cooperate with him (the sheriff) in capturing and bringing to justice these outlaws. In conversing with the deputy United States Marshal, Mr. Earp, I find precisely the same spirit of complaint existing against Mr. Behan (the sheriff) and his deputies. And back of this unfortunate fact, rivalry between the civil authorities, or unwillingness to work together in full accord in keeping the peace, I find two daily newspapers published in the city taking sides with the deputy marshal and the sheriff, respectively, each paper backing its civil clique and berating the other; and back of all this unfortunate fact that many of the very best law-abiding and peace loving citizens have no confidence in the willingness of the civil officers to pursue and bring to justice that element of outlawry so largely disturbing the sense of security, and so often committing highway robbery and smaller thefts. . . .[23]

The Governor's assessment that both sides were unable or unwilling to help each other and that the factions were separating down political lines, with each side publicly being supported by the opposing town newspapers, was right on the mark.

Eventually, the reports made their way to the White House. In May 1882, Chester Arthur, the President of the United States, threatened to declare the Arizona Territory to be under martial law if the cowboys committing depredations did not disperse.[24] But the President's declaration came after much of the violence that would make Tombstone forever a Western legend had already occurred.

Newman H. Clanton was killed by Mexicans in Guadalupe Canyon during August 1881.

9

A GAME OF DRAW

In early August 1881, John Ringo rode into a small settlement on the east slopes of the Chiricahua Mountains known as Galeyville, which was "noted as the rendezvous of the festive cowboys."[1] William Breakenridge later claimed that John Ringo, who "was a perfect gentleman when sober, but inclined to be quarrelsome when drinking," maintained a cabin in Galeyville, where he often kept to himself reading from a small collection of books.[2] Nevertheless, the notorious cowboy still caroused and played cards in the town's saloons where local men and other cowboys often congregated to pass the time.

On August 5, 1881, Ringo ventured into Evilsinger's saloon to drink whiskey and take in a few hands of poker with some players. As the poker game progressed, Ringo discovered that it just was not his night to win at poker. After losing all his money and apparently not being extended any credit to continue, Ringo bitterly left the saloon. But, around midnight, Ringo and a companion named Dave Estes returned to the card game. According to Joseph Bowyer, manager of the Texas Consolidated Mining Company in Galeyville, "Estes entered the front door of the saloon carrying a Henry rifle and a six-gun, his pal [Ringo] passed in at the rear of the house, armed in a singular manner."[3] The two men promptly held up the poker game, taking around $500 and a horse. News of the Galeyville robbery was published by the *Nugget* on August 11, 1881:

> A Social Game
>
> Galeyville is noted as the rendezvous of the festive cowboys. It is there he most congregates and joins in the amusements peculiar to his clan. On last Friday one of them known as Ringold entered into a game of poker and not being as expert with the "keards" as he is with his "gun" he soon went broke. But, the Star adds, he returned with a companion named Dave Estes, one being armed with a Henry rifle and the other with a Six Shooter. The players were promptly ordered to hold up their hands and the cowboys proceeded to go through the party securing in the neighborhood of $500.00. Some of the party broke for the woods where they remained concealed until daylight. A well known saloon keeper who was in the room had $500.00 on his person. He dodged the Henry rifle and Six shooter and escaped into the darkness returning shortly with a shotgun, but the bold desperadoes had vamoosed. When the robbers left town they took with them a horse belonging to one of the citizens.

For the first time since his arrival in Arizona, newspapers in the territory, as several Texas newspapers had done five years earlier, were now calling him "Ringold." Most likely, either the person who reported the robbery account to the newspaper knew of Ringo's Texas past or someone at the newspaper was aware of it. Nevertheless, the mix-up of John Ringo's real name by newspapers reporting the Galeyville robbery, caused confusion over the cowboy's identity and background, which lasted throughout the remainder of his life and to the present day.

Shortly after the incident, Deputy Goodman arrested Dave Estes for the Galeyville robbery and Estes was brought before Justice of the Peace G. W. Ellingsworth to answer the charge against him. After a short hearing, Justice Ellingsworth dismissed the charge against Estes. A letter dated September 4, 1881, signed "Clipper," but written by Joseph Bowyer and sent to the Editor of the *Arizona Daily Star*, describes what happened at Dave Estes' hearing:

A Galeyville Dogberry

> How Justice is Sometimes dispensed on the Border
> Editor Star: Perrish me to give you a brief history of a trial before a border Justice of the Peace, known as G.W. Ellingswood. David Estes was one of two men who robbed a game of about four hundred dollars in cash at the midnight hour in the town of Galeyville, as follows: Estes entered the front door of the saloon in which the game was played, armed with a Winchester and a six-shooter, his "pal" passed in at the rear of the house, armed in a singular manner. They ordered the players to throw up their hands and surrender all their cash. . . . Estes proceeded . . . and confiscated a valuable horse, making the total clean up about $500.00. Estes was subsequently arrested by Deputy Goodman and tried before Ellingwood, and discharged. His honor ruled in the examination of the witnesses that they could not testify to the taking of the money ordered by the bandits to be left on the table, unless they of their own knowledge knew whom a particular parcel of money belonged. This could not be proven, as all the occupants of the room were commanded to absquatulate [depart in a hurry] instantly, leaving Estes and his "pard" to take and divide.[4]

Following the dismissal of the charge against Estes, the Galeyville robbery and Ringo's involvement in the incident seemed to be forgotten. A month later, on the evening of September 9, 1881, John Ringo was seen riding his horse at full gallop into Tombstone.[5] Earlier in the day, Sheriff Behan, upon returning to Tombstone from Tucson, had informed Virgil Earp that Pima County Sheriff Bob Paul "had arrested Pony Deal, one of the men who robbed the Globe stage last February."[6] At the time, Pony Deal's accomplice, Sherman McMasters, was known to be at Tombstone. But Paul had asked Virgil not to arrest McMasters until Deal was in custody or his whereabouts was known. After receiving the news of Deal's arrest from Sheriff Behan, Virgil Earp, around six o'clock, telegraphed Bob Paul, "Do you want McMasters? Answer tonight."[7] Earp eagerly waited at the telegraph office for an immediate response to his telegram, but none was seemingly received. It was later learned that Bob Paul had responded to Earp's dispatch by sending a message to Marshal Williams, the Wells, Fargo express agent.

The telegraph operator, without telling Virgil Earp anything about the contents of the message, delivered the dispatch to the express office.[8] Although Williams was nowhere to be found, the man at the express office opened the dispatch, read the message, and started out to find Marshal Earp. The telegraph read:

> To Marshal Williams, Tombstone: Received at 8:30 P.M.
> Tell V. W. Earp, tonight, that I want McMasters.
> (Signed) R. H. Paul.[9]

Around 9 o'clock, someone approached Chief of Police Virgil Earp, who was standing in the doorway of the telegraph office waiting for a response from Bob Paul, and "told him that Ringold, the man who robbed a poker game with a Winchester rifle at Galeyville, about a month ago, had just rode into town with his horse in a lather."[10] Immediately, Virgil asked the man, "Where is he?" "With McMasters," the informant replied.[11] When

Virgil was finally given Paul's message, Earp exclaimed, "I just passed him; have you got a pistol?"[12] Obtaining a pistol from a citizen, Virgil called to his brother James to get armed to assist in arresting McMasters. After searching the saloons for McMasters without any luck, Virgil headed to the OK Corral to tell the corral man not to let McMasters have his horse. Before reaching the corral, however, Virgil saw "a man come loping out on McMasters' horse."[13] Earp ordered the man to stop but the rider paid him no attention. When the marshal fired his pistol the rider came to a stop. But the man was not McMasters and Virgil let him go. A few moments later, Virgil Earp saw McMasters dash out from behind some bushes. Earp chased after him, emptying his six-shooter into the night, but McMasters had successfully escaped. It was later reported that McMasters had stolen two horses from the Contention mine.[14]

Reports from Tombstone of Virgil Earp's failed attempt to arrest Sherman McMasters reached Tucson the following day, and the incident was mentioned by the *Arizona Weekly Star* on September 15, 1881:

> Attempted Arrest.
>
> Tombstone, September 10. – An attempt was made last night about 10 o'clock to arrest McMaster, one of the men who robbed the Globe stage last winter. Owing to McMasters being warned, he escaped. Marshal Earp fired five shots after him, but he got into a deep arroyo north of town and made good his escape. About 1 o'clock two valuable horses belonging to the Contention mine were stolen, supposed by McMasters and confederate, Ringold, the man who robbed the poker game of $1,000 with a Winchester rifle about a month ago at Galeyville, California district, this county. No trace of them yet.

Ringo's latest escapade in Tombstone likely reminded people in Cochise County of the Galeyville poker game robbery a month earlier. Breakenridge later claimed that John Ringo asked Joe Hill to return the money stolen during the Galeyville robbery the following day.[15] Nevertheless, both John Ringo and Dave Estes were indicted for the Galeyville robbery on November 26, 1881.[16] According to court records, four men had filed a complaint against Ringo: Fred Kohler, L. Evilsinger, J. Coggswell, and Roy Stahl.[17] The criminal charge was entered on the court's docket on November 29, and a bench warrant was issued for Ringo's arrest. Deputy Sheriff Breakenridge promptly rode to Galeyville to bring John Ringo to Tombstone to answer the robbery indictment. When Breakenridge arrived at Galeyville he went to the cabin where Ringo was staying and told him he had to take him back to Tombstone.[18] Ringo quickly dressed and the two men had breakfast together that morning. According to Breakenridge, Ringo told him that he had some business to take care of and that he would catch up to him at Prue's ranch in the morning.[19] Breakenridge's reason for agreeing to this arrangement was that John Ringo's word was as good as his bond. Ringo caught up to Breakenridge the next morning at Prue's ranch and both men rode into Tombstone together. Breakenridge later wrote that he let Ringo sleep over at the jailer's house rather than taking him to the jail.[20]

Despite Breakenridge's later assertions, Ringo had stayed at the Grand Hotel. On December 1, 1881 the *Epitaph* reported: "John Ringold was arrested yesterday [November 30] by Deputy Sheriff Neagle on an indictment found by the present Grand Jury." The same day as his arrest, November 30, the court approved Ringo's bail bond. The sureties were George Hill, Isaac Clanton, James Clark, and William Clark.

On December 1, 1881, John Ringo, represented by Robinson and Goodrich as counsel, was arraigned before district court judge William Stilwell. At this point, the controversy over Ringo's name resurfaced, and Ringo was asked if "John Ringgold was his true name."[21] Ringo replied, "that it was not" and "that his true name was John Ringo."[22] Stilwell ordered the indictment be corrected. According to court records, "The indictment charging the defendant with the crime of Robbery was then read to him by the Clerk and a plea of not guilty was entered by the defendant and a true copy of the indictment was handed to him. The defendant was then given one day to prepare for trial."[23] On December 2, 1881, the *Epitaph* announced Ringo's upcoming case: "Territory vs. John Ringo, indicted for felony, pled not guilty; one day given to prepare for trial." Ringo appeared in court as required on December 2, 1881, but no witnesses against him showed up. The proceeding was "continued" (postponed), and Ringo left town.[24]

In mid-January 1882, John Ringo returned to Tombstone, and on January 20 he was placed in jail on the old Galeyville robbery charge.[25] On January 28 the cowboy was arraigned a second time before Judge Stilwell on the poker game offense.[26] His pleading was scheduled for January 31, at which time he pled not guilty. Ringo's bail bond was set at $3,000, and the hearing on the matter was to be held February 2.[27] The *Nugget* of February 1, 1882, reported that "Deputy Sheriff Breakenridge in his recent trip to Galeyville served bench warrants upon Roy Stahl, Loss Evilsinger, Fred Kohl and J. Coggswell, who had previously failed to put in an appearance. They were brought to this city this time by the Deputy Sheriff." But again the witnesses refused to cooperate, and the trial again was postponed. Perhaps the poker players had decided it wasn't healthy to testify against Mr. Ringo.

In May 1882, Ringo came to Tombstone a third time to answer for his Galeyville indiscretions, and for a third time no witnesses appeared to testify against him. At that point the court dropped the case.[28]

William Breakenridge later recalled how he went to Galeyville to arrest John Ringo for the poker game robbery charge.

10

EARP-CLANTON FEUD

On the afternoon of October 26, 1881, four armed men, walking west on Fremont Street in Tombstone, advanced toward a vacant lot where another party was gathered. The four were Chief of Police Virgil Earp, Wyatt and Morgan Earp, and Doc Holliday.[1] As the Earp party drew closer to the vacant lot where five men were standing, they saw Cochise County Sheriff John Behan talking to the men. Sheriff Behan, who had just finished checking the men for weapons, found that Billy Clanton and Frank McLaury had sidearms, but Ike Clanton and Tom McLaury were not armed.[2] Behan turned to unarmed William Claiborne, a friend of Billy Clanton's, and asked him if he was part of the group. Claiborne responded that he was not with the men and was trying to get them to leave town.[3] Upon seeing the Earp party, the sheriff walked toward the approaching men and tried to stop them, but they brushed him aside and strode up to the Clanton and McLaury brothers.

Almost immediately, two shots were fired, followed by a brief pause. Then a flurry of gunshots was heard. When the smoke cleared, Frank McLaury was dead, and Tom McLaury and Billy Clanton lay on the ground mortally wounded. Also wounded in the affray was Morgan Earp, with a serious but not fatal shoulder wound, and Virgil Earp, who was hit in the calf of his right leg.[4] Contemporary newspapers immediately recognized the potential enormity and fame of the street fight in Tombstone. "The 26th of October, 1881, will always be marked as one of the crimson days in the annals of Tombstone, a day when blood flowed as water, and human life was held as a shuttlecock, a day always to be remembered as witnessing the bloodiest and deadliest street fight that has ever occurred in this place, or probably in the Territory," the *Nugget* concluded.[5] Despite occasionally being portrayed as a participant in the Gunfight at the OK Corral, and in more than one instance even being killed in the shootout by Doc Holliday, John Ringo, much to the regret of Western history buffs, was not involved in the most famous gun battle in the annals of the Old West. Nevertheless, the aftermath of the gunfight was the catalyst that brought John Ringo into what later became known as the Earp-Clanton feud.

Immediately following the time of the street fight, many people thought that Chief of Police Virgil Earp and his three "special" deputies, Wyatt and Morgan Earp and Doc Holliday, had legally tried to disarm the men. "The feeling among the best class of our citizens is that the Marshal was entirely justified in his efforts to disarm these men, and that being fired upon they had to defend themselves, which they did most bravely," the *Epitaph* noted.[6] Nevertheless, two days later, Dr. Henry Matthews, the county coroner, empaneled a jury to investigate the deaths of the three men. Much of the testimony given at the coroner's inquest was published in its entirety in the newspapers, and it began to cast doubt as to the correctness of the Earps' conduct before and during the fight.[7] The day the coroner's inquest ended, Ike Clanton filed a formal murder complaint against the Earps and Holliday.

Wyatt and Doc were arrested and placed in the jail, but Morgan and Virgil Earp were permitted to remain free while they recuperated from their gunshot wounds. That same day, Mayor Clum and the Tombstone common council suspended Virgil Earp as chief of police, naming James Flynn as his temporary replacement.[8] On October 31, a hearing was commenced before Justice Wells Spicer to determine whether there was sufficient evidence against the Earps and Holliday to refer their cases to the grand jury. As the testimony progressed, it appeared that the prosecution's case was strong. The town began to read testimony from eyewitnesses who testified that the Clantons and McLaurys were fired upon while their hands were in the air and that they were attempting to surrender. As a result, many people in Tombstone began to think that the gunfight was closer to murder. "The trial of the Earps and Doc Holliday for killing the cowboys is progressing slowly. . . . Public feeling, which at first was for the Earps and Holliday, seems to have taken a turn, and now nearly all the people of Tombstone condemn the murderers," wrote the *San Francisco Examiner.*[9] When news reached John Ringo of the Tombstone street battle that left Billy Clanton and Tom and Frank McLaury dead, the cowboy made his way to the boom town to learn first hand what had happened. Once in Tombstone, there is little doubt that Ringo went straight to Ike Clanton to personally find out the details of the gunfight. Ike's version was likely the account that Ringo accepted as true.

The day after the gunfight took place, the local newspapers quickly pointed out what was reportedly the origin of the dispute between the two groups. The *Epitaph* wrote, "Since the arrest of Stilwell and Spence for the robbery of the Bisbee stage, there have been oft repeated threats conveyed to the Earp brothers - Virgil, Morgan and Wyatt - that the friends of the accused, or in other words the cowboys, would get even with them for the part they had taken in the pursuit and arrest of Stilwell and Spence. The active part of the Earps in going after stage robbers, beginning with the one last spring where Budd Philpot lost his life, and the more recent one near Contention, has made them exceedingly obnoxious to the bad element of this county and put their lives in jeopardy every month."[10] The *Nugget* concurred, "The origin of the trouble dates back to the first arrest of Stilwell and Spencer for the robbery of the Bisbee stage. The cooperation of the Earps and the Sheriff and his deputies in the arrest caused a number of cowboys to, it is said, threaten the lives of all interested in the capture."[11] But, the *Nugget* added, "Still, nothing occurred to indicate that any such threats would be carried into execution."[12]

On November 16, 1881, Wyatt Earp took the stand as the first witness for the defense. Rather than present evidence by answering questions posed by his counsel and being cross-examined by the prosecutor, Wyatt chose to read a prepared statement into the court record.[13] In his statement, Earp alleged that "the Mclowrys and Clantons have always been friends of Stilwell and Spencer, and they laid the whole blame of their arrest [for the Bisbee stage robbery] on us . . . ."[14] Wyatt Earp went into further details about the so-called threats from the cowboys:

> Frank McLowry took Morgan Earp into the street in front of the Alhambra, when John Ringgold, Ike Clanton, and the two Hicks boys were also standing by, when Frank McLowry commence to abuse Morgan Earp for going after Spencer and Stilwell; Frank McLowry said he would never speak to Spencer again for being arrested by us; he said to Morgan: "If you ever come after me you will never take me;" Morgan replied, if he ever had occasion to go after him he would arrest him; Frank McLowry then said to Morgan: "I have threatened you boys' lives, and a few days ago had taken it back, but since this arrest it now goes;" Morgan made no reply and walked off; before this and after this Marshall Williams, Farmer Daly, Ed Byrnes, Old Man Winter, Charley Smith and three or four others had told us at different times of threats to kill us made by Ike Clanton, Frank McLowry, Tom McLowry, Joe Hill and John Ringgold; I knew all those men were desperate and dangerous men; that they were connected with outlaws, cattle thieves, robbers and murderers; I knew of the McLowrys stealing six government mules and also cattle, and when the owners went after them - finding his stock on the McLowry's ranch - that he was driven off, and they would kill him, and he has keep his mouth shut until several days ago

FOR FEAR OF BEING KILLED

> I heard of Ringold shooting a man down in cold blood near Camp Thomas; I was satisfied that Frank and Tom McLowry had killed and robbed Mexicans in Skeleton Canyon three or four months ago, and I naturally keep my eyes open, for I did not intend that any of the gang should get the "drop" on me if I could help it. . . .[15]

With his prepared statement, Wyatt accused the Clantons, McLaurys, Ringo, and others of having repeatedly threatened to kill the Earps. Nonetheless, not one of the men that Wyatt identified as having told the Earps of the prior threats, testified at the hearing to corroborate Earp's allegations. Yet, Wyatt's prepared statement succeeded in painting a dark picture of the Clantons, McLaurys, and Ringo as "desperate and dangerous men," who were "connected with outlaws, cattle thieves, robbers and murderers."[16] Prior to the Gunfight at the OK Corral, none of the cowboy participants had been accused of a serious crime in Arizona or was considered, at least publicly, to be part of the cowboy depredations that were occurring in the area. Only John Ringo had a past with provable serious allegations of criminal conduct.

Wyatt's claim that he had "heard of Ringold shooting a man down in cold blood near Camp Thomas" can neither be proved nor refuted.[17] Other than Wyatt's accusation, the only account of Ringo shooting someone at Camp Thomas is the popular story of the killing of Dick Lloyd.[18] William Breakenridge later claimed that John Ringo and a group of cowboys playing poker in O'Neil's saloon at Camp Thomas killed Dick Lloyd, who moments earlier had shot a saloon keeper named Mann when he recklessly rode Joe Hill's horse into the saloon.[19] A contemporary account noted: "The killing of Lloyd, the cow-boy, at Maxey's on the 8th, was what might have been expected. He was a reckless character, and it is reported that he had several times taken the town in, putting the people of that place in mortal fear. He sought the and met.'"[20] Another old-timer, Melvin Jones, maintained that he witnessed the incident. He claimed that the whole group, which included Ringo, who he described as "a over bearing, loud talking, dangerous man when drinking," fired at Lloyd.[21] Afterwards, according to the account, Jack O'Neil claimed that he alone had shot Dick Lloyd. The *Arizona Weekly Star* confirmed that O'Neil took responsibility for the killing:

> **A Dead Cow-Boy**
>
> Maxey, March 8. - Dick Loyed [sic], a cow-boy shot E. Mann this evening. After the shooting he rode into Oneil [sic] & Franklin's Saloon, where some person shot him dead. Oneil gave himself up as the party who shot him. We have no Justice to act as coroner. I summoned seven persons to investigate the case. It was justifiable. Mann will survive. Will abide instructions.
>
> Collins[22]

Other than old-timers' recollections, there is no proof that John Ringo and the other poker players shot the rambunctious cowboy. Officially O'Neil claimed responsibility for the killing of Dick Lloyd.

After a month of testimony, on November 30, 1881, Justice Wells Spicer rendered his verdict in the case. "The evidence taken before me in this case would not, in my judgment, warrant a conviction of the defendants by a trial jury of any offense whatever."[23] Spicer's decision absolving the Earps of wrongdoing during the O.K. Corral gunfight was not a popular one. Despite Spicer's ruling, Virgil Earp was not reinstated as Tombstone's chief of police. Rumors began to spread through Tombstone that friends of the Clantons and McLaurys had prepared a hit list that included the Earps, Doc Holliday, Tom Fitch, Wells, Fargo agent Marshall Williams, Judge Spicer, and John Clum.[24]

On December 14, 1881, John Clum boarded a stage to Benson, the first leg of a trip to Washington, D.C., to visit his parents and son. After traveling about four miles, the stage was ordered to "Halt," and several shots rang out.[25] Immediately the six horses pulling the stage were frightened by the shooting and they burst into a gallop. About half a mile later, the driver gained control over the stage. Clum feared that the holdup was simply a sham and that its real purpose was to assassinate him. He quietly jumped from the coach and ran into the desert. Taking no chances, Clum hiked alone through the desert to the Grand Central Mill, near Contention City. Meanwhile, back in Tombstone it was feared Clum may have been killed, but the mill superintendent contacted Tombstone by telephone, advising people there that the mayor was safe. Nevertheless, the *Epitaph* claimed, "That the affair of Wednesday night was intended for the murder of John P. Clum, we are fully satisfied."[26] But the *Nugget* thought that it was more likely that Clum overreacted to a botched stage robbery.[27]

Whether the attackers wanted to assassinate Clum or were robbers who intended to take the cashbox, is not known - the perpetrators were never identified. Occasionally John Ringo is named as one of the assailants who attacked the stage carrying Clum. Stuart Lake, Wyatt's biographer, later claimed that "Frank Stilwell, Ike Clanton, and John Ringo were recognized in a gang of twenty which attempted to assassinate Mayor Clum" that night.[28] But no evidence has ever been found or presented that linked Ringo to the incident or identified the actual the men that attacked the stage that night.

While some threats had been made to Wells Spicer in a letter that was signed "A Miner," there was no indication that the cowboys had made out a death list that included the Earps, Doc Holliday, Tom Fitch, Wells, Fargo agent Marshall Williams, Judge Spicer, and John Clum.[29] Spicer felt the threats were from a rabble coming from within the city, and not the cowboys.[30] About the rumored death threats, Tom Fitch commented that he had "never received a warning or menace from 'cow-boys' or anybody else" and felt perfectly safe.[31] Nevertheless, on the night of December 28, 1881, deputy U. S. Marshal

Virgil Earp was shot twice from ambush while walking along a Tombstone street.[32] It was thought at first that he might die from his injuries. He survived, but, with a large section of bone removed from his arm, he would be crippled for life. The next day the *Tombstone Epitaph* commented that "five shots were fired in rapid succession by unknown men."[33] Immediately following the shooting, three men were seen running past the Ice House of Tough Nut Street, but they were never identified. The *Epitaph* noted, "This further proves that there is a band of assassins in our midst, who having threatened the lives of Judge Spicer, Mayor Clum, Mr. Williams, the Earp brothers and Holliday, have attempted on two occasions to carry their threats to execution, first upon Mayor Clum and second upon Virgil Earp."[34]

With little evidence available to determine the assailants' identity, rumor and innuendo spread throughout Tombstone concerning who had done the shooting. George Parsons, a friend of Mayor John Clum and an Earp supporter, was in town at the time Virgil was shot. "It is surmised that Ike Clanton, Curly Bill, and [Will] McLaury did the shooting," wrote George Parsons in his diary.[35] Parsons' comments, however, were nothing more than unsubstantiated rumors. Will McLaury had left Tombstone two days earlier.

Nothing had been heard of Curly Bill since the *Nugget* had reported that he was leaving the territory three weeks before.[36] The natural suspect, of course, was Ike Clanton. Years later, Wyatt Earp provided another suspect when he asserted that Virgil saw Frank Stilwell going into the vacant building from which the shots were fired. Wyatt further claimed, "We found Ike Clanton's hat, that he dropped in getting away from the rear end of the building."[37] It was later learned that Ike Clanton had been in Charleston at the time of the shooting, and several people would provide him with a rock solid alibi.[38]

Despite the fact that John Ringo was not implicated at the time, he is occasionally listed as one of the assailants of Virgil Earp. Stuart Lake wrote, "John Ringo had been recognized as one of the two gunman who had run down Allen Street."[39] Although the notorious cowboy's whereabouts at the time are unknown, there is no evidence that he was involved in the murder attempt. Decades later,

Fred Dodge, who asserted that he came to Tombstone as an undercover detective for Wells, Fargo, would claim, categorically and without corroboration, that Johnny Barnes, a young cowboy, was also a shooter.[40] Nothing in the contemporary record has been found to support Dodge's claim.

The day after his brother was wounded, Wyatt sent a message to U. S. Marshal Crawley Dake. "Virgil Earp was shot by concealed assassins last night. The wound is considered fatal. Telegraph me appointment [as deputy U.S. marshal] with power to appoint deputies. Local authorities have done nothing. Lives of our citizens have been threatened."[41] In response, Dake immediately "telegraphed an appointment as Deputy marshal to Wyatt Earp, instructing him to spare no pains or expense in discovering the perpetrators of the deed."[42]

Two days following the attempt on Virgil Earp's life, the *Epitaph*, on December 30, 1881, published a lengthy article with information attributed to Mrs. J. C. Colyer, who had recently been in Arizona, that purportedly originated from the *Kansas City Star*. According to the article, Mrs. Colyer claimed that she and her husband became intimate with Ike Clanton and John Ringo during their residence in Tombstone. Mrs. Colyer declared that Ringo and Clanton were the "Chiefs of the Cow-boy's gang,"[43] and that Ringo and Clanton had planned the raids that other cowboys carried out. Mrs. Colyer claimed that the night before she left town, the cowboys intended to raid the Earps at the Oriental Saloon, but their plans were abandoned when a fire broke out near the hotel. The *Epitaph* published a companion article in the same issue which alleged that Milt Hicks, John Ringo, and four other men were closeted in the Grand Hotel where they plotted to attack Earp partisans.[44] But the cowboys' plans were thwarted by a fire that broke out near the Grand Hotel.

A fire had occurred in Tombstone near the Grand Hotel on December 9, 1881. But it is likely that the basis for the rumored attack was only speculation and innuendo. Milt Hicks had busted out of the Tombstone jail on October 24, 1881.[45] It seems unlikely that an escapee like Hicks would stay in Tombstone and take a chance of being arrested. Regardless of the accuracy of the reports, the article added to Tombstone's perception that John Ringo was a desperate and dangerous man who was a leader of the cowboys.

The Tombstone municipal election scheduled for January 3, 1882, was openly billed as a referendum on the Earps as the town's law enforcement team. The *Nugget* commented: "Doc Holliday and the Earps are solid for Blinn and Flynn. So is the Daily Strangler."[46] The *Epitaph* was supporting Lewis Blinn for mayor and James Flynn for chief of police. John Carr was the *Nugget's* choice for mayor, and Dave Neagle was their choice for police chief. The paper went on to note: "The election will to-day decide whether Tombstone is to be dominated for another year by the Earps and their strikers. Every vote against the People's Independent Ticket is a vote in favor of the Earps. Miners, business men, and all others having the welfare of our city at heart should remember this."[47]

The voters got the message, as they elected John Carr, Dave Neagle, and the *Nugget*-backed candidates for common council by large majorities.[48]

Frank McLaury was armed with a pistol during the gunfight at the OK Corral, but likely was already shot before he drew the weapon during the shootout.

Tom McLaury was unarmed during the gunfight at the OK Corral and died without firing a shot.

Virgil Earp was shot and seriously wounded by unknown assailants during the night of December 28, 1881.

11

CHAMPION OF THE COWBOYS

Tombstone's city election brought change to the boom town's political environment, and many people thought that the new officials would put an end to the hostilities of the past few months, but the animosity between the Clantons and the Earps only increased in the new year. Seven years earlier, similar tensions in Texas had resulted in a seemingly unknown John Ringo quickly acquiring with his participation in the Hoodoo War, a reputation as a desperate and dangerous man throughout much of that state. The stage was now set for Ringo's second transformation from a notorious man, now suspected of outlawry in Arizona, to the fearless and undisputed champion of the cowboys.

Three days after the polls closed, on January 6, three bandits stepped from the brush along the road between Hereford and Bisbee intent on stopping the Sandy Bob stage.[1] At seventy-five yards the men, two wearing silk handkerchiefs covering their faces and the other wearing no mask at all, began shooting in an attempt to stop the Bisbee stagecoach. After a short cat-and-mouse game between the robbers and shotgun messenger Charles Bartholomew, which included the exchange of gunfire, the bandits finally succeeded in stopping the stage three miles from Hereford around three o'clock in the afternoon; whereupon they looted the treasure box. Before riding off with "$6,500 in specie [coin] and currency, being sent over to pay the Copper Queen miners and workmen" in Bisbee, the unmasked outlaw, who throughout the robbery did all the talking, threatened to kill the driver of the stagecoach if he did anything to identify any of the men.[2]

A day later, two masked men robbed a second stage as it traveled between Contention City and Tombstone. This time the desperadoes rode off with $1500 and a fancy pair of pistols owned by James Hume, Wells, Fargo's chief detective.[3] When newspaper reports failed to identify any of the bandits that had committed these two robberies, suspicion and blame swiftly fell upon the usual suspects - the cowboys.

Regardless of whether any evidence was available or not, the term "cowboys" now was synonymous with men like Ike Clanton and John Ringo, who had been accused publicly by the *Tombstone Epitaph* of being the leaders of the cowboys. Rumors later even spread to California, where the *Los Angeles Times* reported that Ringo was "one of the ringleaders of the cowboys" and that he was "suspected of being one of the party who lately robbed the stage near Bisbee."[4] January 1882 proved to be a tumultuous time for Tombstone. While both the Clanton and Earp factions were seemingly ready for another confrontation, Ringo brazenly tried to provoke a showdown on Allen Street all by himself.

On the afternoon of January 17, 1882, John Ringo was walking on Allen Street in Tombstone, when in front of the Occidental Saloon he encountered Doc Holliday, whom Wyatt and Morgan Earp closely followed.[5] Ringo and Holliday reportedly "had been on bad terms for some time past," and upon meeting on Allen Street, their bad feelings toward each other were again expressed.[6] As the argument became more heated, "both parties stepped back, placing their hands on their weapons with the intention of drawing and using them."[7] Townspeople crowded the streets and a shooting might have injured innocent bystanders. "Fortunately chief of police Flynn was at hand and placed both parties under arrest."[8] On January 22, 1882, the *Weekly Arizona Citizen* published an account of the incident that was based on an earlier *Nugget* article:

Almost a Tragedy

A difficulty occurred yesterday afternoon [January 17] in front of the Occidental Saloon, Allen street, between John Ringo and Doc Holiday, that very nearly terminated in bloodshed. The parties had been on bad terms for some time past, and meeting yesterday morning words were exchanged and both parties stepped back, placing their hands on their weapons with the intention of drawing and using them. Fortunately chief of police Flynn was at hand and placed both parties under arrest. They were taken to Judge Wallace's court and fined $32 each for carrying deadly weapons. Some little occurrence, which fortunately died out before anything serious occurred. The streets were crowded at the time, and had the shooting commenced it is probable that more than one life would have paid the penalty and another serious tragedy enacted on our street.

Although the encounter appears to have been mainly between Ringo and Holliday, Flynn also arrested Wyatt Earp, and the officer brought the three men to A. O. Wallace's Police Court. Chief of Police Flynn charged each man with carrying a concealed weapon. Despite the potential deadly consequences that a gunfight in the crowded streets might have caused, the *Epitaph,* on January 18, 1882, only briefly mentioned the Ringo-Holliday encounter on Allen Street: "Chief of Police Flynn yesterday, in the gentle zephres that occurred on Allen street, by his prompt action, gave unmistaken proof that he thoroughly understands his business and is fearless in its execution."

Interestingly, rather than discuss the near gunfight between John Ringo and Doc Holliday, which was the real story, the *Epitaph*, instead, praised Flynn's abilities as chief of police. Nevertheless, the *Epitaph* did report on the results of what occurred in A. O. Wallace's Police Court: "J. H. Holliday, Wyatt

John Ringo confronted Doc Holliday and possibly Wyatt Earp on Allen Street, but no gunshots were exchanged. Courtesy Dave Johnson.

Earp, Ringo, arrested for carrying concealed weapons. Earp discharged, Holliday and Ringo fined $30 each."[9] Both Ringo and Holliday were fined, but Wallace dismissed the charge against Wyatt Earp because his appointment as a deputy U.S. marshal entitled him to carry a concealed weapon in Tombstone.[10]

It is only natural to wonder why the *Epitaph,* which supported the Earps, failed to fully cover the details of the near gunfight. Perhaps the reason the *Epitaph* downplayed the incident and used the situation to show Flynn in a positive light, was because the public in Tombstone saw the encounter as more favorable to Ringo and not so flattering to Wyatt or Doc. Years later that's how some old-timers would remember Ringo's confrontation with Earp and Holliday. Robert Boller, an old-timer, later commented that Bull Lewis and Fred Ward told him how Ringo "cowed Doc Holliday and three of the Earps singlehanded."[11] "Ringo gave those fellows every opportunity to fight it out but when he found them to be only a bunch of cowards he ignored them," recalled one old-timer.[12]

Tombstone legend generally tells how Ringo brazenly walked up to Wyatt and Doc, and challenged them to a gunfight to settle their differences once and for all. Wyatt refused, saying that he was a candidate at the next election for sheriff and would not engage in a gunfight. Ringo then turned to Holliday, flipping him the end of a handkerchief to grab hold of to fight it out at close quarters. As Holliday reached for the bandana to shoot it out with the notorious cowboy, Chief of Police James Flynn intervened, grabbing Ringo from behind. Meanwhile, Wyatt escorted Doc from the scene.

It is even possible that more than one confrontation between Ringo and Earp or Holliday had occurred. Ringo proposed "to shoot it out" with Holliday, according to Breakenridge, to end the feud. "This arrangement, however, was not acceptable to the Earp party, and they all went into the saloon."[14] Another account alleges that on one occasion Ringo challenged Wyatt Earp to a knife fight. "Wyatt went pale and backed out of the saloon," recalled the grandson of Joe Hill, Ringo's close friend.[15] Boller recalled how Ringo "made them [the Earps] take water in their dumps in Tombstone, when Fred Ward and Bull Lewis went into the saloon and led Ringo out telling him the Earps would shoot him in the back."[15] Nonetheless, the precise details of what happened between Ringo and Holliday or Earp in Tombstone on January 17, 1882, or during some other brief encounter, have been lost by time and buried under exaggerated tales that have little, if any, corroboration. What is known is that an encounter that almost resulted in a shooting between Ringo and Holliday, and possibly Wyatt Earp, did occur in mid-January 1882.

In any event, the substance of the dispute is not known for sure, but reportedly Doc was a belligerent man, and he may have made some insulting remark just to be nasty. Also, Wyatt did not treat Ringo kindly in his O.K. Corral hearing statement, and Ringo could not have been pleased with Wyatt's comments. It is also conceivable that Doc may have been trying to implicate Ringo in the two recent stagecoach robberies that occurred earlier in the month. Another possibility is that the argument may have been about Big Nose Kate, Doc Holliday's woman, who, if we can believe an account later told by a woman claiming to be Kate, may have shared some time with John Ringo while Doc was sitting in jail during the Spicer Hearing in November 1881.[16] Underlying the climate of animosity, of course, was the fact that Ringo was a friend of Ike Clanton, a deadly enemy of Doc Holliday and the Earps. Whatever the reason for the encounter, one Earp biographer would later write: "This face-off between two of the most feared shootists in town could only serve to exacerbate the already tense situation."[17]

Diarist George Parsons also witnessed the Ringo-Holliday encounter and he recorded in his diary his observations of what happened during the Allen Street encounter:

> . . . Ringo and Doc Holiday came nearly having it with pistols. . . . Bad time expected with cowboy leader and D.H. I passed both not knowing blood was up. One with hand in breast pocket and the other probably ready. Earps just beyond. Crowded

> street and looked like another battle. Police vigilant for once and both disarmed.[18]

As the diary entry clearly shows, Parsons, like most of Tombstone, now publicly perceived Ringo to be a leader of the cowboys committing depredations in Arizona. The notorious cowboy had already received newspaper attention in the territory for the December 1879 Safford shooting of Louis Hancock, who survived the incident, and the August 1881 Galeyville poker game robbery. In addition, in September 1881, the *Epitaph* identified Ringo as the man who warned Sherman McMasters of his impending arrest by Virgil Earp in time to allow him to avoid capture. More recently, the *Epitaph* had published articles that accused John Ringo and Ike Clanton of being the leaders of the cowboy gang that was committing depredations in Arizona and across the border in Mexico.[19]

The published mid-January 1882 newspaper accounts of the confrontation between the reputed cowboy leader and Holliday, clearly provided John Ringo with recognition and notoriety in Arizona. Indeed, it may have been the memory of an incident like the Ringo-Holliday encounter in January 1882 that caused some Arizona newspapers after Ringo's death to make statements that the notorious cowboy was a "recklessly brave man"[20] and "fearless in the extreme."[21] After this incident, it is likely that many people in Tombstone and Arizona considered John Ringo to be the chief antagonist of the Clanton faction that opposed the Earps and Holliday - the champion of the cowboys.

Doc Holliday appeared willing to fight it out with John Ringo, but Chief of Police James Flynn intervened by grabbing Ringo from behind before any shooting started.

12

RINGO AND THE COWBOY WAR

A day after Ringo and Holliday almost shot it out in the streets of Tombstone, Judge William H. Stilwell decided that Ringo's existing $3000 bond for the Galeyville robbery indictments was insufficient, and he issued a warrant for the cowboy's arrest.[1] Ringo's Allen Street encounter with Holliday likely caused Judge Stilwell to seek the increased bond. Two days later, Friday, January 20, 1882, possibly the next time John Ringo was in town, Cochise County authorities arrested Ringo and placed him in the jail.[2] Locked up on a Friday, the cowboy had no choice but to remain in jail until Judge Stilwell set his bond the following Monday morning. Meanwhile, on the same day that authorities arrested Ringo, United States Marshal Crawley Dake placed $3,000 provided by Wells, Fargo & Co. in a special account in the Hudson & Co. Bank.[3]

Dake advised his deputy, Wyatt Earp, that he could use the money to "arrest all parties committing crimes against the United States." Marshal Dake told reporters that the operation was to "have nothing to do with the cow-boy element, farther than to arrest those committing stage coach robbery and raiding the border."[4] Dake asserted that "he did not wish his deputies connected with any outside local troubles not in the line of their duties."[5] What happened next in Cochise County started what the United States government would later fallaciously label the "Cowboy War," which, more realistically, was simply a continuation of the personal feud between the Clantons and the Earps that started with the gunfight at the O.K. Corral. Nevertheless,

James Earp filed an affidavit with the court alleging that John Ringo had escaped from the jail and that the cowboy intended to obstruct the execution of warrants held by Wyatt Earp.

years later the term "Cowboy War" would be used to describe the actions taken by Deputy United States Marshal Wyatt Earp and his posse in suppressing the cowboy raids.

While Ringo was still in custody at the county jail, Wyatt and a posse rode out of Tombstone toward Charleston with federal warrants issued by Judge Stilwell vaguely described as for "divers persons."[6] Despite Dake's restrictions, Wyatt's underlying purpose was not to find stage robbers or cross-border raiders, but rather to find Ike and Phin Clanton, whom he suspected of ambushing his brother Virgil. At the Tombstone jail, John Ringo became aware of Wyatt's departure and the lawman's plan to go after the Clantons. He summoned his attorney, Briggs Goodrich, and told him to arrange for his bail right away.[7] Ringo knew he must warn his friends that Wyatt and his posse were on their trail. Wyatt had a badge to hide behind and private wrongs to avenge, so bloodshed was a distinct possibility. Goodrich went to Sheriff Behan and told him that his client's bail was imminent, so the sheriff released Ringo before the court formally accepted his bond.[8] Upon his release, Ringo went to the stable, saddled his horse, and rode off to alert the Clanton brothers that Wyatt and his men were coming with deadly purpose.

James Earp saw Ringo gallop out of town and surmised that he was intent on foiling Wyatt's effort to surprise the Clantons. He quickly filed an affidavit with the court alleging that Ringo had, in effect, escaped from jail, noting that the court had not yet approved his bail bond. James went on to contend that "the purpose and intent of said Ringo is to intercept one Wyatt S. Earp a marshal intrusted with the execution of warrants for divers persons charged with violations of the laws of this Territory."[9] James concluded that "the purpose of said Ringo is to obstruct the execution of said warrants."[10]

Some later accounts insist, without corroboration, that when the Earp party reached the bridge that straddled the San Pedro River just before Charleston, they were surprised to find Ringo, who they thought was still locked up in the jail at Tombstone.

Instead of proceeding into Charleston, the Earp party, realizing that the men they held warrants for had been forewarned by Ringo, turned and rode away.[11] Nevertheless, the *Nugget* later reported that after the Earp party left Tombstone on January 23, they "went into camp near the Merrimac mine, about three miles from here, where they remained until Wednesday night [January 25]."[12]

After Ringo rode out of Tombstone, a second group of men led by John H. Jackson, left the town at four o'clock the next morning with a warrant issued by Judge Stilwell for John Ringo's arrest.[13] Jackson's party carried no official authority, although Judge Stilwell later implied that he was a deputy U.S. marshal.[14] These events caused much consternation in Tombstone, and the newly elected mayor, John Carr, issued a proclamation urging the citizenry to allow Deputy U. S. Marshal Earp to proceed without hindrance. Concerning Ringo's departure from the city, Mayor Carr further explained: "Yesterday, after the marshal's posse left the city, a bail bond is prepared for Ringo and without its having been approved or filed or any order issuing from the court releasing the prisoner, without color of law, and in face of the fact that the sheriff had been informed that the bail bond accepted in December MUST BE RENEWED, AND THAT HE MUST HOLD THE PRISONER UNTIL THE SAME IS DONE, the prisoner is allowed to deliberately walk to a corral, mount his horse, appear upon one of the principal streets, and ride out of town."[15] Carr's commentary had a clear message, Sheriff Behan should not have released Ringo.

The *Tombstone Epitaph*, capitalizing on the sheriff's predicament of releasing Ringo before his bond was approved, continued to stir controversy about the cowboys and in regards to the sheriff's actions. On January 25, the *Tombstone Epitaph* published the following article about the posse sent out to return John Ringo to Tombstone:

> Up to the time of going to press nothing has been heard from the posse that went out with Marshal Earp. After the escape of Ringo it was decided to send out

another posse to bring him in, as the marshal of course had no warrant for his arrest. Accordingly, yesterday morning about 4 o'clock a posse of eight, led by Mr. J. Jackson, left town with a warrant for his arrest. Arriving at Charleston at daybreak they put their horses in the corral to grain and after leaving their arms at a convenient place proceeded to the Occidental hotel to get their breakfast. Upon passing the threshold they were intercepted by Isaac Clanton and another man with drawn weapons, while the barrels of other Winchesters suddenly gleamed over the adobe wall. Mr. Jackson stated his errand. After a few words by some of the party that nobody would be arrested unless they wanted to be, Clanton stated that Johnny had always acted the gentleman towards him and he would see what could be done, the result of his efforts being that Ringo should return with the posse to Tombstone. A little While afterward Mr. Ringo's lawyer [Briggs Goodrich] rode up and took Ringo [to] one side for conversation. A few moments afterward Clanton informed Mr. Jackson that Ringo had left but would [be] in Tombstone within an hour or an hour and twenty minutes at most, and in just about the allotted time he appeared, gave himself up and was placed in the county jail. The posse returned to town about four o'clock, the intent of their mission having been achieved by the voluntary act of Ringo. They report about twenty-five cow-boys congregated at Charleston, and from a gentleman who came in late from the southern country we learn that he was passed by a quartet about four miles above Charleston, who were making excellent time in the direction of Hereford [located fifteen miles south of Charleston].

When Jackson's posse arrived at Charleston at daybreak, they put their horses in the corral and left their arms at a safe place; whereupon they went to the Occidental Hotel to have breakfast. Before Jackson's party had made their way to the eatery, Ike Clanton and another man with drawn weapons intercepted them. At the same moment, Jackson's party could see barrels of other Winchester rifles suddenly protruding over an adobe wall. Without hesitation, Jackson immediately informed the men that he had a warrant for John Ringo's arrest. In response, someone in the other group remarked that "nobody would be arrested unless they wanted to be."[16] Acting as an intermediary, Ike told Jackson, "Johnny had always acted the gentleman towards him and he would see what could be done."[17] After talking the matter over with Ike, Ringo initially agreed to return with the posse to Tombstone. However, a short time later Ringo's attorney appeared and discussed the matter with his client. Clanton then informed Jackson that Ringo had left town but would be in Tombstone within an hour and twenty minutes at most.

On January 24 John Ringo voluntarily returned to Tombstone, surrendered to the sheriff, and was placed in the county jail.[18] Throughout the day rumors that the Earp boys and the cowboys were hunting each other and that a fight was imminent, spread upon the streets of Tombstone. With two armed factions with known animosity toward each other out in the countryside, a deadly encounter was seemingly a very real possibility. Meanwhile, the day after Ringo surrendered to the sheriff, a third group led by Charles Bartholomew and consisting of thirty men, left Tombstone heading for Charleston to help Wyatt Earp.[19] Once Bartholomew's party met with the Earp posse, both groups proceeded into Charleston. On the road to Charleston they met Ben Maynard, a known friend of the Clantons, and forced him to go to Charleston with them. After arriving at the town, the Earp party at gunpoint made Maynard point out houses and knock on doors where the Clantons might be staying. Unsuccessful in finding the men they wanted, the Earp party continued to patrol the streets of Charleston the remainder of the night but left the following morning.

After receiving assurances that no Earps would be involved, on January 30, 1882, Isaac and Phineas Clanton surrendered to a "neutral" posse led by Charles Bartholomew, a Wells, Fargo shotgun guard. Pete Spence guided the posse to the Clantons, and they were brought to Tombstone without incident.[20] There the brothers learned, to their surprise, that they were not being accused of stage robbery or cattle rustling, as they had been led to believe, but were being charged with assault to commit murder on Virgil Earp. A preliminary hearing was promptly convened and Ike and Phin were released on bail.[21]

On January 31, 1882, John Ringo pled not guilty for a second time for the Galeyville robbery, and Stilwell released him on a $3,000 bond.[22] The same day, Deputy Breakenridge returned to Tombstone from Galeyville, bringing with him four witnesses that were to testify against Ringo. "Deputy Sheriff Breakenridge in his recent trip to Galeyville served bench warrants upon Roy Stahl, Loss Evilsinger, Fred Kohler and J Coggswell, who had previously failed to put in an appearance. They were brought to this city this time by the Deputy Sheriff," the *Tombstone Nugget* noted.[23]

As January 1882 came to a close, the various posses folded their tents and came home. No bloody battles with "cowboys" took place, and Wyatt's posse returned empty handed largely due to the advance warning that the Clantons had received from Ringo. A week after news of Ringo's brush with Holliday in the streets of Tombstone, the local newspapers once again had published stories involving John Ringo. The notorious cowboy's escape and role in the latest confrontation between the Clantons and the Earps likely was a lively topic in Tombstone and added much to his notorious reputation.

Intersection of Fifth and Allen Street in Tombstone.

13

ARREST WARRANTS AND BORDER PATROLS

Wyatt Earp's reckless and ill-conceived raid on Charleston for the ostensible purpose of arresting cowboy border raiders and stagecoach bandits, which caused much commotion with few results, was a public relations disaster for the Earps, succeeding only in further eroding the standing of Virgil and Wyatt Earp with the people of Cochise County. By now it was apparent to many people that the Earps had personal wrongs to avenge, and the majority of citizens wanted them dismissed as deputy marshals.

At a meeting between prominent Tombstone Republicans and Marshal Dake for the purpose of airing their displeasure with the Earps, Councilman James Nash noted that the unacceptable difficulties of recent weeks arose from the fact that the men who held the office of deputy U.S. marshal had private wrongs to avenge.[1] The people at the meeting wanted Dake to appoint a new deputy marshal, stressing their belief that there was no need for more than one. At the conclusion of the meeting it was decided that a committee would confer with Marshal Dake at four o'clock the next day at the Grand Hotel, at which time they would make their recommendations for a new appointee.

The next day the committee suggested that John H. Jackson or Silas Bryant would be a suitable replacement for the Earps as deputy marshal. "After a thorough review of the situation the committee were informed by the marshal that he would, in proper time, place one of the gentlemen suggested in the position of deputy marshal," reported the *Epitaph*.[2] In response to the citizen meetings where their ouster as deputy marshals was discussed, Virgil and Wyatt Earp wrote an open letter to their boss, U.S. Marshal Crawley Dake, which was published in the February 2 *Epitaph*:

Resignation of Virgil W. Earp and Wyatt S. Earp as Deputy Marshals.

Tombstone, February 1, 1882.
Major C. P. Dake, United States Marshal, Grand Hotel, Tombstone - Dear Sir: In exercising our official functions as deputy United States marshals in this territory, we have endeavored always unflinchingly to perform the duties entrusted to us. These duties have been exacting and perilous in their character, having to be performed in a community where turbulence and violence could at almost any moment be organized to thwart and resist the enforcement of the process of the court issued to bring criminals to justice. And while we have a deep sense of obligation to many of the citizens for their hearty cooperation in aiding us to suppress lawlessness, and their faith in our honesty of purpose, we realize that, notwithstanding our best efforts and judgment in everything which we have been required to perform, there has arisen so much harsh criticism in relation to our operations, and such a persistent effort having been made to misrepresent and misinterpret our acts, we are led to the conclusion that, in order to convince the public that it is our sincere purpose to promote the public welfare, independent of any personal emolument or advantages to ourselves, it is our duty to place our resignations as deputy United States marshals in your hands, which we now do, thanking you for your continued courtesy and confidence in our integrity, and shall remain subject to your orders in the performance of any duties which

may be assigned to us, only until our successors are appointed.

Very respectfully yours,

Virgil W. Earp.
Wyatt S. Earp.

The day after Dake received the Earps' letter of resignation, the marshal appointed John Henry Jackson to be his new deputy in Cochise County.[3] The same day, the examination of Ike and Phin Clanton before Judge William H. Stilwell on the charge of attempting to murder Virgil Earp was held.[4] With little evidence of the defendants' guilt being produced by the prosecution, and seven people providing a rock solid alibi defense by testifying that the Clantons were in Charleston when the crime was committed, the court discharged the defendants.[5] The men who attempted to assassinate Virgil Earp were never brought to justice. While John Ringo is occasionally listed as one of the men involved in the shooting of Virgil Earp, he was not publicly charged or implicated at the time.[6]

Seven days later, on February 9, 1882, Ike Clanton refiled murder charges against the Earps and Holliday, this time in Contention City, a small settlement ten miles west of Tombstone.[7] Responding to Ike's complaint, Justice of the Peace James B. Smith issued warrants for the arrest of the accused men.[8] Upon receiving the warrants, Sheriff John Behan took Wyatt Earp, Morgan Earp, and Doc Holliday into custody. (Virgil Earp was still recuperating from the injuries he received December 28 and was allowed to remain at home.)[9] Ironically, John Ringo, Ike Clanton's chief ally and perceived champion of the cowboys, was also arrested and placed in the jail around this time, but he was released on bond on February 11, 1882.[10]

On the same day that Ringo was released from custody, the counsel for the Earps and Holliday filed a writ of habeas corpus on their behalf asking that they be released, arguing that Justice Smith had no authority to order their arrest.[11] U.S. Court Commissioner Thomas J. Drum, however, recused himself, explaining that, since he had represented Holliday and the Earps during the O.K. Corral gunfight hearing, he had a conflict of interest.[12] Probate Judge John Lucas later denied the appeal for the release of the Earps and Holliday, ruling that Justice Smith indeed had the authority to issue the arrest warrants.[13] Judge Lucas then remanded the prisoners to the custody of the sheriff.

Following Judge Lucas' decision, Ike Clanton jubilantly wrote a letter to Billy Byers, one of the two survivors of the August 1881 Guadalupe Canyon massacre in which Ike's father was killed. Ike remarked, "I have got the Earps all in jail and am not going to unhitch. I have got them on the hip and am going to throw them good."[14] On the day of the proposed hearing, Sheriff Behan and a strong posse took Wyatt, Morgan, and Doc to Contention City. A dozen men, friends of the Earps and Holliday, also accompanied the sheriff to protect against any problems from the opposing faction.[15] Upon viewing the courtroom, it was readily apparent to all parties that the "the meager and uninviting accommodations offered by the justice's court" simply were not adequate to conduct a trial that might take several days to complete.[16] After a short meeting, both parties requested Justice Smith, who granted their motion, to adjourn the hearing and rescheduled the case to be heard the following day in Tombstone.[17]

Tombstone diarist George Parsons took note of the excitement: "Wednesday, 15th: Yesterday Earps were taken to Contention to be tried for killing of [Billy] Clanton. Quite a posse went out. Many of Earp's friends accompanied armed to the teeth. They came back later in day, the good people below beseeching them to leave and try case here. A bad time is expected again in town at any time. Earps on one side of street with their friends and Ike Clanton and Ringo with theirs on the other side - watching each other. Blood will surely come. Hope no innocents will be killed."[18] Parsons' fears of bloodshed proved to be unfounded. At Tombstone, Justice Smith heard opening arguments in the case, but later in the day Judge Lucas, faced with another habeas corpus request, ruled that the arrest warrants issued by Smith were no longer valid because he had not committed the defendants to jail after transferring the case to Tombstone. Lucas then dismissed the charges against the Earps and Holliday once and for all. In his ruling the judge noted that a full hearing had already taken place on the matter, and the grand jury had declined to indict the defendants. He could see no valid reason for reconsidering the case.[19]

Following the dismissal of the latest murder complaint against the Earps, Tombstone residents were surprised when, on February 17, 1882, Wyatt led yet another posse out of town. The *Nugget* on February 18, 1882, made the following comments:

Once More Into The Breach

> Wyatt and Morgan Earp, Doc Holliday, "Texas Jack," - Smith, McMasters, and one or two others left the city yesterday afternoon for - where, no one apparently knows, but when in the vicinity of Waterville [about two miles west of town], they separated, four of the party going in the direction of San Simon Valley, to arrest, it is claimed, Poney Dehl and one or two other well known characters, and the remainder to Charleston. It is supposed they are acting in the capacity of U.S. Deputy Marshals, their resignations not having been accepted or their appointments revoked by U.S. Marshal Dake, as was generally supposed some time ago.[20]

Four days earlier, Justice Wells Spicer had issued arrest warrants on February 13, 1882, for Pony Deal (or Diehl), Al Tiebot, and Charles Haws.[21] However, at the time it was believed that the men were under arrest in Cisco, Texas. Wells, Fargo & Co. employee Charles Bartholomew had named the three as being the highwaymen who stole $6,500 from a stagecoach on January 6.

When news reached Tombstone that Dake had authorized the formation of posses to patrol the Mexican border, the *Nugget* commented:

> One of the peculiarities of Major Dake is, that he says one thing and does another. When the posse referred to, consisting of the Earp party, left this place for the Mexican border he telegraphed to certain parties in this place that he knew nothing of their movements, but supposed they desired to serve some old warrants, and further, that John H. Jackson was his deputy at this place. When he was here some time ago, he made many promises to reform in his management of this portion of the Territory, none of which he has fulfilled; but then it requires something more than the average man to make a good and efficient United States Deputy Marshal, especially on the frontier.[22]

The *Nugget*, on February 28, 1882 further commented: "Major Dake informs us that his deputies, with a posse, are out on the Mexican border patroling and trying to capture certain outlaws who committed outrages last fall in southern Arizona. The Marshal has organized this posse on his own responsibility, trusting to Congress for reimbursement.- Prescott Miner." In actuality, Dake had been cut off from additional government funds in 1881 due to his failure to balance his books.

In June 1882, when Dake left officc he was under investigation by federal authorities for gross malfeasance. In attempting to defend himself against the allegations, Dake redirected the blame onto Wyatt Earp, who he claimed had not submitted vouchers to him before he was forced to leave Arizona. Dake claimed that the money had gone to suppress the cowboys, but the money had gone missing long before his office had taken any action whatsoever. In 1885, examiner Leigh Chalmers reported that Dake had "admitted to having 'feloniously converted' over $50,000 in federal monies to his private account and that he had drawn 'upon it as his individual money.'"[23] About the $3000 that Wells, Fargo had supplied Dake, Chalmers commented, "Dake spent some $300 of that sum in a drunken celebration with the posse in the sporting houses of that notorious community."[24] After conducting his investigation, Chalmers wrote, "The Books [of the Bank] show that Wyatt Earp drew but $536.65 of this amount. The examiner concluded, "This is all the 'large sum of money' which the U. S. Attorney 'believes' was spent by the deputy Marshal Earp in suppressing the 'Cow boy raids' and all that Dake ever deposited in Tombstone for said purpose."[25]

Nonetheless, like Wyatt Earp's Charleston foray in late January 1882, Earp came back to Tombstone from his February patrols with nothing in hand other than some additional expense vouchers to be paid by Wells, Fargo. No fights with outlaws took place; no one was arrested; no loot recovered - the invariable outcome of Wyatt's scouting trips during his so-called "war" against the "cowboys." Perhaps Mayor Carr was right when he surmised after Wyatt's Charleston raid that the real purpose of the posses authorized by Dake and led by Earp was to soak up public funds, not catch criminals.[26] Later in the month Marshal Dake was asked about the status of the Earps as far as his office was concerned. The *Prescott Democrat* reported that, "We are informed by Marshal Dake that the resignations of the Earps, as Deputy United States Marshals, have not yet been accepted, owing to the fact that their accounts have not yet been straightened up. As soon as that is done they will step down and out."[27] Against the stern wishes of many prominent Tombstone Republicans, Virgil and Wyatt Earp remained in possession of deputy U.S. marshal badges until their departure from Arizona.

Following the Earp posse's return from its latest excursion after suspected criminals in late February, the tension in Tombstone seemed to subside somewhat. Clara Brown noticed that the situation had cooled, and on March 13, 1882, the *San Diego Union* published her comments about the state of affairs in Tombstone:

> The turbulent condition of affairs which was prevailing at the time of my last letter has been for some time subdued, though exactly in what manner I cannot say, as the movements of the posses sent from here almost

> daily at that time were secret. The presence of United States Marshal Dake on the field of action is undoubtedly the principal cause of so speedy a change for the better, and Judge Stilwell of the District Court is commended for the part he has played in the secret drama. There being a lull in cowboy criminality (which we hope is something more than temporary), and the Indians apparently having left the Dragoons, Tombstone people have been obliged to look to other causes of excitement."[28]

Despite Clara Brown's hope that the subdued condition in Tombstone would be more than temporary, it proved to be only a lull in the storm, as the turbulent conditions in Tombstone were about to return with deadly fury.

During the evening of Saturday, March 18, 1882, Wyatt Earp ran into John Ringo's attorney, Briggs Goodrich, on the street. Earp was suspicious that something was about to happen. Wyatt told Goodrich, "I think they were after us last night. Do you know anything about it?"[29] Goodrich did not know anything but thought that someone could make a move against the Earps at any time. The attorney then commented to Earp, "By the way, John Ringo wanted me to say to you, that if any fighting came up between you all that he wanted you to understand he would have nothing to do with it; that he was going to look out for himself, and everybody else could do the same.'[30] Ringo's comments suggest that he may have known that someone was going to make an attempt to murder the Earps, but he wanted no part in it.

A few hours later Wyatt and Morgan were at "Campbell & Hatch's billiard parlor, on Allen street between Fourth and Fifth," when a shot blasted through the window pane of the back door hitting Morgan.[31] "The bullet entered the right side of the abdomen, passing through the spinal column, completely shattering it, emerging on the left side, passing the length of the room and lodging in the thigh of Geo. A. B. Berry, who was standing by the stove, inflicting a painful flesh wound," the *Epitaph* later reported.[32] A second shot hit the wall above Wyatt Earp's head. Morgan fell instantly and died within an hour.

The day after the shooting, Coroner H. M. Matthews empaneled a jury to investigate the circumstances of Morgan's death. After hearing testimony from several witnesses, the jurors determined that the killer was most likely one of a group of conspirators - Pete Spence, Frank Stilwell, "John Doe" Freeze or Freis (later identified as Frederick Bode), and two Indians or half-breeds, one named Charlie, the other unknown.[33] This conclusion was based in large part on damning statements made by Marietta Spence, Pete Spence's wife, who obviously wanted to see her husband behind bars. The jury did not determine which of the conspirators actually pulled the trigger on the revolver from which the fatal bullet was fired, nor did they propose a motive for the attack. The Earps had been involved in the arrest of Spence and Stilwell for stage robbery the previous September, and this could have inspired the accused parties to assault the lawmen. It is also reasonable that the same parties that killed Morgan were responsible for shooting Virgil in late December 1881.

John Ringo is often accused of participating in Morgan Earp's killing even though there is no evidence linking him to the murder. Over forty years later, Wyatt Earp identified the men that he believed had murdered his brother:

> The men who murdered my brother were Curly Bill, Ringo, Stillwell, Hank Swelling, and the Mexican Florentine. I was told by their lawyer that I must be careful that they were going to assassinate us all. I don't care to tell who the lawyer was who told me as he was a good friend of mine. And at the same time was handling the other side.[34]

Wyatt's claim is questionable considering John Ringo's lawyer, Briggs Goodrich, testified before a coroner's jury about the conversation that he had with Earp. The *Tombstone Epitaph* reported Goodrich's testimony on March 23, 1882:

> . . . By the way, (Goodrich speaking to Earp) John Ringo wanted me to say to you, that if any fighting came up between you all, he wanted you to understand that he would have nothing to do with it; that he was going to look after himself, and anybody else could do the same. I think that from what Frank Stilwell said, that there would be trouble. He said there was some boys in town who would toe the mark, and the worst of it was the Earps would think he was in it, as they do not like him. I told him I would tell them the same for for him as I had for John Ringo, and he said, no, that he would rather die than let them know he cared a damn what they thought. I advised him to keep off the streets at night, and then he would be able to prove an alibi.

In contrast to Wyatt's claim, Goodrich's sworn testimony indicates that he did not tell Earp the names of anyone who he suspected might attempt to kill the Earps. Thus, it is unlikely that Briggs Goodrich told Wyatt Earp that John Ringo was involved in the murder of Morgan Earp.

Virgil Earp and his wife Allie boarded a train at Contention City, with Colton, California, as their ultimate destination. They were escorted as far as Tucson by Wyatt Earp, Warren Earp, Doc Holliday, Sherman McMasters, and "Turkey Creek" Jack Johnson, all heavily armed. When their train reached Tucson on the evening of the 20th, the Earp party came upon Ike Clanton and Frank Stilwell at the station. Ike Clanton, who had been in Tucson for over two weeks, was expecting Milt McDowell of Charleston to arrive in town to testify as a witness in Jerry Barton's trial before the district court. Stilwell had been subpoenaed by the district court.[35] After seeing the Earp party, Clanton told Stilwell that the Earps were at the station and that he should make a run for it. However, Frank Stilwell could not evade the Earps, and his body was found the next day shot several times.[36]

The Earp party quickly traveled back to Tombstone where Wyatt Earp was informed that an arrest warrant from Tucson had been issued for him and the rest of his party. The men packed some things and prepared to leave the town. Sheriff Behan attempted to stop Wyatt Earp and his party. However, Wyatt Earp refused to surrender and Sheriff Behan was forced to back down.[37]

When the Earp party rode out of Tombstone on March 21, 1882, they were fleeing from justice, not riding out to serve warrants or patrol the border as they had claimed they had done the previous two months. Rather than galloping their horses for the safety of the border, Wyatt Earp and his men the next morning rode over to Pete Spence's wood camp looking for Spence and a man named Indian Charlie.[38] Wyatt Earp had personal wrongs to avenge and he was intent on settling the score with the men who he believed had killed his brother Morgan.

Four decades later, Wyatt Earp curiously told writer Walter Nobel Burns that Pete Spence did not kill his brother Morgan. "I am satisfied that Spence had nothing to do with the assassination of Morgan," Wyatt recalled.[39] Yet, if Wyatt did not believe Pete Spence was involved in the killing of his brother Morgan, why was the Earp party looking for Spence on March 22, 1882? Wyatt's own actions at the time seem to contradict his later story.

The Earp party reached Pete Spence's wood camp the next day before noon, and the first man they encountered was Theodore Judah, a hired hand at the wood camp. After talking to Judah, the party learned that Spence was probably in Tombstone, but a Mexican named Florentino Cruz was nearby. Judah watched as the Earp party rode toward Florentino's location. Moments later, Judah heard several gunshots echo in the distance. The next day Cruz's lifeless body was found riddled by gunshots.

Morgan Earp was killed playing billiards in Campell and Hatch's billiard parlor.

United States Marshal Crawley Dake accepted the resignations of Virgil and Wyatt Earp as his deputies, but never officially removed them from the position.

14

THE POSSE

The same morning that Cruz was killed by the Earp party, Sheriff Behan led a large posse, which included Ringo, out of Tombstone in pursuit of Wyatt Earp. "Wednesday, 22nd: Excitement again this morning. Sheriff went out with a posse supposedly to arrest the Earp party, but they will never do it. The cowboy element is backing him strongly, John Ringo being one of the party. There is a prospect of a bad time and there are about three men who deserve to get it in the back of the neck. Terrible thing, this, for our town, but the sooner it is all, over with the better," George Parson noted in his diary.[1]

Despite Goodrich's claim to Earp that Ringo "was going to look out for himself, and everybody else could do the same," the cowboy joined Behan's posse.[2] Breakenridge later claimed that he let Ringo use his rifle and horse. "He [Behan] asked me to loan my horse and rifle to John Ringo, who had left his rifle at a ranch close to town, and who with several others of the cowboys and rustlers made up the posse."[3] The make-up of Behan's posse, which included cowboys as well as some permanent residents of Tombstone, was questioned by some at the time. Breakenridge later defended Behan's selection of some of the cowboys as posse members: "He took these men knowing that the Earp party would resist arrest, and, on account of the feud between them, he believed the cowboys would stay and fight."[4]

The posse left Tombstone around eleven o'clock in the morning, following the trail of the Earp party which had headed toward Contention City the previous evening. At Contention they met Sheriff Bob Paul, who had arrived by the western train. Behan and Paul together returned to Tombstone around four o'clock that afternoon. Later that evening the remainder of the posse returned to town. Some people had thought that the Earp party would head straight for Tucson to turn themselves in to Pima County Sheriff Bob Paul. However, it appeared that the Earp party had "left the Contention road and went in the direction of Sycamore Springs, where they camped Tuesday night." Rumors spread that a "wagon load of provisions was sent to that place for their use," the *Nugget* reported.[5]

After the posse's return to Tombstone, information was received that provided confirmation that the Earp party was at Sycamore Springs. Hoping to effect the arrest of Wyatt Earp and his party, Sheriff Behan led his posse, which consisted of about "seventeen men, all heavily armed," out of Tombstone at eleven o'clock that night. Sheriff Paul remained in Tombstone. Meanwhile rumors spread on the streets that the Earp party had visited Pete Spence's ranch, where they were "holding the Mexicans up," and threatening "them with death if they did not reveal the whereabouts of Spence."[6] Tombstone had not yet learned of the death of Florentino Cruz at Pete Spence's wood camp.

Behan and his posse reportedly "went as far as Dragoon mountains, where they struck the trail of the Earp party, and followed it back to within three miles of town, where it was covered by the surrounding travel."[7] The sheriff's posse returned to Tombstone the morning of March 23, 1882.[8]

The sheriff's posse played cat-and-mouse with the Earp gang for several days but did not manage to locate them. While the sheriff and his quarry were galloping about the countryside, Pete Spence and Frederick Bode were arrested in Tombstone for the murder of Morgan Earp.[9] The Cochise County jail, however, was the safest place for them to be at this time. In early April the murder charges against Spence and Bode were dropped for lack of evidence.[10] Using Contention City as somewhat of a base camp, Behan's posse searched the area with no success. Sometime around four o'clock in the afternoon on March 24, the posse left Contention City, heading for Kinnear's ranch in the Whetstone Mountains.[11] Meanwhile, as Behan's posse was riding toward the far side of the Whetstone Mountains, the Earp party was about to have an encounter twelve miles from Contention City with some men at a spring in the Whetstone Mountains. The next day rumors began to spread that the Earp party had a fight with four men from the sheriff's posse.

The *Tombstone Epitaph* reported that it had received information that a fight had taken place at Burleigh Springs between the Earp party and a group of cowboys lead by Curly Bill.[12] The story claimed that Curly Bill had been killed. This story would evolve over the next few days and details would be altered with each new story. Finally, it was claimed that Wyatt Earp had killed Curly Bill in the fight.[13]

Around eight o'clock the night after Wyatt Earp's party had a shootout in the Whetstone Mountains, Behan's posse returned to Contention City. Behan would report that the men that had encountered the Earp party were not members of his posse.[14] After the initial claims of Curly Bill's death were reported, many people were undecided on which story to believe. Rumors began to spread that the Earp party had received $1000 dollars for his death. The *Nugget* on March 31, 1882, published a story describing the rumored payoff: "It is said, by parties who claim their ability to sustain it, that the reward of $1000 dollars, offered by the Stockraisers Protective Association for Curly Bill, was claimed by Wyatt Earp, and the amount in horses and money, paid to him by H.C. Hooker last Monday. Possibly this is true; but it is rough on the party who paid the reward, as the notorious and Wily William is beyond question of doubt alive in New Mexico, keeping his weather eye open for a fresh saddle horse. Any how it was a neat job."

The *Nugget* steadfastly denied that the reports of Curly Bill's death were credible and offered a $1000 reward to anyone who could prove that Curly Bill was dead. The *Epitaph* countered by doubling the reward amount to $2000, offering to give the money to charity if Curly showed himself in town. Neither reward was ever claimed.[15]

Wyatt Earp told his story of how he killed Curly Bill on different occasions over the next several years.[16] Yet, Wyatt was firing and fleeing at the same time during the encounter, making it almost impossible for him to know the results of his shot from a distance of thirty yards.[17] He did not walk up to a dead victim, roll the body over, and confirm the man was Curly Bill. Wyatt may have believed that Curly was there, and he may have believed that he killed Curly Bill; however, he could not have known for sure.

At the time, there were claims that Curly Bill had left the territory well before Wyatt Earp supposedly killed him.[18] Curly Bill was even reported to be dead over a month prior to the Earp party's supposed battle with the notorious cowboy.[19] After his reputed death at the hands of Wyatt Earp at Iron Springs on March 24, 1882, reports began to surface in newspapers in Texas, New Mexico, and Arizona that Curly Bill was alive. "Curley Bill, a cowboy who obtained an unenviable notoriety in Tombstone a couple of years ago, and has been reported killed several times since, is said to have discovered, in connection with another party, some very rich silver mines in Chihuahua," reported the *Clifton Clarion* in 1883.[20] Old-timers told stories about one person or another seeing Curly years later, and that Curly settled down in Chihuahua, Mexico. But no confirmation has ever been found conclusively confirming his presence anywhere after March 1882.[21] Nonetheless, there are too many reports of Curly Bill's residence in Chihuahua after 1882 to dismiss out of hand the possibility that the notorious cowboy may have lived for many years in the Mexican state.

Contrary to popular accounts that claim Ringo hid out in Mexico until Wyatt Earp and his party left Arizona, Ringo was with Behan's posse the entire time. After ten days in the saddle, Sheriff John Behan's posse returned to town in early April of 1882, and John Ringo rode out of Tombstone.[22]

Early in May 1882, the United States government finally took overt steps to address the so-called cowboy problem in Arizona. President Chester A. Arthur issued an order for "evil-disposed persons who are banded together to oppose and obstruct the execution of the laws" to "disperse and retire peaceably to their respective abodes on or before noon of the 5th day of May."[23] But the troubles in Arizona had largely ended with the departure of Wyatt Earp and his party a month earlier. When the Arizona Legislature met the following year, they passed a joint resolution thanking the President for his "promptness in taking steps for the suppression of lawlessness" in Arizona.[24]

Three days after the President's deadline had passed, John Ringo returned to Tombstone. "Jack Ringold is in town," noted the *Epitaph* on May 8. Ringo had returned to Tombstone to settle the criminal charges based on the Galeyville robbery that were still ongoing. Judge Stilwell scheduled Ringo's trial to be heard on May 12th. The trial was postponed by the judge two additional times apparently because no witnesses could be found to testify against the notorious cowboy.[25] While waiting for his case to proceed, Ringo's name was entered into the Cochise County Great Register and his occupation was listed as "Speculator," on May 16, 1882.[26] Finally, on May 18th, with no witnesses available or apparently willing to testify against Ringo, the court dismissed the charges.[27]

Meanwhile, Doc Holliday, who had been arrested in Colorado, was fighting an extradition attempt by Arizona officials to bring him back to Tucson to answer for the Stilwell killing. While in jail, Holliday made several accusations to reporters concerning what had happened in Tombstone. Doc accused Ringo of recently robbing a woman in Tombstone of all of her jewelry:

> "He [Behan] always hated me after that, and would spend money to have me killed. He has always stood in with the Rustlers and taken his share of their plunder, and in consequence he is in their power, and must do as they say. This is shown by the fact that he has five deputies. One of these men is John Ringo, who jumped on the stage of a variety theater in Tombstone one night about three weeks ago, and took all the jewels from the proprietors wife in full view of the audience."[28]

Was Holliday simply repeating some wild rumor or fabricating a story that he had heard that had no basis in fact? Or, was the accusation against Ringo true? Unfortunately, Doc's allegation against Ringo can be neither proved nor disproved. Nonetheless, the newspapers of the time did not mention Ringo taking jewels from anyone. Likewise, no complaint was ever filed in Tombstone against Ringo for a robbery that occurred in May 1882. When the news report from Colorado made its way back to Tombstone, the *Epitaph* immediately stated its opinion of Doc Holliday's statement: "If the statement before us is a specimen of Doc's veracity, there is no questioning the strength and power of his imagination."[29]

Doc Holliday had also declared that the *Epitaph* had been taken over by the cowboy element and its editor was run out of town. However, Charles Reppy, the *Epitaph's* former editor denied this allegation:

> An Epitaph reporter met Mr. Reppy after reading the interview and inquired if he had seen it. An affirmative answer, accompanied by a laugh, was given, supplemented by the statement that Holliday was the most thoroughly equipped liar, and smoothest scoundrel in the United States. The reporter then enquired if Mr. Reppy was not a friend of the Earps and Holliday, and was immediately answered in the negative.[30]

The *Epitaph* had been sold and was under new management. Consequently, some writers have theorized that the lack of newspaper coverage concerning Ringo's supposed latest outrage, may have been the result of a more sympathetic manner of dealing with the cowboys of Arizona, and that Samuel Purdy, a staunch Democrat, may have refrained from printing any bad press about Ringo.

Regardless, sometime in May 1882, John Ringo left Tombstone at the peak of his notoriety in Arizona. Similar to the end of the Hoodoo War, Ringo had survived the Earp-Clanton feud or the so-called Cowboy War, which had its beginnings with the gunfight at the O.K. Corral. The hostilities ended with at least six men dead largely from private animosities rather than skirmishes between outlaws and lawmen. He emerged as a major figure in the events that had occurred. For the first time in six months, Ringo was free from all criminal charges that had been filed against him. His main antagonist over the past six months, Wyatt Earp, had left the territory with Doc Holliday and the rest of the core of the Earp faction. Seemingly, the reputed cowboy leader had everything going his way.

Two months later he would be dead.

George Parsons saw Sheriff John Behan's posse ride out of Tombstone and noted that the cowboys were backing him strongly because John Ringo was one of the posse members.

Sheriff John Behan assembled a posse to go after Wyatt Earp that included John Ringo and some other cowboys.

Pima County Sheriff Bob Paul mistakenly thought that Wyatt Earp and his party would voluntarily surrender to him once he came to Tombstone after Frank Stilwell was killed.

15

LAST RIDE FROM TOMBSTONE

On a hot Sunday afternoon, two days before Independence Day of 1882, John Ringo rode into Tombstone for the first time in several weeks. At the peak of his notoriety in Tombstone, the *Epitaph* was quick to mention the notorious cowboy's arrival in the town, "John Ringo arrived in town Sunday afternoon."[1] Known to suffer from fits of melancholy, Ringo began to drink heavily, starting an "extended jamboree" that lasted several days.[2] Upon seeing Ringo sipping his sorrows away, *Epitaph* Editor, Samuel Purdy, engaged in a conversation with the reputed cowboy leader. Finding Ringo to be morose, possibly even suicidal, Purdy later recalled, "Two weeks ago last Sunday in conversing with the writer, he [Ringo] said he was as certain of being killed, as he was of living then. He said that he might run along for a couple of years more, and may not last two days."[3] Six days later, on July 8, 1882, John Ringo left the boom town on what would be his last ride from Tombstone.[4] The notorious cowboy was subsequently found dead on July 14, 1882.[5]

On July 9, Ringo stopped at Dial's ranch in the Dragoon Mountains to have dinner, then he continued to Galeyville.[6] Along the trail, Ringo apparently encountered deputy William Breakenridge in the south pass of the Dragoon Mountains. Breakenridge claimed that Ringo was reeling in his saddle, drunk, and that the cowboy stubbornly refused to temporarily stop his journey to Galeyville.

> I met John Ringo in the South Pass of the Dragoon Mountains. It was shortly after noon. Ringo was very drunk, reeling in the saddle, and said he was going to

> Galeyville. It was in the summer and a very hot day. He offered me a drink out of a bottle half-full of whiskey, and he had another full bottle. I tasted it and it was too hot to drink. It burned my lips. Knowing that he would have to ride nearly all night before, he could reach Galeyville, I tried to get him to go back with me to the Goodrich Ranch and wait until after sundown, but he was drunk and stubborn and went on his way. I think this was the last time he was seen alive.[7]

Breakenridge placed the date of his encounter with Ringo around noon, the day before Ringo's death, which was on July 13. If Breakenridge's claim is true, considering the distance from the Dragoon Mountains to Galeyville and that Ringo reportedly passed through the area on July 9, it's more likely that the deputy met the notorious cowboy in the Dragoon Mountains a few days earlier. Nonetheless, late on the evening of July 9, Ringo arrived in Galeyville and persisted in tossing down more whiskey. At some point, Ringo left Galeyville, possibly heading for Morse's Canyon.[8]

On July 14, 1882, teamster John Yoast found John Ringo's dead body in the midst of a clump of oak trees. Yoast, having known Ringo for years in both Arizona and Texas, instantly recognized the notorious cowboy. Immediately, he called for help and within a few minutes several men had arrived at the scene. After conducting an informal inquest at the death scene and preparing a statement for the information of the coroner and county sheriff, they buried the body at the spot it was found.[9] Two days later, news of John Ringo's death reached Tombstone. By the following day, a special dispatch was received in Tucson about Ringo's death. Tucson's *Arizona Daily Star*, printed an announcement of the reputed cowboy leader's death on the front page of the paper's Tuesday, July 18, issue:

HIS LAST SHOT.
The "King of the Cowboys,"
Sends a Bullet Through His Brain.

Special Dispatch to the Star.
TOMBSTONE, July 17. - John Ringgold [Ringo], one of the best known men in southwestern [southeastern] Arizona, was found dead in Morse's canyon, in the Chiricahua mountains last Friday. He evidently committed suicide. He was known in this section as "King of the Cowboys," and was fearless in the extreme. He had many staunch friends and bitter enemies. The pistol, with one chamber emptied, was found in his clenched fist. He shot himself in the head, the bullet entering on the right side, between the eye and ear, and coming out on top of the head. Some members of his family reside at San Jose California.

Newspapers in Arizona, and as far away as California and New Mexico, printed accounts of Ringo's death after seeing news reports from Tucson.[10] Ironically, even in death, the cowboy could not shake off the mistaken belief that his real name was John Ringgold, which started in Texas seven years earlier. On Tuesday, July 18, 1882, the *Tombstone Epitaph* published a more detailed account of John Ringo's demise:

DEATH OF JOHN RINGO

His Body Found In Morse's Canyon.-
Probable Suicide.

Sunday evening intelligence reached this city of the finding of the dead body of John Ringo near the mouth of Morse's canyon in the Chiricahua mountains on Friday afternoon. There was few men in Cochise county, or southeastern Arizona better known. He was recognized by friends and foes as a recklessly brave man, who would go any distance, or undergo any hardship to serve a friend or punish an enemy. While undoubtedly reckless, he was far from being a desperado, and we know of no murder being laid to his charge. Friends and foes are unanimous in the opinion that he was a strictly honorable man in all his dealings, and that his word was as good as his bond. Many people who were intimately acquainted with him in life, have serious doubts that he took his own life, while an equally large number say that he frequently threatened to commit suicide, and that event was expected at any time.

The circumstances of the case hardly leave any room for doubt as to his self destruction. He was about 200 feet from water, and was acquainted with every inch of the country, so that it was impossible for him to lose himself. He was found in the midst of a clump of oaks, springing from the same stem, but diverging outward so as to leave an open space in the center. On top of the main stem [at ground level] and between the spreading boughs, was a large stone, and on this pedestal he was found sitting, with his body leaning backward and resting against a tree. He was found by a man named Yost [John Yoast] who was acquainted with him for years both in this Territory and Texas. Yost is working for Sorgum Smith, and was employed hauling wood. He was driving a team along the road, and noticed a man in the midst of the clump of trees, apparently asleep. He passed on without further investigation, but on looking back, saw his dog smelling of the man's face and snorting. This excited curiosity and he, stopped the team, alighted and proceeded to investigate.

He found the lifeless body of John Ringo, with a hole large enough to admit two fingers about half way between the right eye and ear, and a hole correspondingly large on top of his head, doubtless the outlet of the fatal bullet. The revolver was firmly clenched in his hand, which is almost conclusive evidence that death was instantaneous. His rifle rested against a tree and one of his cartridge belts was turned upside down. Yost immediately gave the alarm and in about 15 minutes eleven men were on the spot. The Subjoined Statement was made by eye witnesses to Coroner [Henry M.] Matthews:

TURKEY OR MORSE'S MILL, CREEK

Statement for the information of the Coroner and Sheriff of Cochise County, Arizona: there was found by the undersigned, John Yost, the body of a man in a clump of oak trees, about 20 yds. north from the road leading to Morse's mill, and about a quarter of a mile west of the house of B. F. Smith. The undersigned viewed the body and found it in a sitting posture, facing west, the head inclined to the right. There was a bullet hole on the top of the head on the left side. There is, apparently, a part of the scalp gone, including a small portion of the forehead and part of the hair. This looks as if cut out by a knife. These are the only marks of violence visible on the body. Several of the undersigned identify the body as that of John Ringo, well known in Tombstone. He was dressed in light hat, blue shirt, vest, pants and drawers. On his feet were a pair of hose and an undershirt torn up so as to protect his feet. He had evidently traveled but a short distance in this foot gear. His revolver he grasped in his right hand, his rifle resting against the tree close to him. He had on two cartridge belts, the belt for revolver cartridges being buckled on upside down.

The undernoted property was found with him and on his person: one Colt's revolver, calibre 45, No. 222, containing five cartridges; one Winchester rifle octagon barrel, calibre 45, model 1876, No. 21,986, containing a cartridge in the breech and ten in the magazine; 1 cartridge belt, containing 9 rifle cartridges; 1 cartridge belt, containing 2 revolver cartridges; 1 silver watch of American Watch company, No. 9339, with silver chain attached; two dollars and sixty cents ($2.60) in money; 6 pistol cartridges in pocket; 5 shirt studs; 1 small pocket knife; 1 tobacco pipe; 1 comb; 1 block matches; 1 small piece tobacco. There is also a portion of a letter from Messrs. Hereford & Zabriskie, attorneys at law, Tucson, to the deceased, John Ringo. The above property is left in the possession of Frederick Ward, teamster between Morse's mill and Tombstone.

The body of the deceased was buried close to where it was found. When found deceased had been dead about twenty-four hours.

Thomas White, John Blake, John W. Bradford, B. F. Smith, A. E. Lewis, A. S. Neighbors, James Morgan, Robert Boller, Frank McKenney, W. J. Dowell, J. C. McGray, John Yoast, Fred Ward.

* * *

From Fred Ward, who arrived in this city on Sunday evening, an EPITAPH reporter learned that the general impression prevailing among people in the Chiricahuas is that his [Ringo's] horse wandered off somewhere, and he started off on foot to search for him; that his boots began to hurt him, and he pulled them off and made moccasins of his undershirt. He could not have been suffering for water, as he was within 200 feet of it and not more than 700 feet from Smith's house. Mrs. Morse and Mrs. Young passed by where he was lying Thursday afternoon [July 13], but supposed it was some man asleep, and took no further notice of him. The inmates of Smith's house heard a shot about 3 o'clock Thursday evening, and it is more than likely that that is the time the rash deed was done.

He was on an extended jamboree the last time he was in this city, and only left here ten days ago. He had dinner at Dial's in the South Pass of the Dragoons one week ago last Sunday, and went from there to Galeyville, where he kept on drinking heavily. We have not heard of his whereabouts after leaving Galeyville, but it is more than likely that he went to Morse's canyon. He was subject to frequent fits of melancholy and had an abnormal fear of being killed. Two weeks ago last Sunday in conversing with the writer, he said he was as certain of being killed, as he was of living then. He said he might run along for a couple of years more, and may not last two days.

He was born in Texas [Indiana] and is very respectably connected. He removed to San Jose, California, when about sixteen years old, and Col. Coleman Younger, one of the leading citizens of that town is his grandfather. Ringo was a second cousin to the famous Younger brothers now in the Minnesota penitentiary, for their partnership with the James boys. He has three sisters in San Jose, of whom he was passionately fond. He was about thirty-eight [thirty-two], though looking much younger, and was a fine specimen of physical manhood. Many friends will mourn him, and many others will take secret delight in learning of his death.

A telegraph dispatch was sent to San Jose informing that town that John Ringgold, the "King of the Cowboys," was dead. The local newspaper made a brief inquiry before reprinting the *Star's* account of the cowboy's death, adding that his real name was "Ringo," and that his sisters, who had been orphaned at a young age, had lived with a relative.[11] Responding to the notice, John Ringo's sister, Enna Ringo, wrote to the *Epitaph* in an attempt to clarify some statements made about her brother:

> The Epitaph yesterday received a letter from Miss Emma [sic] Ringo, sister of the late John Ringo, in which she says that John Ringo was born in Indiana, in 1850, and was thirty-two years old at the time of his death, Col. Younger was an uncle by marriage, and consequently Ringo was no relative of the Younger boys.[12]

If the early writers or researchers would have found the above article, which provides key information about the notorious cowboy's background, the debate over John Ringo's true name, his age, place of birth, and connection to the Younger brothers, would have been resolved years ago.

For more than a century, mystery and controversy have circulated about the details of Ringo's demise, making his passing one of the most hotly debated deaths in Old West history. The *Epitaph's* initial article provided the fodder that commenced this dispute when it commented, "Many people who were intimately acquainted with him in life, have serious doubts that he took his own life, while an equally large number say that he frequently threatened to commit suicide, and that event was expected at any time."[13]

Despite the opposing views, the *Epitaph* concluded, "The circumstances of the case hardly leave any room for doubt as to his self destruction."[14] Other newspapers concurred, proclaiming that John Ringo, or as some reports proclaimed, "John Ringgold," had "evidently committed suicide."[15] Nonetheless, the official coroner's report, filed on November 3, 1882, was not quite as conclusive: "Cause of death 'unknown' but presumed from gunshot wounds."[16] Today, those writers and historians that do not accept that the reputed cowboy leader committed suicide, often cite the strange circumstances surrounding Ringo's death, before concluding that someone may have killed him.

The main points of controversy focus on the description of items listed, and more importantly, what was not listed by the citizen's impromptu "Statement for the information of the Coroner and Sheriff."[17] One of the first points often raised is that John Yoast and the other men that held the informal inquest noted that Ringo's Colt .45 caliber pistol, serial number 222, contained five cartridges.[18] Some people have speculated that this suggests that the cowboy had not fired his pistol. In the Old West, it was customary for people to only load five cartridges into their weapons for their own safety. The pistols of that day, if suddenly jarred, could accidently go off when the firing pin was resting on a live cartridge. However, while it may have been customary, there are provable incidences where people loaded six cartridges in their pistols. One such example occurred in Tombstone when Curly Bill Brocius shot Fred White. At a hearing later conducted in Tucson on the matter, Wyatt Earp stated, "I examined the pistol afterwards and found only one cartridge discharged, five remaining."[19] Ironically, Wyatt Earp in Wichita once had his pistol, which presumably contained six cartridges, discharge when it fell from his belt and hit the floor.[20] Since some men did carry pistols fully loaded with six cartridges at times, it is likely that the coroner's jury simply failed to state that one of the rounds had been fired because it was so obvious. Considering that the men examined Ringo's pistol, it is hard to imagine that they would not have realized that it had not been fired if there were no exploded cartridges in the six-shooter.

Another issue often raised is the supposed fact that there were no powder burns on his temple, suggesting that he was shot at a distance.[21] The coroner's jury made no mention of the absence or presence of powder burns. However, we should remember that these men were not professional coroners, they were simply trying to quickly

Samuel Purdy talked with Ringo during his last visit to Tombstone and later reported that the cowboy suffered from fits of melancholy and had an abnormal fear of being killed.

record some details of the scene. Ringo's body had been lying in the hot sun for a day and it was decomposing rapidly. Powder burns and powder residue would have been hard to detect in these messy conditions. In any case, if the muzzle of the revolver was against Ringo's head when fired, and it most likely was, the exploding powder would have been projected into the wound and external powder burns would have been minimal. In actuality, these men were probably more concerned with burying the body, than making sure every item had been covered in their statement. It did not occur to them then that more that a century later, people would be debating the particulars of their descriptions. Years later, Robert Boller, one of the men on the coroner's jury, wrote a letter to Frank M. King in 1934, describing the scene of Ringo's death. The letter was published in Frank King's, *Wranglin' with the Past* (1935). Boller wrote:

> I showed him [Yoast] where the bullet had entered the tree on the left side. Blood and brains [were] oozing from the wound and matted his hair. There was an empty shell in the six-shooter and the hammer was on that. I called it suicide fifty-two years ago, I am still calling it suicide. I guess I'm the last of the coroner's jury.[22]

Despite the fact that Robert Boller's recollections were made over a half century later, and old-timer accounts are often not completely reliable, he was, at least, provably present at the scene of Ringo's death. Thus, we must give his reminiscences some weight. A more curious circumstance noted by the coroner's jury was that on Ringo's feet "were a pair of hose and an undershirt torn up so as to protect his feet."[23] The men also noticed that Ringo's belt for revolver cartridges was "buckled on upside down."[24] An even stranger observation was that the body appeared to have a small part of the forehead and scalp gone, including part of the hair, which looked as if someone had cut it with a knife.[25] But these factors did not give the jurors pause in coming to their suicide determination.

Because of his sudden and mysterious death, people have questioned whether Ringo committed suicide. Many theories have developed regarding John Ringo's passing, and several candidates have emerged as possible suspects in the notorious cowboy's death. Popular proposed killers of Ringo include Buckskin Frank Leslie, Wyatt Earp, and Mike O'Rourke, alias "Johnny-Behind-The-Deuce," the killer of Phillip Schneider in Charleston.[26]

For nearly forty years, Ringo's mysterious death was considered a suicide, but rumors that he was murdered by one man or another persisted. One early article published by a San Francisco newspaper in 1893, provided an interesting story about a man who was tracking down rustlers in Arizona for vengeance. According to this tale, the avenger's last act was killing Ringo.[27] While it is a good story, there is no evidence to corroborate it whatsoever. Over three decades later, a writer published an interesting but obviously impossible account of a Mexican sheepherder who claimed to have seen Frank Leslie shoot Ringo near the location his body was found.[28] After Ringo was shot by Leslie, the notorious cowboy would have needed amazing strength and willpower to climb down from his horse, take a few steps, then collapse at the tree where he was found - quite a feat for someone who, in actuality, had a wound to the head that must have caused instantaneous death. Nevertheless, rumors that Leslie and Ringo were on bad terms at the time, had been involved in an argument, and that Leslie was seen in the area where Ringo was found dead, helped to fuel the theory that he killed John Ringo.[29] By 1922, Buckskin Frank easily emerged as the leading candidate for possibly having killed Ringo, although there was little evidence to prove the claim.

It appears that Frank Leslie was the first man to claim that he killed Ringo. While Leslie was in the Yuma Territorial Prison for killing his wife in the 1890s, Frank King, then a guard at the prison, later declared that Leslie had told him that he had killed Ringo.[30] At the time, Leslie's claim was not seriously believed by anyone. Some thought that Leslie had simply tried to take credit for the killing for whatever notoriety it might bring him. Breakenridge also later claimed that "Frank

Leslie tried to curry favor with Earp sympathizers by claiming that he had met Ringo and had to kill him in self-defense, but the evidence proved to be a lie. We all knew that Leslie would not care to tackle him even when he was drunk."[31] Apparently, Breakenridge's comments were based on conversation made in San Francisco bars during the 1920s. Leslie biographer Don Chaput wrote, "There is evidence to suggest that in the 1920s, Frank Leslie would tell anyone anything, so long as it led to a free drink."[32] Buckskin Frank's biographer dismissed his claim as idle boasting, an activity for which Leslie was famous.[33]

If Leslie did kill Ringo, then it was a cowardly act, similar to the craven killings of other Old West characters like Wild Bill Hickok and John Wesley Hardin.[34] The notorious cowboy would likely have been passed out drunk, sleeping off the effects of alcohol, when Leslie supposedly murdered him. To believe this theory, we would have to accept that Leslie used Ringo's gun to do the deed and then stage a suicide scene. But why? If no one saw him slay the cowboy, he would have been in the clear even if it was later obvious that a homicide had occurred. Rather than wasting time using Ringo's pistol and arranging the body in a suicide-like pose at three o'clock in the afternoon (the time a single shot was heard at the nearby Smith house[35]), Buckskin Frank would have been better off simply shooting the cowboy from a safe distance, then quickly riding off. Another popular rumor with no basis in fact is the claim that Billy Claiborne came to Tombstone to revenge Ringo's death and was killed by Leslie in a gunfight.[36] While Buckskin Frank did kill Claiborne in a gunfight in November 1882, newspaper accounts of the testimony following the killing show that the shooting was the result of a political argument.[37] The stories that Claiborne implicated Leslie in Ringo's death before he died appear to be tall tales.

During the 1920s, Stuart Lake contacted Fred Dodge for information for a future book about Wyatt Earp. Dodge was a former resident of Tombstone, who later claimed, categorically and without corroboration, that he came to the boom town during 1879 as an undercover agent for Wells, Fargo.[38] In September of 1929, after Wyatt Earp had died, Stuart Lake wrote to Dodge and asked him directly if Wyatt Earp had killed Ringo.[39] Dodge replied, "No Wyatt had not killed Ringo. You are right Wyatt had left Arizona some little time ago."[40] Fred Dodge went on to state:

> John Ringo was found dead sitting up with his back to a tree, where he had been placed. Johnny-behind-the-deuce Murdered him. There was bad blood between the two and Johnny-behind-the-deuce was afraid of Ringo. Johnny was not in the same class as Ringo. So Johnny made a sure thing of it and Murdered Ringo.[41]

Mike O'Rouke, alias Johnny-Behind-the-Deuce, one of the more colorful figures in Tombstone folklore, is best known as the killer of mining engineer Philip Schneider in Charleston on January 14, 1881.[42] After his arrest in Charleston, a mob formed, and vigilante justice seemed a distinct possibility. Johnny was quickly brought to Tombstone, where Virgil Earp, town marshal Fred White, deputy John Behan, and others, which probably including Wyatt Earp, kept a mob led by mining man Dick Gird at bay.[43] Years later the incident reached legendary proportions with Wyatt Earp boldly saving O'Rourke from a blood thirsty lynch mob.[44] For his own safety, O'Rouke was taken to Tucson to be lodged in the Pima County jail to await his opportunity to answer for the killing of Schneider.[45] Yet, the Pima County jail proved to not be secure as the agile and quick Johnny-Behind-the-Deuce, with the aid of other prisoners, managed to get over the yard wall and make his escape during April 1881.[46]

Fred Dodge later claimed that O'Rourke, after escaping from the Pima County jail, maintained a camp near the location where Ringo's body was found. According to Dodge, he had seen O'Rourke several times "trying to arrange to use him in getting hold of some things I wanted to know in my under cover work for Wells, Fargo."[47] After Ringo's lifeless body was found, Dodge and Frank Leslie (Dodge, for what it is worth, claimed Leslie was with him when Ringo was killed) supposedly went to O'Rourke's camp, finding that camp was "stripped

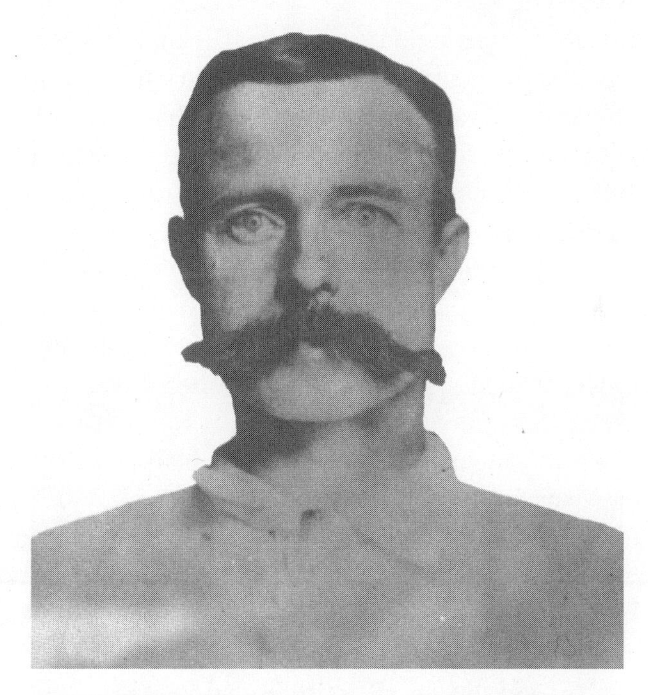

Frank Leslie later claimed to have killed John Ringo, but nobody believed his story.

quite recently."[48] From these details the self-proclaimed undercover agent for Wells, Fargo deduced that "Johnny had seen Ringo riding in the vicinity and probably thought he was looking for him - Johnny - and got scared up."[49] Dodge surmised, "Johnny made a sure thing of it and Murdered Ringo."[50]

Fred Dodge's assertions that Johnny-Behind-the-Deuce killed John Ringo is based on absolutely no evidence whatsoever, and his claim that O'Rourke was hanging around the Chiricahua Mountains following his escape from the Pima County jail is hard to believe. Johnny-Behind-the-Duece was wanted for murder, and a possible death sentence or life imprisonment in the Yuma Territorial Prison awaited the young gambler if Arizona authorities captured him - thus providing, it seems, two very good reasons why O'Rourke would not have stayed for fifteen months camping in Arizona after he escaped from jail. The wanted fugitive was last reported by one newspaper "on the eve" of departure for Texas.[51]

The first known published writing to claim that Wyatt Earp killed Ringo was from Frank Lockwood's *Pioneer Days in Arizona* (1932). Lockwood asserted that "Earp told me in circumstantial detail [with careful attention to detail] how he killed both Curly Bill and John Ringo."[52] According to Lockwood, Earp claimed to have killed both men during his hurried escape from Arizona. But Curly Bill, if he were killed by Earp, was killed in March 1882, and John Ringo was found dead four months later on July 14, 1882. Many writers have recognized this error and the account is generally considered not credible. Two unpublished manuscripts from Earp interviewers and earlier biographers, Forrestine Hooker (1919) and John Flood (1926), also contain the account that Wyatt Earp killed both Curly Bill and John Ringo during his departure from Arizona.[53] Thus, it is reasonable to infer that the story of Earp killing Ringo originated with Wyatt Earp himself. Nonetheless, some Earp biographers maintain that Earp never made the claim to have killed Ringo to Lake and that during a 1893 interview Wyatt Earp commented that he did not kill John Ringo.[54]

In recent years a few writers have argued that Wyatt Earp and Doc Holliday secretly returned to Arizona from Colorado and assassinated Ringo.[55] These writers have attempted to show that Wyatt and Doc, whose presence in Colorado was documented from time to time by court records and newspaper accounts, had a window of opportunity to surreptitiously travel to Arizona, find and kill Ringo, and return to Colorado and safety in time for their next interview with a reporter. The origin of the "Wyatt and Doc returned to Arizona and killed Ringo" scenario is not certain, but Earp researcher John Gilchriese gave the fantasy a big boost in the 1960s in remarks he made to Bob Thomas, a Tucson newspaper reporter. A fragment of Thomas' January 26, 1964, *Arizona Daily Star* article, based on Gilchriese's comments on the death of Ringo, is reprinted here:

> **Did Wyatt Earp Kill Ringo?**
> **Historian Says It's Possible**
>
> ... A field historian and head of special collections for the U of A's library, Gilchriese plans to detail the killing of Ringo in a chapter of his book, "The Man Called Wyatt Earp," to be published next year. "I am convinced that Earp could have traveled from Colorado to the Chiricahuas, killed Ringo and traveled back again without being recognized," Gilchriese said....
>
> Earp could have taken the old Atlantic and Pacific Railroad (later the Santa Fe) through the Raton Pass to East Las Vegas, N.M. That would be a day and a night by train. Then he could have ridden horseback from there to Roswell, N.M., skirting the Mescalero country and the western fringes of the Staked Plains.
>
> "From Roswell another horseback ride would take him to Lordsburg and from there he would ride straight to the Chiricahuas.
>
> "That means," continued Gilchriese, "about six days [and five bundred miles] by horse and one by train. It could be done."

Wyatt Earp told a reporter in 1893 that he did not kill John Ringo, but Earp interviewers Forrestine Hooker and John Flood wrote that Earp did kill Ringo. University of Arizona Professor Frank Lockwood also claimed that Wyatt Earp told him how he had killed John Ringo on the way out of Arizona.

Decades later Gilchriese denied that he meant to imply to Thomas that he was convinced that Wyatt performed the feat, only that he thought there was a block of time during which he could have accomplished it. Gilchriese insisted that he did not believe that Ringo died at Wyatt's hand.[56]

Another flaw in the "Wyatt and Doc came back and knocked off Ringo" concept is that Wyatt would have had to have spent a considerable amount of time hunting for his quarry. The "King of the Cowboys" himself did not know where he would be from one day to the next, so Earp could not simply go to his abode and accost him there. Wyatt was still wanted in Arizona for murder and thus could not travel about Cochise County at will.[57] Lastly, it would appear that Pete Spence and Ike Clanton would have been much higher on Wyatt's enemies list than John Ringo. If Wyatt were to risk arrest by coming to Arizona, it seems more reasonable that he would have done so to search for one or both of these men.

The assertion that Doc Holliday accompanied Wyatt to Arizona on a mission to annihilate Ringo is refuted by the historical record. Ringo died on July 13, 1882. On July 11 the grand jury in Pueblo, Colorado, indicted Holliday for larceny and a warrant for his arrest was issued. On the same day as the indictment, Holliday was brought before the court and arraigned:

> Tue. July 11, 1882
>
> The People, &c.
> vs. Larceny
> J. H. Holliday.
> This day come the said People by Robert A. Quillbrau, Esq.,
> District Attorney, and the said defendant **in his own proper person** [emphasis added] as well as by his counsel, W. G. Hollins, Esq., also come.
> And being ready to plead to the indictment said defendant says he is not guilty in manner and form as charged in said indictment and of this he puts himself

> upon the country; and the said People, by their said attorney, say they do the like.[58]

Two days after Doc Holliday was in court in Colorado, John Ringo perished in the Chiricahua Mountains in Arizona. Holliday could not have traveled to Morse's Canyon from Pueblo, Colorado, in such a short time. Nevertheless, a few writers have suggested that the term "in his own proper person, as well as by his attorney," could be interpreted to mean that Holliday's attorney appeared for him on July 11, 1882.[59] These writers argue that since a capias warrant for his arrest was issued by the court following the indictment, it shows that Holliday was not in Pueblo at the time. Yet, this was normal court procedure. Before the county sheriff could arrest Holliday on the indictment, an arrest warrant had to be issued authorizing the sheriff to take Holliday into custody to answer the charge against him.

In July 1882, the prevailing view was that Ringo's 1000 pound bay horse "wandered off somewhere, and he started off on foot to search for him."[60] When his "boots began to hurt him, he pulled them off and made moccasins of his undershirt."[61] Eventually, he made his way to the tree where he was found, killing himself around three o'clock that afternoon.[62] Although both Ringo's boots and horse were not at the tree when his body was found, there was no evidence that he made such a hike through the area in search of his horse. According to the coroner's jury, "He had evidently traveled but a short distance in this foot gear."[63] Even if he had made such a walk, why would he kill himself once he was close to water or within a short distance to two ranches?

The story became more elaborate as old-timers offered conjecture to explain the circumstances of Ringo's death. William Breakenridge speculated that Ringo had stopped the night before to sleep off the effects of the whiskey he had been drinking, taking off his boots and throwing them over his saddle, but his horse wandered off at night in search of water. "When Ringo awoke, he must have been crazed for water and started out afoot. He was within sound of running water when he became crazed with thirst and killed himself,"

Breakenridge surmised.[64] To support his theory that Ringo was "crazed with thirst" when he killed himself, Breakenridge presented the following information:

> The report that came to the Sheriff's office at the time was that one of the cartridge belts was on bottom side up and all the cartridges had dropped out of it, while in the other belt were several cartridges that the lead of which had been chewed up showing that the tried to get moisture in his mouth. His boots were gone and he had taken off his undershirt and torn it in two, and wrapped it around his feet, and when he was found the shirt had worn through, showing that he had walked for some distance.[65]

Despite the former deputy's guesswork involving Ringo's death, he was not present when Ringo was found and his comments concerning the findings of the coroner's jury are not accurate. No mention of cartridges having "dropped out" of one of the cowboy's belts was recorded, or that the cartridges in Ringo's other belt showed signs of being chewed up to create moisture in his mouth. Finally, Breakenridge's claim that the wrapping around Ringo's feet "had worn through, showing signs that he had walked for some distance," was a considerable distance from the truth. In reality, the statement to the coroner said that Ringo had "traveled but a short distance in this foot gear,"[66] and nothing in the report suggests that Ringo had stumbled about the area searching for his horse or water, or that he was crazed with thirst.

While the missing boots and the feet wrapped in a shirt to protect them seem odd, considering the coroner jury's observation that the wrapping was in fairly reasonable condition it seems highly unlikely that John Ringo trudged for any real distance in search of his horse or water. In the rugged terrain of Turkey Creek canyon, his newly fashioned leggings likely would have shown obvious signs of such a trek. Indeed, one could imagine that they might even have been ripped and torn, filthy with dirt, possibly even blood-stained from the journey through the rough topography. It is far more likely that Ringo rode directly to the spot where he was later found. Of course, murder conspiracy theorists might argue that the cowboy could also have been brought to the location by some unknown killer or assailants. But why? Such a deed would require the killer or killers to risk detection of the crime by hauling Ringo's dead body to the tree, which is along a fairly-well-traveled dirt road and in close proximity to at least two ranches; then arrange the body is a suicide-like pose; fire another pistol shot; and leave before being discovered.

There is absolutely no evidence that this is what occurred. The only things supporting this scenario are bogus claims later made in an attempt to fit the known facts and wild conjecture in order to come up with a suspected killer. More importantly, the *Tombstone Epitaph* reported that "Mrs. Morse and Mrs. Young passed by where he was lying Thursday afternoon, but supposed it was some man asleep, and took no further notice of him."[67] Later that day, "a shot was heard about 3 o'clock Thursday evening, and it is more than likely that that is the time the rash deed was done," noted the *Epitaph*.[68] Mrs. Morse and Mrs. Young gave no indication of having seen a man or a group of men around the tree where Ringo was apparently asleep sometime before the presumed fatal shot was fired at three o'clock later that day.

Ringo's horse wandered throughout the area apparently unseen and unmolested until July 25, 1882, when a son of B. F. Smith found him about two miles from the spot the cowboy was found dead. "His saddle was still upon him with Ringo's coat upon the back of it. In one of the pockets were three photographs and a card bearing the name of 'Mrs. Jackson' [Ringo's sister], reported the *Epitaph*.[69] No mention was made of Ringo's boots at the time, but Rosa Smith, a daughter of B. F. Smith, later claimed that one of the boots had been found.[70]

The men on the coroner's jury also noticed that Ringo's belt for revolver cartridges was buckled on upside down. Like the missing boots and torn undershirt wrapped around Ringo's feet, this finding is peculiar, but still does not deflate the conclusion that John Ringo committed suicide. It is more than possible that Ringo, who was known to be drinking heavily for about ten days, could have put the belt on backwards in a state of alcoholic confusion. But it is also possible that, for whatever reason, Ringo may have intentionally buckled on the cartridge belt in that manner. While wearing an upside down cartridge belt may seem quirky to some people, Ringo may have had some preference for wearing the belt in that manner.

Even the most puzzling aspect of Ringo's death, the observation that the body appeared to have a small part of the forehead and scalp gone, including part of the hair, which looked as if someone had cut it with a knife, can be reasonably explained absent the need of a murderer. Ringo's body had been lying in the heat for an estimated twenty-four hours. It is conceivable that a bird or other wild animal may have caused the damage after his death, or that the cowboy fell down at some point in a drunken stupor, causing a gash on his scalp. Some writers have speculated that the lock of hair removed from Ringo's head may have been taken as a sort of trophy.[71] Even if someone did cut a part of Ringo's hair as a keepsake, it does not mean he was murdered. It is hard to imagine that a man who had just killed Ringo, who had the presence of mind to arrange his body in a suicide-like pose, would then disrupt his own efforts to deflect blame onto Ringo by taking a trophy that might raise suspicion over the cowboy's death. If someone did take a piece of John Ringo's hair as a keepsake, one possible suspect likely could have been John Yoast, the man who initially found the cowboy's dead body. Considering Yoast knew Ringo for several years in Arizona and Texas, he is a good candidate for taking a souvenir from the notorious cowboy's dead body. Obviously, he was well aware of the John Ringo's reputation - both in Arizona and in Texas - and he might have considered Ringo noteworthy enough to take a memento of the notorious cowboy.

No matter who their favorite perpetrator might be, all of the murder theorists must somehow account for the appearance of a suicide at the death site. Their explanation is that the killer or killers adroitly faked a suicide scene. But why? If no one saw the slaying, the slayer would have been in the clear even if it was later obvious a homicide had occurred. Once Ringo was dead, the killer was better off leaving the area as quickly as possible, rather than wasting time arranging the body in a suicide-like pose. Ringo's corpse was found near a road and not far from an occupied dwelling - not a place where a murderer would want to spend time fooling around with his victim's remains at three o'clock in the afternoon. Of fundamental importance is the steep upward path taken by the bullet through Ringo's head. It would be virtually impossible for an assailant's bullet to achieve this trajectory. No, the murder plots just aren't plausible. Consequently, this writer is convinced that the jurors were right -John Ringo had lost all interest in life, and in a state of alcoholic despair the young man shot himself.

John Ringo's grave near Turkey Creek.

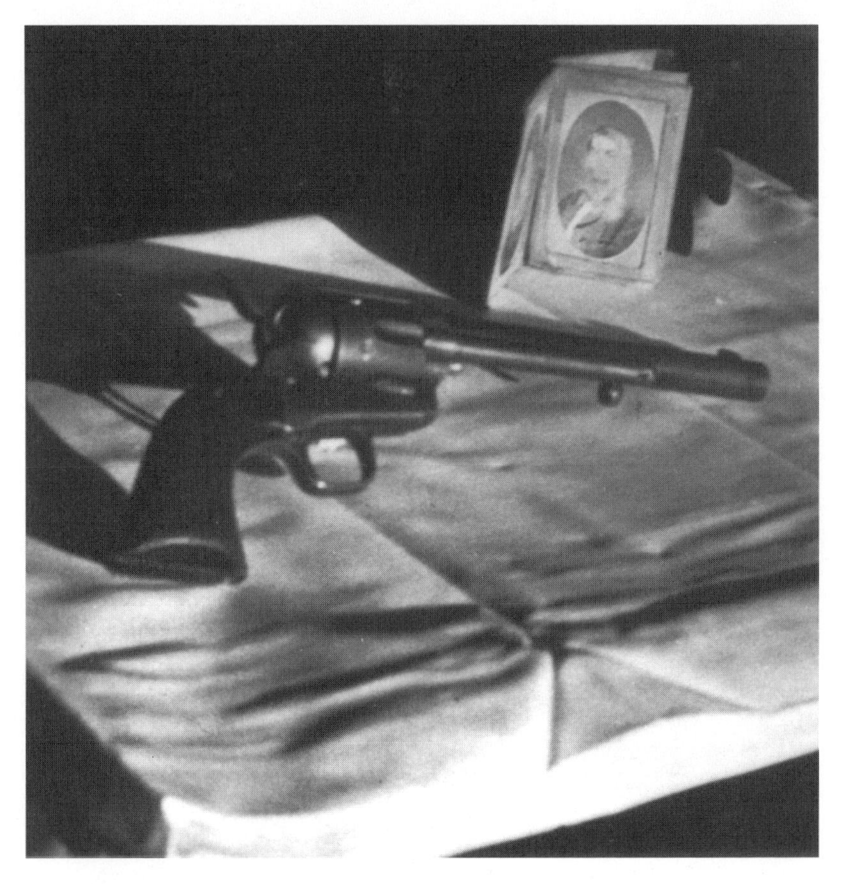

The pistol and wallet that were found when John Ringo's lifeless body was discovered. Arizona Historical Society, #17629.

16

LEGEND OF JOHNNY RINGO

On July 18, 1882, just four days after John Ringo's dead body was buried near Turkey Creek, the seed that would later turn into the legend of Johnny Ringo, the "classic cowboy-gunfighter," began to slowly sprout and take root.[1] Ringo's death had been announced in the *Tombstone Epitaph* and the *Arizona Daily Star*, and the news of Ringo's demise was repeated in newspapers in California and New Mexico.[2] John Ringo's moody and melancholy disposition, his suicidal tendencies, and his recklessly brave behavior were reported in these newspapers and these descriptions laid the foundation that writers would use for the notorious cowboy's disposition.

Described as a "strictly honorable man," whose "word was his bond," the *Tombstone Epitaph* proclaimed that Ringo "would go any distance, or undergo any hardship to serve a friend or punish an enemy."[3] On anointing Ringo with the title "King of the Cowboys," an obvious reference to his perceived role in Arizona as the leader of a so-called cowboy gang, the *Star* noted that he "was fearless in the extreme" and that he had "many staunch friends and bitter enemies."[4]

The traits and descriptions of John Ringo that were published in these early articles were later used by Western writers, along with recollections from old-timers, to forge the cowboy's legendary image. But it was a New Mexico newspaper article, published four days after the Arizona accounts, that foretold that John Ringo, or more precisely John Ringgold, as the account called him, should be forever remembered in the history of our nation:

ANOTHER GREAT SOUL FLOWN

It is with much regret that we chronicle the demise of one of the illustrious men of the southwest. Had the much lamented deceased lived in antiquity his fame might have surpassed that of Hector or Ulysses; but alas, republics are ungrateful, and no public honor was ever shown to the king of the cowboys. Born of poor but honest parents, John Ringgold surmounted all the obstacles thrown in his path and made for himself a name that should live in the history of the nation. Gentleman like and pleasant in his manner, even easy going in many ways, he was a rigid observer of the old fashioned frontier code of honor that unfortunately is fast disappearing. During the past few years thirty-two men dared to doubt his honor. They now fill thirty-two graves. He distinguished himself when at Shakespeare by his fine and effective shooting, and is kindly remembered in that burg. Although he had many competitors in his line, he had no true rivals, and Curly Bill and Billy the Kid will not bear comparison with him. His body was found last week in the Chiricahua mountains with a bullet hole through his head. The supposition is that he was crossed in love and ended his sufferings in this tragic manner. Thus passed away in the flower of his youth a man who, had he lived, might have aspired to almost any eminent position. Alas! 'Twas not to be:

Car il etait du monde ou les plus belles choses
Ont le destin
Et Ringgold a vecu ce que vivent les roses
L'espace d'un matin.[5]

Forty years after the death of Ringo, Western writer Frederick Bechdolt, mainly using old-timer recollections and stories, published his book *When the West Was Young* (1922),[6] starting the process that led to the rediscovery of the Tombstone story, the recollections of Ringo's exploits, and the eventual legend of Johnny Ringo. Like the Silver City newspaper account in July 1882, Bechdolt's inferences were based on stories about Ringo from old-timers, and Bechdolt distinguished Ringo from the cowboys of Tombstone with whom he rode. He asserted that Ringo was a man not unlike "Don Quixote," who adhered to a strong code of honor.[7] Although Bechdolt's book did not receive wide acclaim or distribution, it did serve as a great influence for the book that brought the Tombstone saga back to life five years later.

Walter Noble Burns' highly successful book, *Saga of Billy the Kid*, had resurrected the Billy the Kid story from oblivion in 1922, and the writer, able to recognize a cookie-cutter formula for success in writing books about Old West figures, approached Wyatt Earp to publish his story.[8] But Earp was already trying to push his own badly written manuscript penned by a friend. After Burns convinced Wyatt that he would, instead, write about Doc Holliday's life, Earp provided the writer with some information.[9] In 1927, Burns released his book, *Tombstone, An Iliad of the Southwest*, which was an instant success and gave the Tombstone story a much needed boost in publicity.[10] Burns was greatly influenced by Bechdolt's earlier book and he "borrowed" heavily from the work.[11] Like Bechdolt, Burns used descriptions of John Ringo to paint a picture of someone mysterious and vague:

> An introspective man, tragic figure, darkly handsome, splendidly brave, a man born for better things . . . . tall, sculpturesque physique and lean, saturnine face, he was a silent man of mystery who, in moods of bitter melancholy, sometimes spoke of suicide.[12]

Many of Burns' descriptions are similar to the news accounts that were published after Ringo's death. Burns declared that Ringo was reckless because of the low value he placed on his own life. The writer declared that Ringo was an "honorable outlaw," and that his "word once given was kept inviolately."[13] Burns wrote:

> Old-timers still tell of his quixotic ideals regarding women. Womanhood to him was like an icon before which he bowed in reverence. No woman was so bad that she was ever outside the pale of his knightly chivalry. A man who in his presence made a disparaging remark about a woman, be she irreproachable maid or matron or red-light siren, had to eat his words or fight. That was John Ringo's way.[14]

One old-timer that provided Burns with recollections and descriptions of John Ringo was William Breakenridge, who lived in Tombstone and worked as a deputy sheriff during the boom town's early years. The year after Burns' *Tombstone* was printed, Breakenridge's *Helldorado: Bringing the Law to the Mesquite* (1928) was published. Breakenridge's descriptions of Ringo seem to indicate that he was in awe of the notorious cowboy:

> Ringo was a mysterious man. He had a college education, but was reserved and morose. He drank heavily as if to drown his troubles; he was a perfect gentleman when sober, but inclined to be quarrelsome when drinking. He was a good shot and afraid of nothing, and had great authority with the rustling element. Although he was their leader on their trips to Mexico after cattle and in their raids against smugglers, he generally kept by himself after they returned to Galeyville. He read a great deal and had a small collection of standard books in his cabin.[15]

The early books of Bechdolt, Burns, and Breakenridge set the stage for John Ringo's legendary reputation. However, John Ford's 1939 classic western movie *Stagecoach*, which provided acting legend John Wayne with his first big role starring as the "Ringo Kid," gave the Ringo name a major lift in popularity. The final showdown scene where Ringo kills the three Plummer brothers to avenge the murder of his father and brother is reminiscent of the tale in Burns' book that John Ringo killed three men to avenge the murder of his brother.

Another book that later became instrumental in creating the legend of Johnny Ringo was Eugene Cunningham's *Triggernometry: A Gallery of Gunfighters* (1941). Cunningham's book provided a brief sketch of men noted in the West for their ability with a gun - gunfighters, or more precise, gunmen. Cunningham described the term *gunman* in the following way:

> When you said of a man that he was a gunman, you meant not only a pistol man - a man bearing one of more pistols. You meant to designate (and were understood to designate) a man specially skilled in the use of a pistol - and much more than normally ready to demonstrate that in blazing homicidal gunplay. The word gunman had flexed to neatly take into account, not only the weapon, but the character, of the man you were discussing.[16]

Cunningham also discussed various techniques, complete with illustrations, used by many of the so-called gunfighters of the Old West. Cunningham's book discussed Breakenridge's role in the Tombstone saga and much of the discussion mirrors the accounts of Tombstone and Ringo that were portrayed in Breakenridge's book.

Around the time of the publication of Cunningham's book, Hollywood mogul Daryl Zanuck, head of 20th Century Fox, was looking for a new Western movie, and he assigned Andre De Toth to come up with a story line that would receive critical acclaim but with broad appeal. According to Richard Slotkin, author of *Gunfighter*

Nation, The Myth of the Frontier in Twentieth-Century America (1992), "De Toth went to history for his story, but to a source and a subject that were distinctly marginal. Eugene Cunningham's *Triggermonetry: A Gallery of Gunfighters* (1934) was a collection of brief biographies of Westerners noted for their skill with weapons."[17] De Toth was drawn to Cunningham's focus on the "technique of the fast-draw."[18] From Cunningham's book, De Toth chose for his subject, John Ringo, who Slotkin considered "one of the most obscure figures" in the work.[19] "De Toth was intrigued by the idea that Ringo's killer could gain stature by claiming to be 'the man who killed Johnny Ringo'."[20]

De Toth's efforts produced, *The Gunfighter* (1950), starring Gregory Peck as "Jimmy Ringo," a tired but notorious gunman seeking a way to escape his fate and to live a different life with his wife and son. The film was part of a new subgenre - the gunfighter Western, which portrays the gunfighter as "physically troubled and isolated from normal society by something 'dark' in his nature and/or his past."[21] About the gunfighter Western genre Slotkin wrote, "Fittingly, the seminal film in the development of this new subgenre was *The Gunfighter*."[22]

We will never know for sure why De Toth chose John Ringo as his subject rather than other more popular figures such as Bill Longley, Ben Thompson, Billy the Kid, or John Wesley Hardin, who is widely considered the greatest gunfighter of them all. But it probably had nothing to do with the tonal quality of Ringo's name. It is likely the manner in which Ringo was prominently portrayed by Cunningham in the Tombstone saga, which was, of course, based on Breakenridge's accounts of the notorious cowboy, that drew De Toth to him as a subject. Cunningham proclaimed, "John Ringo was a man with whom everyone in that part of Arizona must reckon, the fastest gunfighter and the deadliest, a man who courted trouble, with the thoughtless courage of a bulldog."[23] Cunningham then published the following portion of a conversation that he had with William Breakenridge:

> "Who-" I was asking Breakenridge one day "- was the outstanding expert, both mechanically and

> temperamentally, among all the gunfighters you have encountered?"
>
> "John Ringo!" Breakenridge replied without hesitation.
>
> "Better than Wyatt Earp? Better than yourself, say?"
>
> "Ringo would have made me look like an amateur," Breakenridge answered. "As for Wyatt Earp, certainly I had no reason to like the man, but I wouldn't deny that he must have been an expert with a six-shooter. And if Earp had been given the job of gathering in Ringo, I think that he would have gone out and tried to bring Ringo in. So would I. But probably it is just as well that I never had to go up against Ringo in a gunplay and my opinion is that Earp felt the same way."[24]

As noted by Slotkin, De Toth was particularly intrigued that a person might attempt to gain stature by claiming to be the man that killed John Ringo, and this later was the film's underlying theme. Imagine what De Toth would have thought if Cunningham's book would have mentioned, as some sources assert today, that Wyatt Earp later claimed to have killed John Ringo.[25]

Following Hollywood's big-screen release of *The Gunfighter* (1950), the character of Johnny Ringo began to appear frequently on televison. *Stories of the Century*, a television series Western that used newspaper files of notorious characters from the Old West, had its debut in 1954. The television series won an Emmy in 1955 for Best Western or Adventure Series, and one episode featured the notorious Johnny Ringo.[26] A year after *Stories of the Century* was broadcast, the *Buffalo Bill, Jr.* (1955) show aired the episode, *The Death of Johnny Ringo*, and the popular televison series *The Life and Legend of Wyatt Earp* (1955), which was based largely on Stuart Lake's book, included Johnny Ringo in its cast. Two years later, Hollywood again used the Johnny Ringo character in a number of gunfighter Westerns like *Gunfight at the OK Corral* (1957), *The Last of the Fast Guns* (1958), and *Toughest Gun in Tombstone* (1958).[27]

The following year the televison series *Johnny Ringo* (1959) starring Dan Durant as Johnny Ringo, made its debut. The show produced 38 episodes, but was cancelled after the first year. Nevertheless, the show became somewhat of a marketing bonanza, flooding the consumer market with a variety products that included a *Johnny Ringo* (1959) comic book, *Johnny Ringo* holster and gun sets, action figures, and an assortment of licensed *Johnny Ringo* toys and games. Johnny Ringo was now a commercial product.[28]

By 1960, cinema and television had made Johnny Ringo a popular Western character known throughout the United States and in parts of Europe. Of course, the legendary Johnny Ringo, "the fastest gun in all the West, the quickest ever known," now completely overshadowed the real John Ringo's exploits.[29] Audiences simply did not care that the historical John Ringo, at least those that knew there was an Old West character by that name, could not match the fictional exploits of the legendary Johnny Ringo.

The next stage in the evolution of the Ringo legend occurred in 1964. Actor Lorne Greene, whose television series Western *Bonanza* was at the peak of its popularity, released a hit song, actually a spoken-word recording, entitled *Ringo* (1964), based loosely on the fictional story line of a sheriff who had once saved the life of Johnny Ringo.[30] Greene's narrative voice proclaimed: "And hour on hour I watched in awe. No human being could match the draw of Ringo."[31] The song went up the charts and spent a week at number one, before going on to become an international best seller. The following year, Duccio Tessari's popular spaghetti Western, *A Pistol for Ringo* (1965), which was inspired by Lorne Greene's hit song, was released in Europe.[32] Tessari followed up *A Pistol for Ringo* the next year with the highly successful hit sequel, *Return of Ringo* (1966), which many critics believed was better than the first.[33]

The success of *A Pistol for Ringo* caused a huge sensation overseas, popularizing the Ringo name throughout Italy and Europe. A press book released by Embassy Pictures to market *A Pistol for Ringo* to American audiences asked the following question: "What's the most popular American name in Italy? It's Ringo!"[34] About the Ringo phenomenon in Europe one writer later commented, "There were also many unofficial 'sequels' quick to capitalize on the 'Ringo' name, among them: Sergio Corbucci's *Ringo and his Golden Pistol* (originally filmed under the title *Johnny Oro*), *Kill or Die* starring Robert Mark as the 'famous' Ringo, plus *Ringo and Gringo Against All*; *Ringo, It's Massacre Time*; *Ringo, Pray to Your God*; *Ringo the Lone Rider*, *Ringo's Big Night*; *Ringo: Face of Revenge* and, of course, the forgettable 'Franco and Ciccio' comedies, *Two R-R-Ringos from Texas* and *Two Sons of Ringo*."[35] Not to mention the Italian film *Kill Johnny Ringo* (1966) and the German film *Who Killed Johnny R.* (1966).[36]

The same year that Italian and German films were killing off Johnny Ringo, the popular English television series *Dr. Who* aired four episodes (*A Holiday for the Doctor; Don't Shoot the Pianist; Johnny Ringo; The OK Corral*) which concluded with Ringo being killed by the Earps and Holliday at the OK Corral. Three years later, in 1969, the Johnny Ringo character appeared in two episodes of the popular American television series *High Chaparral*.[37]

While the Ringo character and name was a box office hit in Europe and made television appearances on both sides of the Atlantic Ocean, little was being done by Western writers or historians in the United States to flesh out the real story of John Ringo. Instead, writers seemed content to write historical Western novels like Leslie Scott's *Tombstone Showdown* (1957) and Ray Hogan's *The Life and Death of Johnny Ringo* (1963) (Released in 1964 in England as *Johnny Ringo: Gentleman Outlaw*). These books were not intended as biographies. They were fictional accounts, novels really, that were loosely based on the Ringo story as told by early writers like Burns, Breakenridge, and Stuart Lake, but with an increased emphasis on the gunfighter image that was created by the movies and television.

Western writers often exaggerated Ringo's exploits or made claims for him that were not supported by the facts. Historians did not do much better. Rather than researching John Ringo's life, many simply repeated the often exaggerated accounts that were being repeated by writers based on the earlier books. Where and when the notorious cowboy was born, and even whether his true name was Ringo or Ringgold, remained unknown, despite his sister's letter to the *Tombstone Epitaph* during July 1882, which told where and what year the cowboy was born.[38] In actuality, few people were seriously researching John Ringo's background and it was easier to rely on the works of others for information.

Jack Burrows' *John Ringo: The Gunfighter Who Never Was* (1987) was the first serious attempt to write a biography of John Ringo. Instead of concentrating on John Ringo's life and exploits, however, Burrows compared and contrasted the writings of others to show how inaccuracies had evolved in books and articles about the legendary gunman. Thanks to a distant Ringo relative, Burrows did manage to pin down John Ringo's birth and true name, and provide some information about the Ringo family's journey across the plains.[39] Unfortunately, rather than make an attempt to flesh out more details of Ringo's life and activities, especially in Texas, Burrows was content to simply expose the inaccuracies of Western writers who repeated earlier works, which were often taken from old-timer accounts at face value without corroboration. These writers frequently exaggerated claims for Ringo, and the authors did little primary research at all.

Although acknowledging that "there lies buried a substratum of truth beneath the myths that engulf" John Ringo, Burrows concluded, "John Ringo's image was created for him by inaccuracies of innumerable writers, and I believe that he remains a western figure largely because of the mellifluous tonal quality of his name."[40] Unfortunately, Jack Burrows' book missed the mark. He did show how Western writers had exaggerated John Ringo's deeds, but this phenomenon was not solely directed at Ringo. Virtually all Western figures were exaggerated beyond their mere mortal status. There is no question that many writers embellished John Ringo's exploits and image, and that cinema, television, and radio have popularized the name Ringo - creating the legendary Johnny Ringo. Still, long before 20th century writers wrote stories about him, and film and televison made his name a household word, John Ringo had attained a notorious reputation as a desperate and dangerous man in the Old West. He just was not "the fastest gun in all the West, the quickest ever known."[41]

Burrows further theorized that Ringo's family was largely to blame for the innaccuracies and exaggerations of writers because they attempted to conceal facts that would have resolved many of the issues regarding the notorious cowboy's life. "To be concise, John's immediate family - those 'dear little sisters' - felt bitterly shamed and disgraced by their gunman-outlaw brother, and they labored with an unswerving single-mindedness and no little success to suppress all information and facts about him; in so doing, they perverted the natural course of history," Burrows concluded.[42]

In 1995, this author published *John Ringo: The Reputation of a Deadly Gunman*, which was an attempt to chronologically present Ringo's life to understand what his reputation was at the time of his death. Of course, to fully understand what John Ringo's reputation was during his life requires extensive research into contemporary sources, especially in Texas and about the Hoodoo War, areas that Burrows seemingly failed to thoroughly investigate. A deeper look into Ringo's activities in Texas, as illustrated by contemporary newspapers of the day, shows that John Ringo was considered a notorious, desperate, and dangerous man in Texas by 1878. The *Austin Weekly Statesman* in November 1876, declared that John Ringo was "one of the most desperate men in the frontier counties." Over a year later an Austin paper considered John Ringo "famous for the devilish deeds" he had done.[43] In actuality, in parts of Texas, the notorious John Ringo was already a household name before he even headed to Arizona in 1879.

More information about John Ringo's life came out with the publication of David Johnson's *John Ringo* (1996). Johnson discussed in detail the Ringo family's lineage in America and their early days in Indiana and Missouri. He also provided an in-depth analysis on the

HoodooWar and John Ringo's role in the feud, which for decades remained obscure because descendants in the area preferred not to speak of it. More importantly, he clarified that John Ringo's sisters, while he was alive, had no idea whatsoever about his activities in Texas and Arizona.[44]

The movie *Tombstone* (1993) re-introduced the legendary Johnny Ringo to new audiences throughout the world. Actor Michael Biehn's portrayal of Ringo was lauded as a fine performance and likely will remain the image of the legendary Johnny Ringo for years to come. *Tombstone* featured a verbal Latin duel between Johnny Ringo and Doc Holliday, portrayed by Val Kilmer, that already has Western fans proclaiming the scene to be a classic. At the end of the movie Holliday outdraws Johnny Ringo in a deadly gunfight. Thus, ensuring for years to come from Old West neophytes that saw *Tombstone,* the answer to the following question: "Who Killed Johnny Ringo?" - "Doc Holliday," of course.

Appendix

Court Documents

In the Name and by the Authority of the State of Texas.

THE GRAND JURORS OF ~~WILLIAMSON~~ Burnet COUNTY in said State, at the April Term, A. D. 1875, of the DISTRICT COURT, of said County, on their oaths in said Court, present that John Ringo with force and arms, in said County and State, on the 25th day of December A. D. 1874, did then and there unlawfully discharge a pistol in and across the public square & in & across a public street in the town of Burnet said street & square not then and there being the outer town or suburbs of said town against the peace & dignity of the State

And the grand jurors aforesaid on their oaths aforesaid in said Court do further present that John Ringo in the county of Burnet State of Texas on the 25th of December A.D. 1874 did then and there unlawfully rudely displaying a pistol in a public place [illegible] so as to disturb the inhabitants of said place in the preservation of their lawful business "against the peace and dignity of the State."

Norton Moses

Foreman of the Grand Jury.

John Ringo's first known indictment for disturbing the peace in the town of Burnet, Texas, on Christmas Day 1874. District Court Clerk's Office. Burnet, Texas.

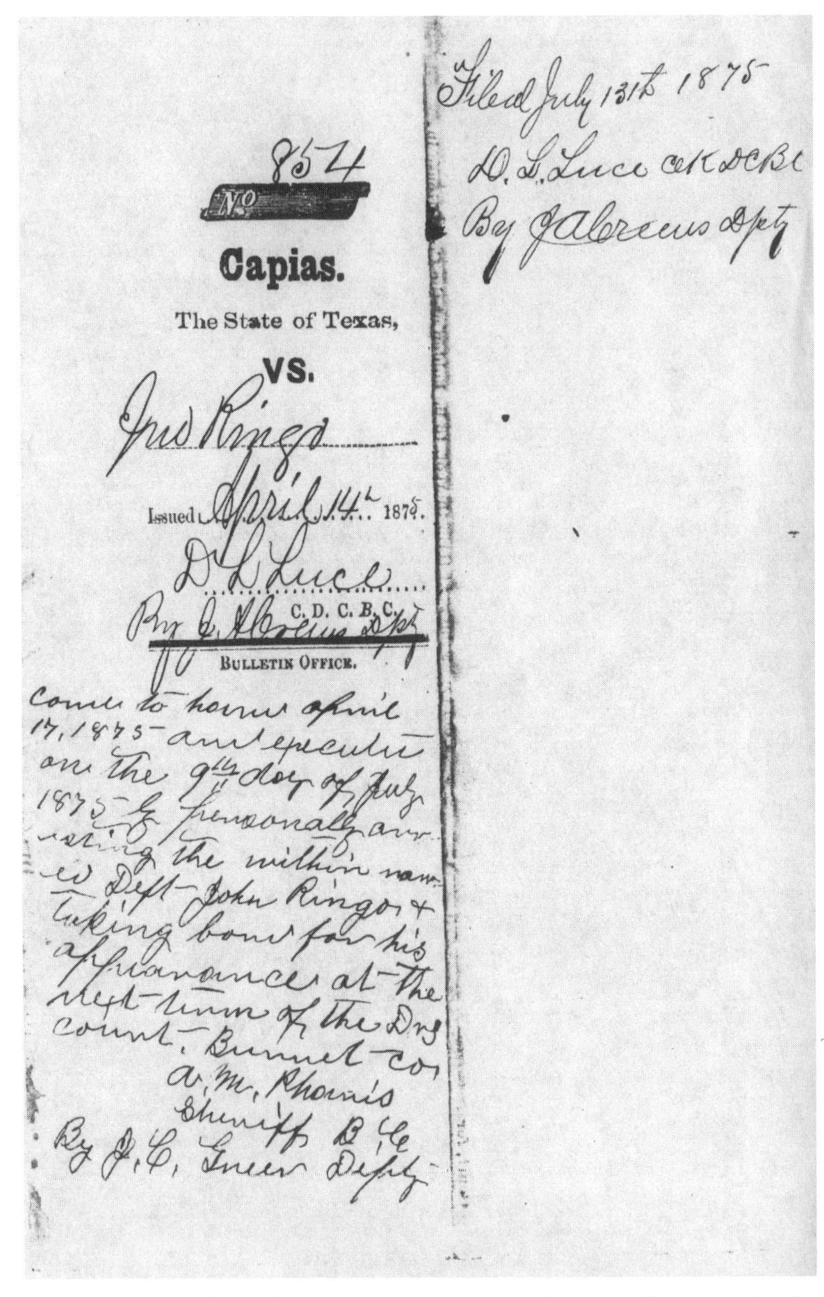

Filed July 13th 1875
D. L. Luce Clk DCBC
By J Abrens Dpty

854
No.
Capias.
The State of Texas,
VS.
Jno Ringo
Issued April 14th 1875.
D L Luce
C. D. C. B. C.
By J. Abrens Dpty
BULLETIN OFFICE.

Came to hand April 17, 1875 and executed on the 9th day of July 1875 by personally arresting the within named Deft John Ringo & taking bond for his appearance at the next term of the Dis Court, Burnet Co.
A. M. Rhoanis
Sheriff B. C.
By J. C. Greer Depty

Arrest warrant for John Ringo issued by the Burnet County District Court on April 14, 1875. District Court Clerk's Office, Burnet, Texas.

The State of Texas--- COUNTY OF BURNET.

Know all Men By These Presents that we John Ringo

as principal, and J R Baird & Geo Gladden

as sureties, do acknowledge ourselves to owe, and be indebted unto the State of Texas, jointly and severally in the sum of One hundred and fifty Dollars, for the payment of which well and truly to be made, we bind ourselves, our heirs, and legal representatives, firmly by these presents. Nevertheless to be void upon the condition that the aforesaid principal, John Ringo shall make his personal appearance before the Honorable District Court of Burnet County, at the next term thereof, to be begun and holden at the Courthouse in the town of Burnet, County and State aforesaid, on the first Monday after the 4th monday in jan A. D. 1876, then and there to remain in attendance upon said Court from day to day, and term to term thereafter, to answer the State of Texas, and stand trial upon a bill of indictment preferred against him the said John Ringo by the Grand Jury of Burnet County for Disturbance of the peace

and not depart the Court without leave.

Witness our hands on this the 6 day of Dec A. D. 1875

Approved by John C. [illegible] Sheriff B. C.

This 6 day of Dec A. D. 1875

John Ringo
J. R. Baird
G. W. Gladden

Burnet County bond signed by John Ringo, George Gladden, and John Baird. District Court Clerk's Office, Burnet, Texas.

And now at this time comes into Court
the Grand Jury, a quorum being
present and present into open Court
the following Indictments, to-wit;

The State of Texas
vs
Jno Ringo &
Scott Cooley
Seriously threatening to
take the life of a human
being

The State of Texas
vs.
Jno Ringo &
Scott Cooley
Seriously threatening to take
the life of a human being

On February 1, 1876, John Ringo and Scott Cooley were indicted on two counts of seriously threatening to take the life of a human being.
District Court Clerk's Office, Burnet, Texas.

THE STATE OF TEXAS,
To the Sheriff or any Constable of Mason County—GREETING:
You are Hereby Commanded, to take the body of John Ringo
and him safely keep, so that you have him before the Honorable District Court of Mason County, Texas, at the Court House thereof, in the town of Mason, on the 12th day of November A. D. 1877, then and there to answer the State of Texas, in a charge by Indictment, wherein the said John Ringo
charged with the offence of Murder

Herein fail not, but due service and return hereof make as the law requires.
WITNESS, Wilson Hey Clerk of the District Court of Mason County, aforesaid, with the Seal of the Court hereon impressed, this day of October A. D. 1877
ATTEST: Wilson Hey
Clerk of the Dist. Court of Mason County.
By Ed Anderson Deputy.

Mason County murder warrant for John Ringo. The sheriff was ordered to have Ringo present in court on November 12, 1877, to answer the indictment charging him with the murder of James Cheyney. District Court Clerk's Office, Mason, Texas.

No 21 The State of Texas vs. John Ringo Et al — Murder — May 15th 1878
~~Dismissed on Motion of District attorney for the following reasons to wit~~
Now Comes the State by the district attorney and Moves the Court to dismiss this Case for the reason that testimony Can not now be procured to make out the Case. which being duly Considered by the Court it was ordered that said Case be dismissed

The murder charge against John Ringo for the killing of James Cheyney was dismissed on May 15, 1878. District Court Clerk's Office, Mason, Texas.

San Simon Valley, N.M.
March 3d 1880

Mr. C. Shibel
Dear Sir, being under Bond
for my appearance before the Grand
jury of Pima Co., I write to let you
know why I can not appear—
I got shot through the foot and it is
impossible for me to travel for awhile
if you get any papers for me, and
will let me know, I will attend to
them at once as I wish to live
here I do not wish to put you to
any unnecessary trouble, nor do I
wish to bring extra trouble on myself
Please let the Dist-Atty know why I
do not appear, for I am
that there is know forfeiture taken on the
Bond.

Respcty yours.
John Ringo

John Ringo wrote this letter to explain why he could not appear before the Pima County grand jury in March 1880. Robert N. Mullin Collection, Nita Stewart Haley Memorial Library, Midland, Texas.

#170 Turkey or Morse's Mill Creek
14th July 1882.

Statement for the information of the Coroner and Sheriff of Cochise Co. A. T.

There was found by the undersigned John Yoast the body of a man in the a clump of oak trees about 20 yards north from the road leading to Morse's mill and about a quarter of a mile west of the house of B. F. Smith. The undersigned viewed the body & found it in a sitting posture, facing west, the head inclined to the right. – There was a bullet hole in the right temple, the bullet coming out on the top of the head on the left side. There is apparently a part of the scalp gone including a small portion of the forehead and part of the hair, this looks as if cut out by a knife. – These are the only marks of violence visible on the body. – Several of the undersigned identify the body as that of John Ringo, well known in Tombstone. He was dressed in light hat blue shirt, vest, pants and drawers, on his feet were a pair hose and undershirt torn up so as

Statement for the information of the Coroner and Sheriff of Cochise County, A. T. Cochise County Clerk's Office Bisbee, Arizona.

to protect his feet. — He had evidently travelled
but a short distance in this foot gear. — His
revolver he grasped in his right hand, his rifle
rested against the tree close to him. — He had
on two cartridge belts, the belt for the revolver
cartridges being buckled on upside down. —
The undernoted property were found with him and
on his person. —

1 Colt's revolver Cal: 45 No 222, — containing 5 cartridg
1 Winchester rifle octagon barrel Cal: 45 Model 1876
No 21896, containing a cartridge in the breech and
10 in the magazine
1 cartridge belt containing 9 rifle cartridges
1 Do — 2 revolver Do
Silver watch of American watch Co No 9339 with
Silver chain attached
Two dollars & sixty cents ($2 60) in money
pistol cartridges in his pocket
shirt studs
small pocket knife
Tobacco pipe — 1 Comb
Block matches, — 1 small piece Tobacco
ere is also a portion of a letter from Messrs Hereford
Zabriskie, Attorneys at Law, Tucson to the
ased John Ringo. —
e above property is left in the possession of
ederick Ward, Teamster between Morse's Mill

and Tombstone

The body of the deceased was buried close to where it was found

The body of When found deceased had been dead about 24 hours

Thomas White
John Blake
Wm. W Bradfield
B.F. Smith
W.W. Smith
A. E. Lewis
A.S. Neighbours
James Morgan
Robert Boller
Frank McKinney
W. J. Darnal
J. C. McGregor
Jas. Blake
Fred Ward

The names of the men that signed the statement concerning John Ringo's death.

The official cause of John Ringo's death was listed as "unknown." Cochise County Court Clerk's Office, Bisbee, Arizona.

Notes and Sources

Chapter One. THE DISCOVERY

1. *Tombstone Epitaph*, July 18, 1882.
2. Ibid.
3. Ibid.
4. Ibid.
5. Statement for the information of the Coroner and Sheriff of Cochise County. Cochise County Court Clerk's Office, Bisbee, Arizona; *Tombstone Epitaph*, July 18, 1882.
6. On several occasions throughout his life, John Ringo was identified as John Ringgold or John Ringold in private writings or in newspapers. It does not appear that the cowboy used either name as an alias in Texas, New Mexico, or Arizona. While the cause of the confusion is not known for certain, it is likely that it began as an error being reported in the newspapers and over time gained acceptance by people that had no personal knowledge of John Ringo's true name.
7. *Arizona Daily Star*, July 18, 1882.
8. Cochise County Records, MS 180, box 8, folder 83: Sheriff John Behan's financial reports, January - April 1882, Arizona Historical Society, Tucson, Arizona. These papers list the men who joined Behan's posse on March 22, 1882, the number of days each served, and how much each man was paid (at the rate of $5 per day). Eighteen men, including John Ringo, served for ten days. A few others from one to five days. At the time, Wyatt Earp was still considered a deputy U. S. marshal in Arizona when he was indicted for the murder of Frank Stilwell in Tucson.
9. *Tombstone Epitaph*, July 18, 1882.
10. King, Frank M., *Wranglin' With the Past* (Pasadena: Self Published, 1935), pp. 207-208; Chaput, Don, *"Buckskin Frank" Leslie* (Tucson: Westernlore Press,1999), p 54. Although accepting that Leslie

probably did make the claim that he killed John Ringo, Biographer Chaput commented, "There is evidence to suggest that in the 1920s, Frank Leslie would tell anyone anything, so long as it led to a free drink."

11. Hooker, Forrestine Cooper, *An Arizona Vendetta: The Truth about Wyatt Earp* circa 1919-1920 (Riverside: Earl Chafin Press, 1998), pp. 53-54. Based on interviews with Wyatt Earp, the Hooker manuscript tells how Wyatt Earp killed both Curly Bill and John Ringo on his way out of Arizona. This is a feat that was not possible since Wyatt left Arizona by early April 1882 and Ringo did not die until three months later, in July 1882. A similar account is also repeated in the John Flood manuscript (circa 1926), which was also written based on interviews with Wyatt Earp. Flood, John Henry Jr., *Wyatt Earp* (Riverside: Earl Chafin, 1997), pp. 238-242. University of Arizona Professor Frank Lockwood, who met with Wyatt Earp in Los Angeles during 1926, later claimed that Earp told him the same account as is presented in both the Hooker and Flood manuscripts. Lockwood wrote: "Earp told me in circumstantial detail [with careful attention to detail] how he killed both Curly Bill and John Ringo" (Lockwood, Frank C., *Pioneer Days in Arizona* (New York: The MacMillan Company, 1932), p. 283.

12. Cowboy Depredations File, U.S. Documents [microfilm], Record Group 60, University of Arizona Library, Tucson, Arizona. *Tombstone Daily Epitaph*, August 5, 1881; *Arizona Daily Star*, February 15, 1881.

13. *Tombstone Epitaph*, October 27, 1881.

14. *Tombstone Nugget,* March 26, 1882; *Ford County Globe*, May 23, 1882; Nyle Miller and Joseph Snell, *Great Gunfighters of the Kansas Cowtowns, 1867-1886* (Lincoln: University of Nebraska Press, 1967), p. 93. Former Ford County District Attorney Edward Colburn was told by Wyatt Earp the story of how Earp killed Curly Bill. On May 20, 1882, Colburn sent a letter to the *Globe*, and the newspaper published the letter three days later with the details of the conversation. Articles in *Field and Farm*, August 17, 1893, and the *San Francisco Examiner*, August 2, 1896, also contain Wyatt Earp's claim to have killed Curly Bill Brocius.

15. Various newspaper articles throughout the country published dispatches concerning the reported depredations and border raids reportedly committed by cowboys in Arizona. For example, the *Pueblo*

Chieftain (Colorado), on February 17, 1881, noted: "A dispatch from Tucson, Arizona, says: Reliable information has been received from the San Pedro River, below the Sonoran line [Mexico], that San Simon cow boys are depredating fearfully upon Mexican stock raisers in Sonora."

16. *San Francisco Examiner*, May 4, 1882. Quoted in Tefertiller, *Wyatt Earp*, pp. 252-253.

17. John Ringo's participation in the Hoodoo War was public knowledge, and newspapers throughout Texas from 1875 to 1878 published many articles that discussed Ringo's activities in that state, establishing for him a notorious reputation as a desperate and dangerous man. The *Austin Weekly Statesman*, on November 9, 1876, commented that John Ringo was "regarded as one of the most desperate men in the frontier counties" of Texas. A year later, on December 4, 1877, the *Austin Statesman* wrote, "Distinguished Arrivals . . . George Gladden . . . [and] John Ringo . . . The people will be curious to see these two men, famous for the devilish deeds they have done."

18. Theme song of the television show *Johnny Ringo* (1959), written and sung by Don Durant, who starred in the title role. The television show and song portrayed Johnny Ringo as "the fastest gun in all the West, the quickest ever known." Historical fiction books like Leslie Scott's, *Tombstone Showdown* (New York: Pyramid Books, 1957) and Ray Hogan's *The Life and Death of Johnny Ringo* (New York: Signet Books, 1963). Released in 1964 in England as *Johnny Ringo: Gentleman Outlaw* (London: John Long), also presented Johnny Ringo in the gunfighter image.

Chapter Two. GONE TO TEXAS

1. Cause 854, filed on April 5, 1875. Burnet County District Court Clerk's Office, Burnet, Texas.

2. Burrows, Jack, *John Ringo, The Gunfighter Who Never Was* (Tucson: University of Arizona Press, 1987), p. 5.

3. Scott, *Tombstone Showdown*, p. 7; Hogan, *The Life and Death of Johnny Ringo*, p. v.

4. Burns, Walter Noble, *Tombstone, An Iliad of the Southwest* (New York: Doubleday, 1927), p. 133.

5. Breakenridge, William M., *Helldorado, Bringing the Law to the Mesquite* (New York: Houghton Mifflin 1928), p. 134.

6. Hogan *The Life and Death of Johnny Ringo,* pp. v-vi. Hogan concluded that his true name was Ringo because "no man named Ringgold, wishing to conceal his identity, would choose a name so similar, so alike in sound."

7. Ringo's supposed family connection to the Younger brothers was first published by the *Tombstone Epitaph* on July 18, 1882, four days after the cowboy was found dead. A week later, on July 25, 1882, the *Epitaph* published a letter from Ringo's sister, Enna Ringo, that corrected the misconception. The letter confirmed that the notorious cowboy's true name was Ringo and that he was born in Indiana in 1850. But the newspaper article, which would have corrected several issues regarding the cowboy's background, eluded early researchers.

8. Scott, *Tombstone Showdown,* p. 7.; Burrows, *Gunfighter,* p. 50. Burrows cites Bakarich, Sara Grace, *Gunsmoke, The True Story of Old Tombstone* (Tombstone: Tombstone Press 1954), pp. 95-97.

9. Burns, *Tombstone,* p. 134.

10. Reminiscences of a Stranger, Author Unknown, dated July 29, 1927. Arizona Historical Society Library, Tucson, Arizona. The account pre-dates the publication of Burns' *Tombstone (*1927*)* and Breakenridge's *Helldorado* (1928).

11. Ringo, David, *Ringo Family Series,* 1981, p. 11. The Ringo family is listed in the 1850 Indiana Federal Census as living in Washington, Clay Township (now called Green's Fork), Wayne County.

12. The *Liberty Tribune* on September 8, 1848, wrote: "Married on September 4, 1848 by JMC Inskeep, Martin Ringo, Esq., of Washington, Indiana to Mary, daughter of John R. Peters, Esq., of Clay County."

13. Ringo, David, *Ringo Family Series,* p. 11.

14. Johnson, David, *John Ringo* (Stillwater: Barbed Wire Press, 1996), pp. 22-24. Johnson noted that the *Liberty Tribune,* during September 1857, had thanked several people, among them Martin Ringo, for bringing to Liberty "late St. Louis and other eastern papers," thus setting the Ringos' likely arrival in Liberty, Missouri, at that time. According to Johnson, Martin moved his family to Gallatin sometime in 1858.

15. Ringo, David, *Ringo Family Series,* p. 11.

16. Johnson, *John Ringo,* pp. 23-24.

17. 1860 Missouri Federal Census. Thompson was enumerated in

the census in close proximity to the Ringo family. While it is not certain, it seems likely that school teacher Thompson probably taught school to young John Ringo.

18. Burrows, *Gunfighter*, p. 106; Johnson, *John Ringo*, p. 28.

19. Ringo, Mary, *The Journal of Mrs. Mary Ringo* (Santa Anna: Privately printed, 1956), entry for May 18, 1864.

20. Ibid.

21. Ibid

22. Ibid

23. Ibid

24. Ibid

25. Ibid

26. Ibid

27. Ibid

28. *Liberty Tribune*, September 6, 1864. Martin Ringo's grave is located a few miles west of Glenrock, Wyoming. Near his grave is another emigrant, J. P. Parker, who died four years earlier on the same wagon trail. Brown, Randy, "The Death of Martin Ringo." *Overland Journal*, Vol. 7, No. 1, 1989.

29. *Liberty Tribune*, September 16, 1864.

30. Johnson, *John Ringo*, pp. 40-41.

31. Santa Clara County, California, Probate Court Records.

32. Johnson, *John Ringo*, pp. 85-86; citing *Galveston Daily News*, February 9, 1876.

33. Burrows, *Gunfighter*, p. 129. Burrows wrote that Frank Cushing, John Ringo's nephew, had years later told Charles Ringo, a distant cousin, that "John became quite a drunkard and left home at 19 in 1869 . . . [leaving] the family in the lurch."

34. San Jose City Directory for 1870, p. 115. See also Johnson, *John Ringo*, p. 43. The 1870 California Federal Census also enumerated John Ringo and his family.

35. Mattie B. Cushing and Mary Enna Ringo, letter to J. H. Letton, October 5, 1934. Courtesy Dave Johnson, copy in author's files.

36. Bartholomew, Ed, *Jesse Evans, A Texas Hide Burner* (Toyavale, Frontier Press of Texas, 1955).

37. Cause 854, filed on April 5, 1875. Burnet County District Court Clerk's Office, Burnet, Texas.

38. Cause 854, Capias warrant issued on April 14, 1875, and

executed by arresting John Ringo on July 9, 1875. Burnet County District Court Clerk's Office, Burnet, Texas.

39. Ibid.

40. Ibid.

Chapter Three. HOODOO WAR

1. Sonnichsen, C. L., *I'll Die Before I Run* (New York: Harper & Company, 1951).

2. Ibid.

3. *Burnet Bulletin*, September 5, 1874.

4. Ibid.

5. *Burnet Bulletin*, September 5, 1874; Johnson, *John Ringo*, p. 58.

6. *Burnet Bulletin*, September 5, 1874.

7. Gamel, Thomas W., *The Life of Thomas W. Gamel* (Mason: Mason County Historical Society, 1994), p. 21.

8. Holmes, Lucia, *The Diary of Lucia Holmes* (Mason: Mason County Historical Society, 1985), p.3.

9. Johnson, *John Ringo*, p. 63.

10. Roberts, Dan W., *Rangers and Sovereignty* (San Antonio: Wood Printing & Engraving Co., 1914), pp. 87-89.

11. Ibid.

12. Sonnichsen, C. L., *Ten Texas Feuds* (Albuquerque: University of New Mexico Press, 1957), p. 89. About the use of the name "Hoodoo," Sonnichsen further noted: "Negroes used to call the Ku Klux Klan by the same name" and "Lee Hall's Texas Rangers down on the Rio Grande had earned the same title."

13. Gamel, *The Life of Thomas W. Gamel*, p. 17.

14. Holmes, *The Diary of Lucia Holmes*, p. 11.

15. *San Antonio Daily Herald*, August 30, 1875; Gamel, *The Life of Thomas W. Gamel*, p. 20.

16. Gamel, *The Life of Thomas W. Gamel*, pp. 23-24.

17. *Austin Weekly Democratic Statesman,* October 21, 1875.

18. Johnson, *John Ringo*, p. 71; citing Gillett, James B., *Six Years With The Texas Rangers* (Austin: Von Boeckmann-Jones Company, 1921), p. 47.

19. Johnson, *John Ringo*, pp. 71-72; Citing *Dallas Herald*,

February 10, 1872 and Galveston *Christian Advocate*, May 29, 1872.

20. Johnson, *John Ringo*, p. 72; Citing 1870 Mortality Schedule, Jack County, Texas.

21. Johnson, *John Ringo*, p. 71; Citing *Austin Daily Statesman*, November 28, 1874.

22. Starting in January 1876, Texas newspapers on a number of occasions noted that John Ringo and Scott Cooley had been either arrested together, implicated in the same crimes, or busted out of the same jail.

23. Johnson, *John Ringo*, pp. 71-72; Citing *San Antonio Daily Herald*, August 30, 1875.

24. Johnson, *John Ringo*, p. 71; Citing Gamel, *The Life of Thomas W. Gamel*, p. 24.

25. Johnson, *John Ringo*, p. 74.

26. Gamel, *The Life of Thomas W. Gamel*, p. 25.

27. Burrows, *Gunfighter*, p. 135.

28. *Austin Weekly Democratic Statesman,* October 21, 1875.

29. Ibid.

30. Gamel, *The Life of Thomas W. Gamel*, p. 21.

31. Henry Holmes letter to Texas Governor Richard Coke, September 8, 1875, Governor's Papers, Texas State Archives, Austin, Texas.

32. Ibid.

33. O'Neil, James B., *They Die But Once* (New York: Knight Publications, 1935) p. 135.

34. Gamel, *The Life of Thomas W. Gamel*, pp. 21-22.

35. The *Austin Weekly Democratic Statesman,* October 21, 1875, stated, "It was rumored that one Cheney [sic] had beguiled Beard [sic] and Gladden into this unequal fight. . . ." In Gamel, *The Life of Thomas W. Gamel*, p. 21, Gamel claimed that Cheyney was paid $50 to lure Moses Baird and George Gladden toward Mason and into Clark's ambush party.

36. Gamel, *The Life of Thomas W. Gamel*, p. 22.

37. Ibid.

38. Major John B. Jones, Texas Rangers, letter to William Steele, Adjutant General for the State of Texas, October 28, 1875. Adjutant General's Files, University of Texas, Austin, Texas.

39. John Ringo's younger brother, Martin Albert Ringo, died of tuberculosis in San Jose, California, on August 29, 1873. On September 19, 1873, the *Liberty Tribune* published the following notice of Martin Ringo's death: "Died, in San Jose, California, on the 29th of August, 1873, of consumption, Martin Albert Ringo, son of the late Martin Ringo, formerly of Liberty, aged 20 years."

40. Major John B. Jones, Texas Rangers, letter to William Steele, Adjutant General for the State of Texas, September 28, 1875. Adjutant General's Files, University of Texas, Austin, Texas.

41. Gamel, *The Life of Thomas W. Gamel*, p. 23.

42. Ibid., p. 24.

43. Ibid.

44. Ibid.

45. Major John B. Jones, Texas Rangers, letter to William Steele, Adjutant General for the State of Texas, September 30, 1875. Adjutant General's Files, University of Texas, Austin, Texas.

46. *San Antonio Herald*, October 12, 1875.

47. *San Antonio Herald*, November 12, 1875.

48. Johnson, *John Ringo*, p. 72. Case 854, Burnet County District Court Clerk's Office, Burnet, Texas.

49. Case 854, Burnet County District Court Clerk's Office, Burnet, Texas.

50. Ibid.

51. *Galveston Daily News*, November 25, 1875.

Chapter Four. SERIOUS THREATS

1. Alias Capias, arrest warrant, Case 854. Issued on October 19, 1875, and executed by arresting Ringo. Filed on December 14, 1875. Burnet County District Court Clerk's Office, Burnet, Texas.

2. Case 854. Burnet County District Court Clerk's Office, Burnet, Texas. John R. Baird and George Gladden signed as sureties for John Ringo's $150 bond on December 6, 1875.

3. *Austin Statesman*, January 4, 1876; Case 925 and 926, Burnet County District Court Clerk's Office, Burnet, Texas.

4. Testimony of John J. Strickland. State of Texas vs. John C. Carson, Lampasas District Court Clerk's Office, Lampasas, Texas.

5. Ibid.

6. Ibid.

7. *Austin Statesman*, January 4, 1876.

8. Gamel, *The Life of Thomas W. Gamel*, p. 25.

9. *Austin Statesman*, February 1, 1876.

10. Ibid.

11. Docket entry for February 1, 1876, Cause 925 and 926, Burnet County District Court Clerk's Office, Burnet, Texas.

12. Cause 854. Burnet County District Court Clerk's Office, Burnet, Texas.

13. Docket entry for February 3, 1876, Cause 925 and 926, Burnet County District Court Clerk's Office, Burnet, Texas.

14. Ibid.

15. Ibid.

16. *Dallas Herald*, March 16, 1876; reprinting article from *Lampasas Dispatch*.

17. *Galveston Daily News*, February 9, 1876.

18. Cause 380 and 381, Lampasas County District Court Clerk's Office, Lampasas, Texas. Docket entries, March Term 1877.

19. *Fayette County New Area*, May 12, 1876; reprinting article from *Burnet Bulletin*.

20. Testimony of Ed Cavin. State of Texas vs. John C. Carson, Lampasas District Court Clerk's Office, Lampasas, Texas.

21. Ibid.

22. Ibid.

23. Ibid.

24. Johnson, *John Ringo*, p. 87.

25. Testimony of Ed Cavin. State of Texas vs. John C. Carson, Lampasas District Court Clerk's Office, Lampasas, Texas.

Chapter Five. A NOTORIOUS MAN

1. Testimony of A. R. Johnson. State of Texas vs. John C. Carson, Lampasas District Court Clerk's Office, Lampasas, Texas.

2. Testimony of James Randall. State of Texas vs. John C. Carson, Lampasas District Court Clerk's Office, Lampasas, Texas.

3. Ibid.

4. Ibid.

5. Testimony of W. P. Hoskins. State of Texas vs. John C. Carson,

Lampasas District Court Clerk's Office, Lampasas, Texas.

6. Ibid.

7. Ibid.

8. Ibid.

9. Johnson, *John Ringo*, p. 88; citing *The Lucia Holmes Diary,* entry for May 6, 1876.

10. *Austin Daily Statesman*, June 9, 1876.

11. Johnson, *John Ringo*, p. 88; citing Gamel, *The Life of Thomas W. Gamel*, p. 30.

12. *Dallas Weekly Herald*, June 10, 1876; Houston *Daily Telegraph*, June 14, 1876.

13. *Austin Statesman*, August 18, 1876.

14. Johnson, *John Ringo*, p. 88; citing Gamel, *The Life of Thomas W. Gamel*, p. 30.

15. *Austin Statesman*, June 14, 1876.

16. Cause 977. Burnet County District Court Clerk's Office, Burnet, Texas.

17. *Burnet Bulletin*, July 14, 1876.

18. Burnet County District Court Clerk's Office, Burnet, Texas. Cause 967 - State of Texas vs. John Ringo; Cause 966 - State of Texas vs. Scott Cooley; Cause 965 - State of Texas vs. John Baird.

19. Holmes, *The Lucia Holmes Diary*, p. 79. Entry for September 5, 1876.

20. *Austin Statesman*, September 23, 1876.

21. Johnson, *John Ringo*, pp. 95-96, citing report of J. C. Sparks of Company C to William Steele on December 1, 1876.

22. Ibid.

23. Ibid.

24. Cause 21. Mason County District Court Clerk's Office, Mason, Texas.

25. Johnson, *John Ringo* p. 97, citing *Burnet Bulletin*, December 15, 1876.

26. Johnson, David, *G. W. Gladden - Hard Luck Warrior,* National Outlaw and Lawman Association *Quarterly*, Vol. XV. No. 3 (July - Sept., 1991), p. 5.

27. Ibid., p. 5. Citing Clemency Records in the Texas State Archives, Johnson wrote the following about Gladden's pardon: "Then, on December 30, 1884, he [Gladden] was pardoned by the govenor on

'the recommendation of the District Judge, District Atty., County Judge and most other County officials and many citizens'."

28. Hardin, John Wesley, *The Life of John Wesley Hardin* (Sequin, Texas, 1896), p. 126.

29. 2 Texas Appeals 290 (1877).

30. Ibid.

31. Johnson, *John Ringo*, p. 97; citing *Burnet Bulletin*, January 26, 1877.

32. Cause 21. Mason County District Court Clerk's Office, Mason, Texas.

33. Cause 380 and 381, Lampasas County District Court Clerk's Office, Lampasas, Texas.

34. Cause 21. Mason County District Court Clerk's Office, Mason, Texas; Mason County Court Commissioner Book 1, Mason County District Court Clerk's Office, Mason, Texas.

35. Mason County Court Commissioner Book 1, Mason County District Court Clerk's Office, Mason, Texas.

36. Cause 21. Mason County District Court Clerk's Office, Mason, Texas.

37. Ibid.

38. Mason County Court Commissioner Book 1, Mason County District Court Clerk's Office, Mason, Texas.

39. *Austin Statesmen*, December 4, 1877.

40. Cause 21. Mason County District Court Clerk's Office, Mason, Texas.

41. Ibid.

42. Johnson, *John Ringo*, p. 99; citing *Galveston Daily News*, January 17, 1878.

43. Cause 21. Mason County District Court Clerk's Office, Mason, Texas.

44. Adjutant General's File, University of Texas, Austin, Texas.

45. Cause 21. Mason County District Court Clerk's Office, Mason, Texas.

46. Ibid.

47. Ibid.

48. Ibid.

49. *Galveston Daily News*, May 31, 1878.

50. Cause 380 and 381, Lampasas County District Court Clerk's

Office, Lampasas, Texas.

51. Official Election Register, pp. 259-269, Texas State Library at Austin, Texas.

52. Johnson, *John Ringo*, p. 102; citing Mason County Brand and Marks Register, Mason, Texas.

53. Johnson, *John Ringo*, pp. 103-104; citing interview with John Olney.

54. Ibid.

55. Ringgold, Jennie Parks, *Frontier Days in the Old Southwest* (San Antonio: The Naylor Company, 1952), p. 15.

Chapter Six. SAN SIMON COWBOYS

1. Letter from Department of State to Carl Schurz, Secretary of the Interior, dated December 10, 1878, which transcribed a letter written by the Mexican Minister on December 6, 1878. Cowboy Depredations File, U.S. Document [microfilm], Record Group 60, University of Arizona Library, Tucson, Arizona.

2. Letter from E. B. Pomroy, United States Attorney for Territory of Arizona, to Wayne MacVeagh, United States Attorney General, June 23, 1881. Cowboy Depredations File, U.S. Document [microfilm], Record Group 60, University of Arizona Library; Tucson, Arizona.

3. The *Arizona Weekly Star,* on October 7, 1880, noted that four cowboys at San Simon took possession of a locomotive but could not use it because the fire was out in the boiler. About a month later, the *Arizona Weekly Star*, on November 4, 1880, alleged that Curly Bill was one of the four cowboys involved in the San Simon train incident.

4. Letter from Secretary of Interior Charles Schurz to Governor John C. Fremont, dated December 24, 1880. Cowboy Depredations File, U.S. Document [microfilm], Record Group 60, University of Arizona Library; Tucson, Arizona. Schurz wrote: "I enclose herewith a copy of a letter of the Secretary of State, enclosing copies of letters addressed to him by Senor Don Juan N. Navarro, Charge d affaires ad interim of the Mexican Republic to this country, relative to alleged outrages perpetrated upon citizens of Mexico by a party of outlaws headed by one Robert Martin. I have to request that you make inquiry in regard to this matter, and if the lurking place of said Martin be found within the Territory of Arizona, that you will adopt such measures as may be

within your power looking to the breaking up of his band and the preservation and maintenance of peace along the frontier between the two countries."

5. Letter from Governor John C. Fremont to Secretary of Interior Carl Schurz, dated January 6, 1879. Cowboy Depredations File, U.S. Document [microfilm], Record Group 60, University of Arizona Library; Tucson, Arizona. About the allegation of a band of organized men in Arizona, Fremont commented: "This statement greatly surprises me. Except for the occasional crime, relative to a border situation, no mention has come to me of any disturbances on the frontier. The authorities on our side have vigorously followed up every outrage, and Gen. Mariscal, the Governor of Sonora, has shown every disposition to cooperate effectively with us in maintaining good order and a friendly understanding."

6. Ibid.

7. Tays to John B. Jones, letter dated May 31, 1878.

8. Ibid.

9. Ibid.

10. Gatto, Steve, *Alias Curly Bill, The Life and Times of William Brocius* (Tucson: Privately printed, 2000) pp. 4-8. See also Gatto, Steve, *Wyatt Earp, A Biography of a Western Lawman* (Tucson: San Simon Publishing, 1997), pp. 65-66; Gatto, Steve, *Real Wyatt Earp* (Silver City: High-Lonesome Press, 2000), p. 49.

11. Gatto, Steve, *Alias Curly Bill, The Life and Times of William Brocius* (Tucson: Privately printed, 2000) p. 5; quoting an article published in the *Mesilla Valley Independent* on May 25, 1878.

12. Ibid. Cause 300, State of Texas v Robert Martin and William Bresnaham. El Paso County District Court Clerk's Office, El Paso, Texas.

13. Brand, Peter, "The Escape of 'Curly Bill' Brocius," Western Outlaw Lawman Association *Quarterly*, 2000.

14. *Arizona Weekly Star*, December 2, 1880; *Tucson Daily Citizen*, December 7, 1880; *Tucson Weekly Citizen*, December 11, 1880; *Arizona Daily Star,* December 9, 1880.

15. Ibid.

16. *Tombstone Daily Epitaph*, October 28, 1880.

17. Lake, Stuart N., *Wyatt Earp, Frontier Marshal* (New York: Houghton Mifflin, 1931), pp. 234-235. Lake created the "Clanton-Curly

Bill-McLowery" [sic] gang, which he declared had "three hundred outcasts of frontier society," with Curly Bill and John Ringo as Newman "Old Man" Clanton's next in command. Since then, many writers have accepted that there, indeed, was such a gang. While newspapers of the day occasionally did refer to the cowboys in the area as a single unit because they were seen as a common menace, in actuality, few historians today believe that there was one single cowboy gang operating in Arizona. More realistically, there were several small groups of men that may have rode together at times; however, they owed no special allegiance to any single gang or man.

18. Rasch, "The Resurrection of Pony Deal," Phil Rasch Collection, Arizona Historical Society Library, Tucson, Arizona.

19. Ibid.

20. Brand, "The Escape of 'Curly Bill' Brocius," p. 1.

21. 1880 New Mexico Federal Census, Grant County, New Mexico.

22. The *Tombstone Epitaph*, on October 23, 1881, reported that deputy William Breakenridge had arrested Milt Hicks, "who is charged with having in his possession and fraudulently branding cattle belonging to a rancher." On the afternoon of October 24, Hicks and two other prisoners overpowered their guard and escaped from the county jail. On October 25, 1881, the *Tombstone Epitaph* noted the escape and that "Sheriff Behan, Deputies Breakenridge, [Andy] Bronk and [Lance] Perkins, Chief of Police Earp, Morgan Earp, Wyatt Earp and several others started in pursuit" but could not find the escaped men. Milt Hicks fled to New Mexico, joining his brother Will, who had already crossed over to New Mexico to avoid arrest.

23. Hill, Janaloo, *Yours Until Death, William Grounds*, *True West*, April 1973, p. 14.

24. Register of Complaints, Cochise County Court Clerk's Office, Bisbee, Arizona. Like Milt and Will Hicks, Led Moore fled to New Mexico. He was never arrested on the criminal charge.

25. 1880 New Mexico Federal Census, Grant County, New Mexico.

26. *Tombstone Daily Nugget*, November 11, 1881.

27. Reminiscences of Frank and John Stark, 1971. University of Arizona Library, Media Center, Audio Tape 400, Tucson Arizona. According to William Stark's sons: "They [William Stark and Al George] came from Colorado heading to California. They stopped at San Simon because the mule team was tired. They turned the mules loose in a

pasture and went to sleep. When they woke up they couldn't see the mules. So they went up to a house on a hill (it was Chenoweth's), and they knocked on the door. And the fellow who came to the door was John Ringo. Dad didn't know who anybody was at the time. He said that his mules had strayed off. Ringo said, they are around here somewhere, take my horse and go get them."

28. Register of Complaints, Cochise County Court Clerk's Office, Bisbee, Arizona.

29. Breakenridge claimed that cowboy Dick Lloyd woked on a ranch owned by J. B. Collins. Breakenridge, *Helldorado*, pp. 113-114.

30. *Arizona Daily Star,* December 14, 1879. Several newspapers throughout Arizona carried the story of the Hancock shooting.

31. Ibid.

32. 1880 Arizona Federal Census. Hancock is listed as living in Safford with his brother-in-law, James Hayes.

33. Lake, *Frontier Marshal*, p. 235. It appears that Lake was the first writer to discuss the shooting of Louis Hancock by John Ringo. "Ringo, a week after Wyatt Earp reached Tombstone, invited a chance acquaintance in a saloon, one Louis Hancock, to have a drink, and shot his guest through the throat when Hancock ordered beer as Ringo took whiskey," Lake wrote. Since there was no mention of where the event took place or whether Hancock was killed, writers simply repeated the account from Lake's book. Often these later accounts erroneously indicated that Hancock was killed by Ringo in a Tombstone saloon.

34. John Ringo to Charles Shibell, March 3, 1880. Courtesy Robert N. Mullin Collection, Haley Library, Midland, Texas.

35. Pima County Court Record, p. 76. Copy courtesy Ben T. Traywick.

36. New Mexico Land Records. Grant County District Court Clerk's Office, Silver City, New Mexico; Gatto Steve, "Johnny Ringo, Land and Cattle Speculator," National Outlaw Lawman Association *Quarterly* Vol.18, No. 4, 1994, pp. 9-10.

37. Ibid.

38. Hill, Janaloo, *Yours Until Death, William Grounds, True West,* April 1973, p. 14.

39. Johnson, *John Ringo*, p. 117.

40. Letter from J. B. Collins to Barton Jacobs, July 17, 1880, Special Collections Department, University of Arizona Library, Tucson, Arizona.

41. Reminiscences of A. M. Franklin, Arizona Historical Society Library, Tucson, Arizona.

42. Ibid.

43. *Arizona Daily Star,* Fifty Year Anniversary Issue, May 1927.

44. Reminiscences of A. M. Franklin, Arizona Historical Society Library, Tucson, Arizona.

45. Ibid.

46. *Grant County Herald*, July 22, 1882.

47. Reminiscences of James C. Hancock, Arizona Historical Society Library, Tucson, Arizona.

48. Breakenridge, *Helldorado*, p. 134.

49. Traywick, *Clantons of Tombstone*, pp. 11, 41-46.

50. Statement of Wyatt Earp, *Tombstone Nugget*, November 17, 1881.

51. Copy of the appointment document in author's files courtesy Ben T. Traywick.

52. *Dodge City Times*, June 8, 1878.

53. 1880 Arizona Federal Census. Doc Holliday was listed as living in Prescott.

54. Testimony of Ike Clanton. *Tombstone Nugget*, November 15, 1881.

55. *Tombstone Daily Epitaph*, July 30, 1880.

56. Ibid.

57. *Tombstone Weekly Nugget*, August 5, 1880.

58. Statement of Wyatt Earp. *Tombstone Nugget*, November 17, 1881.

59. Appointment document dated July 27, 1880. Pima County Recorder's Office, Tucson, Arizona.

60. *Tombstone Epitaph*, October 28, 1880.

61. *Arizona Weekly Star*, November 4, 1880.

62. Ibid.

63. *Tombstone Epitaph*, October 29, 1880.

64. Ibid.

65. Ibid.

66. *Tucson Daily Star*, December 28, 1880.

67. *Tucson Daily Citizen*, December 27, 1880; *Tucson Daily Star*, December 28, 1880.

Chapter Seven. ELECTION SCANDAL

1. *Arizona Daily Star*, August 31, 1880.
2. Ibid.
3. Ibid.
4. The 1880 Arizona Federal Census listed Louis Hancock as residing in the same household as his brother-in-law, James Hayes, in Safford.
5. *Tombstone Nugget*, October 19, 1880. Record of Pima County Board of Supervisors 1880, Arizona Historical Society Library, Tucson, Arizona.
6. Record of Pima County Board of Supervisors 1880, Arizona Historical Society Library, Tucson, Arizona.
7. Ibid.
8. Ibid.
9. New Mexico Land Records. Grant County District Court Clerk's Office, Silver City, New Mexico; See also Gatto, "Johnny Ringo, Land and Cattle Speculator," pp.9-10.
10. Anderson, "Posses and Politics in Pima County," *The Journal of Arizona History*, 1986, pp. 272-275.
11. Ibid.
12. Ibid.
13. Ibid.
14. Ibid.
15. Record of Pima County Board of Supervisors 1880, Arizona Historical Society Library, Tucson, Arizona.
16. Letter from Mattie Cushing and M. Enna Ringo to Mrs. J. H. Letton, October 5, 1934. Courtesy David Johnson.
17. The Laws of Arizona (1881); Act 7, enacted by Eleventh Legislative Assembly of the Territory of Arizona, p. 4.
18. Judge Charles French's order that all district court cases that had originated in Cochise County must be transfered to that county was based on a sound legal basis. Included within the act creating Cochise County was Section 7, which provided for the cases originating in Cochise County to be transferred to the district court in that county.
19. The substance of the cause of action and the location where the case originated is not known. Yet, since a "nolle pros." was entered in the case only three days after Judge French's order, it seems likely

that the complaint against John Ringo and Ben Schuster was dismissed to transfer the case to another county. If the case was transferred to Cochise County, it appears that it was never filed in that district court.

20. *Austin Daily Statesman*, May 3, 1881.

21. Record of Arrests, Austin, Texas.

22. *Tombstone Nugget*, July 12, 1881.

Chapter Eight. BORDER RAIDS

1. Letter from Department of State to Carl Schurz, Secretary of the Interior, dated December 10, 1878, which transcribed a letter written by the Mexican Minister on December 6, 1878. Cowboy Depredations File, U.S. Document [microfilm], Record Group 60, University of Arizona Library, Tucson, Arizona.

2. *Arizona Daily Star*, December 9, 1880.

3. Ibid.

4. Letter from Secretary of Interior Charles Schurz to Governor John C. Fremont, dated December 24, 1880. Cowboy Depredations File, U.S. Document [microfilm], Record Group 60, University of Arizona Library, Tucson, Arizona.

5. *Arizona Weekly Star*, December 2, 1880; *Tucson Daily Citizen*, December 7, 1880; *Tucson Weekly Citizen*, December 11, 1880; *Arizona Daily Star*, December 9, 1880. None of these contemporary newspapers commented that Bob Martin was a suspected leader of a cowboy gang raiding the Mexican border. While some allegations were made to government officials concerning Bob Martin's suspected role as a cowboy gang leader in the San Simon Valley, the rumors and complaints apparently were not widely known to the newspapers in the territory at the time.

6. One Mexican rancher who apparently tried to recover his losses from stolen livestock from the U. S. government and the Arizona court system was Ramon Lujan. During 1879, two Pima County deputies had "reported to Chihuahua cattle rancher Ramon Lujan that a 'strong and well organized band' of rustlers, mostly Mexican, were selling cattle from Mexico to 'a number of well-known Americans about fifty miles north of the border.'" *Marks, And die in the West*, p. 126. According to Marks, the deputies offered to "trace the rustled stock for six dollars a day," plus expenses and a percentage based on recovered livestock.

Ibid. In September 1880, a Mexican official reported to the U. S. government that the stock was at San Carlos, and that Lujan wanted "reimbursement for the stolen cattle and expenses incurred in trying to locate the thieves." *Ibid.* It is possible that Ramon Lujan also filed a civil suit in Pima County district court to recover damages for his stolen livestock. On November 2, 1880, the *Tucson Daily Citizen* noted that the matter of "Lujan vs. Thompson" was scheduled for jury trial before Judge Silent on November 4, 1880. The trial was apparently postponed and the case was continued [postponed] until the next term. On March 27, 1881, the *Arizona Weekly Citizen* reported: "Ramon Lujan vs. A. H. Thompson - Continued till adjourned term." How the case was settled is not known. A. H. Thompson has been identified as a San Simon rancher, and he was originally one of the election judges for the 1880 vote at the San Simon precinct.

7. *Tombstone Nugget*, June 9, 1881.

8. Johnson *John Ringo*, pp. 103-104; citing letter from Orlando B. Willcox to adjutant General, June 9, 1881. Cowboy Depredations File, U.S. Document [microfilm], Record Group 60, University of Arizona Library, Tucson, Arizona.

9. *Arizona Weekly Star,* June 16, 1881. The *Star* informed its readers that about seventy cowboys had gather near Willcox, Arizona, to prepare for an attack on Fronteras.

10. *Arizona Weekly Star*, June 23, 1881. A letter written in response to an earlier report of cowboys gathering at Willcox was sent to the editor of the *Star*, and it commented, "This is a quiet place - almost too quiet. My opinion of the matter is that it is a hoax. I think the cow-boys have too much sense to engage in anything of that sort, at least on so large a scale." By mid-June, the Army had discovered and reported that there was no "evidence of raiding parties either to or from Mexico." Cowboy Depredations File, U.S. Document [microfilm], Record Group 60, University of Arizona Library, Tucson, Arizona.

11. Letter from J. W. Evans to Crawley Dake, June 18, 1881. Cowboy Depredations File, U.S. Document [microfilm], Record Group 60, University of Arizona Library, Tucson, Arizona.

12. Letter from Luis Torres to J. W. Evan, June 24, 1881. Cowboy Depredations File, U.S. Document [microfilm], Record Group 60, University of Arizona Library, Tucson, Arizona; quoted by Johnson, *John Ringo,* p. 146.

13. John Ringo was in Austin, Texas, on May 2, 1881, where he was arrested by Ben Thompson. *Austin Daily Statesman*, May 3, 1881. Exactly when Ringo left Arizona is not known, but considering that he was in Texas during earlier May, it is reasonable to conclude that he left sometime around mid-April 1881.

14. *Tombstone Nugget*, July 12, 1881.

15. Reminiscences of James C. Hancock. Arizona Historical Society Library, Tucson, Arizona. It should be remembered that Hancock was not present during the incident and his recollections were made years later based on what he claimed he had heard.

16. Walter Noble Burns was one of the first to mistake the attack near Fronteras, Mexico, as occuring in Skeleton Canyon. Burns, *Tombstone*, pp. 95-106. Since then many writers, including this author, have repeated the error. Marks, Paula Mitchell Marks, *And Die in the West* (New York: William Morrow, 1989), p. 170; Erwin, Richard, *The Truth About Wyatt Earp* (Carpinteria: The OK Corral Press, 1993), pp. 196-200; and Tefertiller, Casey, *Wyatt Earp, The Life Behind the Legend* (New York" John Wiley and Sons, Inc., 1997), p. 92. Nonetheless, Skeleton Canyon, which is in the United States, is fifty miles from the Mexican town of Fronteras.

17. *San Francisco Evening Bulletin*, August 13, 1881.

18. *Tombstone Nugget*, August 16, 1881; *Arizona Weekly Star*, August 25, 1881. In recent years some authors have speculated that the Earp brothers and Doc Holliday carried out the Guadalupe Canyon massacre. The historical record shows that scenario is without merit.

19. Ibid.

20. Gatto, *Wyatt Earp*, pp. 92-93, citing Traywick, Ben T., *The Clantons of Tombstone* (Tombstone: Red Marie's Books 1996), p.77. See also Gatto, *Real Wyatt Earp*, pp. 92-93.

21. Ibid.

22. *Arizona Weekly Citizen*, September 4, 1881.

23. Cowboy Depredations File, U.S. Document [microfilm], Record Group 60, University of Arizona Library, Tucson, Arizona.

24. Cowboy Depredations File, U.S. Document [microfilm], Record Group 60, University of Arizona Library, Tucson, Arizona. See also Tefertiller, *Wyatt Earp*, pp. 252-253.

Chapter Nine. A GAME OF DRAW

1. *Tucson Citizen,* April 4, 1881; *Tombstone Nugget*, August 11, 1881; *Arizona Weekly Star*, August 11, 1881.
2. Breakenridge, *Helldorado*, p. 134.
3. Joseph Bowyer to editor *Arizona Daily Star*, September 4, 1881. Secretary of State File, Arizona State Archives, Phoenix, Arizona.
4. Ibid.
5. *Tombstone Daily Epitaph*, September 10, 1881.
6. Ibid.
7. Ibid.
8. Ibid.
9. Ibid.
10. Ibid.
11. Ibid.
12. Ibid.
13. Ibid.
14. Ibid.
15. Breakenridge, *Helldorado*, p. 135.
16. Criminal Register of Actions, Cochise County Court Clerk's Office, Bisbee, Arizona: Territory of Arizona vs. John Ringgold, robbery indictment, November 26, 1881, (cause 53) and Territory of Arizona vs. John Ringo, robbery indictment, December 2, 1881 (cause 81); Criminal Register of Actions, Cochise County Court Clerk's Office, Bisbee, Arizona: Territory of Arizona vs. David Eustis [Estes], robbery indictment, November 26, 1881, (cause 72) and Territory of Arizona vs. David Eustis [Estes], robbery indictment, December 2, 1881 (cause 86).
17. Criminal Register of Actions, Cochise County Court Clerk's Office, Bisbee, Arizona: Territory of Arizona vs. John Ringgold, robbery indictment, November 26, 1881, (cause 53)
18. Breakenridge, *Helldorado*, pp. 134-136.
19. Ibid.
20. Ibid.
21. Court Records, Cochise County Court Clerk's Office, Bisbee, Arizona: Territory of Arizona vs. John Ringgold, robbery indictment, November 26, 1881, (cause 53). The cause was later transferred to Territory of Arizona vs. John Ringo, robbery indictment, December 2,

1881 (cause 81).

22. Ibid.

23. Ibid.

24. Ibid.; *Tombstone Epitaph*, December 2, 1881.

25. *Tombstone Epitaph*, January 21, 1881.

26. *Tombstone Epitaph*, January 25, 1881.

27. Court Records, Cochise County Court Clerk's Office, Bisbee, Arizona: Territory of Arizona vs. John Ringgold, robbery indictment, November 26, 1881, (cause 53). Cause 53 was later transferred to Territory of Arizona vs. John Ringo, robbery indictment, December 2, 1881 (cause 81).

28. Ibid.

Chapter Ten. EARP-CLANTON FEUD

1. *Tombstone Epitaph*, October 27, 1881.

2. Testimony of John Behan published by the *Tombstone Daily Nugget* on October 29, 1881 and November 3, 1881.

3. *Tombstone Daily Nugget*, November 3, 1881.

4. *Tombstone Epitaph*, October 27, 1881.

5. The October 27, 1881, *Tombstone Nugget* is not available. However, the *Nugget's* article on the gunfight was reprinted in Tucson's *Weekly Arizona Citizen* on October 30, 1881.

6. *Tombstone Epitaph*, October 27, 1881.

7. *Tombstone Daily Nugget*, October 29, 1881; October 30, 1881.

8. Minutes of the Tombstone common council, Special Collections department, University of Arizona Library, Tucson, Arizona; Gatto, *Real Wyatt Earp*, p. 30.

9. Tefertiller, *Wyatt Earp*, p. 134; citing *San Francisco Examiner*, November 7, 1881.

10. *Tombstone Epitaph*, October 27, 1881.

11. The October 27, 1881, *Tombstone Nugget* is not available. However, the *Nugget's* article on the gunfight was reprinted in Tucson's *Weekly Arizona Citizen* on October 30, 1881.

12. Ibid.

13. *Tombstone Nugget*, November 17, 1881. The Eleventh Legislative Assembly of the Territory of Arizona (1881) amended Section 133, Chapter XI, Compiled Laws on February 12, 1881, allowing a

defendant a "right to make a statement in relation to the charges against him." Laws of Arizona, 1881, p.22.

14. Ibid.

15. Ibid.

16. Ibid.

17. Ibid.

18. Reminiscences of Melvin Jones. Arizona Historical Society Library, Tucson, Arizona.

19. Breakenridge, *Helldorado*, pp. 113-115.

20. *Arizona Weekly Star*, March 10, 1881.

21. Reminiscences of Melvin Jones. Arizona Historical Society Library, Tucson, Arizona.

22. *Arizona Weekly Star*, March 10, 1881.

23. *Tombstone Epitaph*, December 1, 1881.

24. *Tombstone Epitaph*, December 16, 1881.

25. *Tombstone Epitaph*, December 15, 1881.

26. Ibid.

27. *Tombstone Nugget*, December 15, 1881; December 16, 1881.

28. Lake, *Frontier Marshal*, p. 310.

29. *Tombstone Daily Nugget*, December 16, 1881; *Tombstone Epitaph,* December 18, 1881.

30. *Tombstone Epitaph*, December 18, 1881.

31. *Tombstone Epitaph*, January 13, 1882.

32. *Tombstone Epitaph*, December 29, 1881.

33. Ibid.

34. Ibid.

35. Bailey, Lynn R., ed., *A Tenderfoot in Tombstone: The Private Journal of George Whitwell Parsons - The Turbulent Year, 1880 - 1882* (Tucson: Westernlore Press 1996), pp. 198-199.

36. *Tombstone Nugget*, December 16, 1881.

37. The *Tombstone Epitaph* of February 3, 1881, published the proceedings of the Clanton Trial for the shooting of Virgil Earp. The *Epitaph* commented, "J. W. Bennett was called and stated that he had found a hat in the building - the new drug store - immediately after the shooting. The exit where the hat was discovered being about five feet four inches high. Hat was produced in court."

38. *Tombstone Epitaph*, February 3, 1881.

39. Lake, *Frontier Marshal*, p. 310. Ringo was neither implicated

in the crime at the time by the local newspapers that reported the incident nor was he later charged with the crime as the Clanton brothers were in late January 1882.

40. Lake, Carolyn, ed., *Undercover for Wells Fargo: The Unvarnished Recollections of Fred Dodge* (Boston: Houghton Mifflin, 1969), p. 243; reprinting letter from Fred Dodge to Stuart Lake, September 30, 1929. About Virgil's shooting, Dodge asserted: "The night that Virgil was shot in Tombstone, Johnny Barnes and Pony Deal were there; and Johnny Barnes was the man who fired the shot that tore up Virg's arm." Many of Fred Dodge's statements made decades later cannot be confirmed, and many people have questioned the veracity of his claims. He asserted that he came to Tombstone as an undercover man for Wells, Fargo. According to Dodge, the only man who knew of his undercover position was Wells, Fargo president, John J. Valentine - the man who hired him. No Wells, Fargo employment records for Fred Dodge for the years he was in Tombstone have ever been found. Dodge was later employed by Wells, Fargo in Texas. It seems that Dodge in his later years extended his term of employment with Wells, Fargo and appointed himself an undercover man for the company. Robert Chandler, historian and senior researcher for Wells Fargo Bank, made the following statement after reveiwing Fred Dodge's claim that he was a secret agent for Wells, Fargo: "I do not believe it." Chandler concluded, "In my opinion, Fred Dodge idolized the older Wyatt Earp. When Stuart Lake brought them together in 1928, Dodge - the former faro dealer - romanticized his disreputable arrival in Tombstone. Claiming to have been a Wells Fargo detective was a ploy that place him in the forefront of the action and made him a peer of the great Wyatt." Chandler, Robert J. "Under Cover for Wells Fargo: A Review Essay." *Journal of Arizona History*. Volume 41, Number 1, Spring 2000, pp. 83-96.

41. Reproduced in Traywick, *Clantons of Tombstone*, p. 134.

42. *Arizona Gazette,* December 30, 1881. Some people have suggested that Wyatt Earp became a deputy U.S. marshal in Arizona several months earlier based on a newspaper accounts in September 1881 that referred to Wyatt Earp as a deputy U.S. marshal. Wyatt did occasional work under the authority of his brother, Virgil, who was a deputy U.S. marshal. However, his work as Virgil's assistant in some instances did not make him a deputy U. S. marshal. On November 17, 1881, the *Tombstone Nugget* published a prepared statement read by

Wyatt Earp to the court during the Spicer hearing concerning the gunfight at the OK Corral. In that statement, Wyatt Earp commented: "am at present a saloon-keeper; also, have been Deputy Sheriff and detective." Since Wyatt Earp failed to mention that he was a deputy U.S. marshal or had held the position in Arizona prior to the gunfight, there is little doubt that he was not officially appointed a deputy U. S. marshal until late December 1881.

43. *Tombstone Epitaph*, December 30, 1881.

44. Ibid.

45. *Tombstone Epitaph*, October 25, 1881.

46. *Tombstone Nugget*, January 1,3, 1882.

47. Ibid.

48. *Tombstone Epitaph*, January 4, 1882.

Chapter Eleven. CHAMPION OF THE COWBOYS

1. *Tombstone Daily Epitaph*, January 10, 1882; Marks, *And Die in the West*, pp. 324-325; Tefertiller, *Wyatt Earp*, pp. 179-181.

2. Ibid.

3. Ibid.

4. *Los Angeles Times*, January 26, 1882; *San Francisco Evening Bulletin*, January 26, 1882; *San Diego Union*, January 26, 1882.

5. *Weekly Arizona Citizen*, January 22, 1882.

6. Ibid.

7. Ibid.

8. Ibid.

9. *Tombstone Daily Epitaph*, January 18, 1882.

10. Ibid.

11. Reminiscence of James C. Hancock. Arizona Historical Society Library, Tucson, Arizona. See also Johnson, *John Ringo*, p. 182.

12. King, *Wranglin' With the Past*, pp. 207-208.

13. In *Tombstone*, Burns' telling of the story, which is about as unreliable as any, has "Mayor Thomas" intervening in the near shootout, not James Flynn. See Burns, *Tombstone*, p. 137-138. Needless to say that James Carr was the mayor at the time of the January 1882 incident and John Clum was the previous mayor. All that is known for sure is that Ringo had a confrontation with Doc Holliday and possibly Wyatt Earp, but no shooting occurred during the encounter.

14. Breakenridge, *Helldorado*, p. 157.
15. Johnson, *John Ringo*, p. 182.
16. King, *Wranglin' With the Past*, pp. 207-208.
17. Tefertiller, *Wyatt Earp*, pp. 162, 184.
18. Ibid., p. 184.
19. Bailey, *Parsons Journal*, pp. 201-202; Gatto, *Real Wyatt Earp*, p. 145.
20. *Tombstone Epitaph*, December 30, 1881; reproduced in Gatto, *Wyatt Earp: A Biography of a Western Lawman*, p. 151-154. See also Gatto, *Real Wyatt Earp*, p. 144.
21. *Tombstone Epitaph*, July 18, 1882.
22. *Arizona Daily Star*, July 18, 1882.

Chapter Twelve. RINGO AND THE COWBOY WAR

1. Court Records, Cochise County Court Clerk's Office, Bisbee, Arizona: Territory of Arizona vs. John Ringgold, robbery indictment, November 26, 1881, (cause 53). Cause 53 was later transferred to Territory of Arizona vs. John Ringo, robbery indictment, December 2, 1881 (cause 81).
2. Register of Complaints; Cause 81, Territory of Arizona v John Ringo. Cochise County Court Records, Court Clerk's Office, Bisbee, Arizona.
3. Report by Leigh Chalmer, Examiner, Dept. of Justice, 1885, Cowboy Depredations File, U.S. Document [microfilm], Record Group 60, University of Arizona Library, Tucson, Arizona; *Arizona Gazette*, January 25, 1882; *Tombstone Epitaph*, January 28, 1882.
4. *Arizona Gazette*, January 25, 1882.
5. Ibid.
6. *Tombstone Epitaph*, January 24, 1882.
7. Ibid.
8. Ibid.
9. Affidavit of James Earp, written January 23, 1882. James Earp File, Arizona Historical Society Library, Tucson, Arizona.
10. Ibid.
11. Lake, *Frontier Marshal*, p.315.
12. *Tombstone Nugget*, January 27, 1882.
13. *Tombstone Epitaph*, January 25, 1882.

14. *Tombstone Nugget*, February 1, 1882.

15. *Tombstone Epitaph*, January 24, 1882.

16. *Tombstone Epitaph*, January 25, 1882.

17. Ibid.

18. Ibid. The *Tombstone Nugget*, on January 25, 1882, commented: "John Ringo was re-arrested yesterday and placed in the county jail."

19. *Tombstone Nugget*, January 26, 1882; Tefertiller, *Wyatt Earp*, pp. 179-181.

20. Ibid.

21. *Tombstone Nugget*, January 31, 1882.

22. Cause 81, Territory of Arizona vs. John Ringo. Docket Sheet for January 31, 1882. Cochise County Court Records, Court Clerk's Office, Bisbee, Arizona.

23. *Tombstone Nugget*, February 1, 1882.

Chapter Thirteen. ARREST WARRANTS AND BORDER PATROLS

1. *Tombstone Epitaph*, February 1, 1882.

2. *Tombstone Epitaph*, February 2, 1882.

3. *Tombstone Epitaph*, February 3, 1882.

4. *Tombstone Epitaph*, February 2, 1882.

5. Ibid.

6. Lake, *Frontier Marshal*, p. 310. Lake wrote: "John Ringo had been recognized as one of the two gunmen who had ran down Allen Street" following the shooting of Virgil Earp. Nonetheless, the *Tombstone Epitap*h, on December 29, 1881, published an account of the shooting that mentioned that some men were seen running away after the shots had been fired, but nobody was identified at the time. In addition, complaints were filed against Pony Deal, and Phin and Ike Clanton for the attempted murder of Virgil Earp in late January 1882. In contrast, John Ringo was not publicly implicated at the time of the shooting or charged with the crime at any time.

7. *Tombstone Epitaph*, February 11, 1882.

8. Ibid.

9. Ibid.

10. *Tombstone Nugget*, February 12, 1882. The *Nugget* wrote: "John Ringo was released on $2000 bail last evening. His bondsmen

are messrs. Ritchie and Brophy."

11. *Tombstone Nugget*, February 12, 1882.

12. Ibid.

13. *Tombstone Nugget*, February 14, 1882.

14. Letter from Ike Clanton to Billy Byers in Leavenworth, Kansas, dated February 14, 1882. Byers file, Arizona Historical Society Library, Tucson, Arizona.

15. *Tombstone Nugget*, February 15, 1882.

16. Ibid.

17. Ibid.

18. Bailey, *Parsons Journal*, p. 206.

19. *Tombstone Nugget*, February 16, 1882.

20. *Tombstone Nugget*, February 18, 1882.

21. *Tombstone Nugget*, February 28, 1882.

22. Ibid.

23. Report by Leigh Chalmer, Examiner, Dept. of Justice, 1885, Cowboy Depredations File, U.S. Document [microfilm], Record Group 60, University of Arizona Library, Tucson, Arizona.

24. Ibid.

25. Ibid.

26. *Tombstone Nugget*, January 27, 1882.

27. *Tombstone Nugget*, February 28, 1882.

28. Quoted in Tefertiller, *Wyatt Earp,* p. 199.

29. *Tombstone Nugget*, March 23, 1882.

30. Ibid.

31. *Tombstone Epitaph*, March 20, 1882.

32. Ibid.

33. *Tombstone Nugget*, March 22, 23 1882.

34. Letter from Wyatt Earp to Walter Noble Burns, March 15, 1927. Walter Noble Burns Collection, University of Arizona Library, Special Collections, Tucson, Arizona.

35. *Arizona Daily Star*, March 22, 1882.

36. Ibid.

37. Ibid.

38. Letter from Wyatt Earp to Walter Noble Burns, March 15, 1927. Walter Noble Burns Collection, University of Arizona Library, Special Collections, Tucson, Arizona.

39. *Tombstone Epitaph*, March 23, 1882.

Chapter Fourteen. THE POSSE

1. Bailey, *Parsons Journal*, p. 213.
2. *Tombstone Epitaph*, March 23, 1882.
3. Breakenridge, *Helldorado*, p. 178.
4. Ibid.
5. *Tombstone Nugget*, March 23, 1882.
6. Ibid.
7. *Arizona Weekly Citizen*, March 26, 1882.
8. Ibid.
9. *Tombstone Nugget*, March 25, 1882; *Tombstone Epitaph*, March 23, 1882.
10. *Tombstone Epitaph*, April 3, 1882; *Tombstone Nugget*, April 4, 1882.
11. *Arizona Weekly Citizen*, March 26, 1882; Carmony, Neil B. ed., *Next Stop: Tombstone - George Hand's Contention City Diary 1882,* (Tucson: Trial to Yesterday Books), 1995.
12. *Tombstone Epitaph*, March 25, 1882.
13. *Tombstone Nugget*, March 26, 1882.
14. Ibid.
15. *Tombstone Nugget*, April 1, 1882; *Tombstone Epitaph*, April 14, 1882
16. *Field and Farm*, August 17, 1893; *San Francisco Examiner*, August 2, 1896.
17. *Tombstone Nugget*, March 26, 1882. Thirty yards was the distance reported by the *Nugget*'s informant, probably Dick Wright who along with Tony Kraker was scheduled to meet the Earp party at Iron Springs. The informant told the *Nugget* that he had a conversation with Wyatt Earp shortly after the encounter at Iron Springs and that Earp claimed to have killed Curly Bill.
18. *Tombstone Nugget*, December 16, 1881.
19. *Tombstone Nugget*, February 21, 1882.
20. *Clifton Clarion*, July 14, 1883.
21. There were a few so-called sightings of Curly Bill that were reported in newspapers during 1883, and a later sighting published in a newspaper in 1902; however, no conclusive evidence has been found of Curly Bill Brocius living after March 1882. Nevertheless, the cowboy was reported to be leaving Arizona in December 1881. Thus, his absence

from Arizona can be explained without the necessity of Curly Bill's death at Iron Springs in March 1882. Since he was reported to be leaving the territory and there were no reports about his presence in Arizona after December 1881 until the day following his "reported" death on March 24, 1882, it is possible that Curly Bill may have simply drifted off into obscurity in some other location rather than having been killed by Earp in March 1882.

22. Cochise County Records, MS 180, box 8, folder 83: Sheriff John Behan's financial reports, January - April 1882. Arizona Historical Society Library, Tucson, Arizon

23. Tefertiller, *Wyatt Earp*, pp. 252-253.

24. Twelfth Legislative Assembly of the Territory of Arizona (1883), Laws of Arizona, Act No. 4, Joint Resolution, p. 238.

25. Cause 81, Territory of Arizona vs. John Ringo. Cochise County Court Records, Court Clerk's Office, Bisbee, Arizona; *Tombstone Epitaph*, May 8, 1882.

26. 1882 Cochise County Great Register. Arizona Historical Society Library, Tucson, Arizona; See also Gatto, *Johnny Ringo, Land and Cattle Speculator*, pp. 9-10.

27. Cause 81, Territory of Arizona vs. John Ringo. Cochise County Court Records, Court Clerk's Office, Bisbee, Arizona; *Tombstone Epitaph*, May 8, 1882.

28. *Denver Republican*, May 22, 1882.

29. *Tombstone Epitaph*, May 24, 1882.

30. Ibid.

Chapter Fifteen. LAST RIDE FROM TOMBSTONE

1. *Tombstone Epitaph*, July 4, 1882.

2. *Tombstone Epitaph*, July 18, 1882.

3. Ibid.

4. Ibid.

5. Statement for the information of the Coroner and Sheriff of Cochise County, Cochise County Court Clerk's Office, Bisbee, Arizona; *Tombstone Epitaph*, July 18, 1882.

6. *Tombstone Epitaph*, July 18, 1882.

7. Breakenridge, *Helldorado*, p. 187.

8. *Tombstone Epitaph*, July 18, 1882.

9. Statement for the information of the Coroner and Sheriff of Cochise County, Cochise County Court Clerk's Office, Bisbee, Arizona; *Tombstone Epitaph*, July 18, 1882.

10. *Tombstone Epitaph*, July 18, 1882; *Arizona Daily Star*, July 18, 1882; *Los Angeles Times*, July 18, 1882; *San Francisco Evening Bulletin*, July 18, 1882; *San Jose Mercury*, July 25, 1882; *Grant County Herald*, July 22, 1882.

11. *San Jose Mercury*, July 25, 1882.

12. *Tombstone Epitaph*, July 25, 1882.

13. *Tombstone Epitaph*, July 18, 1882.

14. Ibid.

15. *Arizona Daily Star*, July 18, 1882.

16. Statement for the information of the Coroner and Sheriff of Cochisee County, Cochise County Court Clerk's Office, Bisbee, Arizona.

17. Ibid.

18. Statement for the information of the Coroner and Sheriff of Cochise County, Cochise County Court Clerk's Office, Bisbee, Arizona; *Tombstone Epitaph*, July 18, 1882.

19. *Tucson Daily Citizen*, December 27, 1880.

20. *Wichita Beacon*, January 12, 1876.

21. Statement for the information of the Coroner and Sheriff of Cochise County, Cochise County Court Clerk's Office, Bisbee, Arizona; *Tombstone Epitaph*, July 18, 1882.

22. King, *Wranglin' With the Past*, pp. 207-208.

23. Statement for the information of the Coroner and Sheriff of Cochise County, Cochise County Court Clerk's Office, Bisbee, Arizona; *Tombstone Epitaph*, July 18, 1882.

24. Ibid.

25. Ibid.

26. While some accounts mention one or two other lesser known individuals, the majority of writers cite Frank Leslie and Wyatt Earp as the most likely suspects to have killed John Ringo.

27. Tefertiller, *John Ringo of Tombstone, Wild West* p. 52.

28. Ibid., p. 56.

29. Burns, *Tombstone*, pp. 261-278.

30. King, *Wranglin' With the Past*, pp. 207-208.

31. Breakenridge, *Helldorado*, p. 189.

32. Chaput, *"Buckskin Frank" Leslie*, pp. 51-54.

33. Ibid.

34. Both Hickok and Hardin were shot by an assailant in the head from behind and without warning or a chance to defend themselves.

35. *Tombstone Epitaph*, July 18, 1882.

36. Burns, *Tombstone*, pp. 272-276; Lake, *Frontier Marshal*, p. 358.

37. *Tombstone Epitaph*, November 18,1882.

38. Other than Fred Dodge's claim that he was an undercover man for Wells, Fargo when he came to Tombstone, no corroborating evidence has been found to support his claim.

39. Wyatt Earp passed away at his Los Angeles home on January 13, 1929, at the age of eighty. He was cremated and his ashes were buried in a cemetery in Colma, California.

40. Lake, *Undercover*, p. 239.

41. Ibid.

42. Gatto, *Johnny-Behind-the-Deuce*, p. 7; *Arizona Daily Citizen*, January 15, 1881.

43. Gatto, *Johnny-Behind-the-Deuce*, p. 7; *Tombstone Epitaph*, January 17, 1881.

44. Lake, *Undercover*, pp. 246-250.

45. Gatto, *Johnny-Behind-the-Deuce*, p. 7; *Arizona Daily Citizen*, January 15, 1881.

46. Gatto, *Johnny-Behind-the-Deuce*, p. 22; *Tombstone Epitaph*, May 13, 1881.

47. Lake, *Undercover*, p. 239.

48. Ibid.

49. Ibid.

50. Ibid.

51. *Tombstone Epitaph*, April 19, 1881.

52. Lockwood, *Pioneer Days in Arizona*, pp. 283, 285.

53. Hooker, *An Arizona Adventure* (1919), pp. 53-54; Flood, *Wyatt Earp* (1926), pp. 238-242. Both Forrestine Hooker and John Flood based their writing on interviews with Wyatt Earp.

54. Tefertiller, *Wyatt Earp*, p. 366, note 40. In an article about John Ringo's death published in *Wild West Magazine*, February 2000, Tefertiller acknowledged that it was impossible for Wyatt Earp to have killed John Ringo on his way out of Arizona. However, he maintained that "Earp did not make the claim to his biographer Stuart Lake, nor did

he make it in an interview with writer Walter Noble Burns." Rather than consider that Wyatt Earp may have fabricated the claim, Tefertiller concludes that "Earp neither killed Ringo nor ever actually made the claim that he did so." But with three independent and separate sources (Hooker - 1919, Flood - 1926, and Lockwood - 1926) corroborating the claim that Earp said he killed Ringo while leaving Arizona, which is provably false, the most reasonable conclusion is that Wyatt Earp did, indeed, make the bogus claim.

55. Boyer, Glenn, *I Married Wyatt Earp* (Tucson: University of Arizona Press, 1976), pp. 107-108, 111; Traywick, *Clantons of Tombstone*, 203-207; and Tanner, Karen Holliday, *Doc Holliday: A Family Portrait* (Norman: University of Oklahoma Press, 1998), pp. 194-195, 292-295.

56. Gatto, *Real Wyatt Earp*, p. 231; Personal conversation between author and John Gilchriese in 1995.

57. Territory of Arizona vs. Doc Holliday, Wyatt Earp, Warren Earp, Sherman McMasters and John Johnson. Arizona Historical Society Library, Tucson, Arizona. On March 25, 1882, the Pima County grand jury indicted Wyatt Earp and the others for the murder of Frank Stilwell.

58. A facsimile of the original arraignment document, along with Holliday's indictment and arrest warrant, appears in Traywick's, *Clantons of Tombstone*, p. 188.

59. Tanner, *Doc Holliday*, pp. 194-195, 292-295.

60. *Tombstone Epitaph*, July 18, 1882.

61. Ibid.

62. Ibid.

63. Statement for the information of the Coroner and Sheriff of Cochise County, Cochise County Court Clerk's Office, Bisbee, Arizona; *Tombstone Epitaph*, July 18, 1882.

64. Breakenridge, *Helldorado*, pp. 188-189.

65. Ibid. One of Breakenridge's more curious statements was that Ringo's "watch was still running, and his revolver was caught in his watch chain with only one shot discharged from it." Frank King, in his book *Wranglin' With the Past*, pp. 207-208, reproduced a letter written in 1934 by Robert Boller, one of the men that found Ringo's body, which seems to corroborate Breakenridge on this issue. About Ringo's pistol and watch chain, Boller wrote, "The sight on his barrel had caught on his watch chain and held his hand from dropping in his lap." Of course,

since Boller's comments were written after Breakenridge's book was in print, it is possible that Boller might have "remembered" the pistol - watch chain information after reading Breakenridge's book.

66. Statement for the information of the Coroner and Sheriff of Cochise County, Cochise County Court Clerk's Office, Bisbee, Arizona; *Tombstone Epitaph*, July 18, 1882.

67. *Tombstone Epitaph*, July 18, 1882.

68. Ibid.

69. *Tucson Weekly Citizen*, July 30, 1882.

70. Reminiscences of Rosa Anna Smith, *Douglas Daily Dispatch,* January 31, 1939.

71. Burrows, *Gunfighter*, p. 193. Burrows comments, "If Ringo was, indeed, scalped - if, as Phil Rasch theorized, 'someone removed a trophy' - it was a badly botched job and a gruesome choice of a trophy."

Chapter Sixteen. LEGEND OF JOHNNY RINGO

1. Burrows, *Gunfighter*, p. 5.

2. *Tombstone Epitaph*, July 18, 1882; *Arizona Daily Star*, July 18, 1882; *Los Angeles Times*, July 18, 1882; *San Francisco Evening Bulletin*, July 18, 1882; *San Jose Mercury*, July 22, 1882; *Grant County Herald*, July 22, 1882.

3. *Tombstone Epitaph*, July 18, 1882.

4. *Arizona Daily Star*, July 18, 1882.

5. *Grant County Herald*, July 22, 1882.

6. Bechdolt, Frederick, *When the West Was Young* (New York: The Century Company, 1922).

7. Ibid., pp. 135-136.

8. Letters, Stuart N. Lake Collection, Huntington Library, San Marino, California. Copies on microfilm, University of Arizona library, Tucson, Arizona, and in the Boyer Collection, MS 0087, Arizona Historical Society Library, Tucson, Arizona.

9. Letter from Wyatt Earp to Walter Noble Burns, March 15, 1927. Walter Noble Burns Collection, University of Arizona Library, Special Collections, Tucson, Arizona.

10. Burns, *Tombstone.*

11. Letters, Arizona Historical Society Library, Tucson, Arizona. Burns' publisher had concern over the similarities between Bechdolt's

When the West Was Young and Burns' manuscript. Burns was asked to provide an acknowledgment of his sources and to change the title of his chapter on John Ringo's death because Bechdolt had used the same title in discussing the "Passing of John Ringo."

12. Burns, *Tombstone*, p. 135.

13. Ibid., p. 134.

14. Ibid., p. 135.

15. Breakenridge, *Helldorado*, p. 134.

16. Cunningham, *Triggernometry*, pp. 2-3.

17. Slotkin, Richard, *Gunfighter Nation, The Myth of the Frontier in Twentieth Century America* (New York: Maxwell MacMillan, 1992), pp. 383-390.

18. Ibid., p. 384.

19. Ibid., p. 384.

20. Ibid., p. 385.

21. Ibid., p. 383.

22. Ibid., p. 383.

23. Cunningham, *Triggernometry*, pp. 99-100.

24. Ibid., pp. 119-120.

25. Hooker, *An Arizona Adventure* (1919), pp. 53-54; Flood, *Wyatt Earp* (1926), pp. 238-242. Both Forrestine Hooker and John Flood based their writing on interviews with Wyatt Earp. Lockwood, *Pioneer Days in Arizona*, pp. 283, 285.

26. Information courtesy of the Internet Movie Database, www.IMDb.com.

27. Ibid.

28. Ibid.

29. Theme song of the television show *Johnny Ringo* (1959), written and sung by Don Durant, who starred in the title role.

30. The song *Ringo,* was recorded by actor Lorne Green in 1964. Words were by Hal Blair and Don Robertson. Music by Don Robertson.

31. Ibid.

32. Weisser, Thomas, *Spaghetti Westerns - The Good, the Bad, and the Violent: A Comprehensive, Illustrated Filmography of 558 Eurowesterns and their Personnel 1961-1992* (Jefferson, North Carolina: MacFarland & Company, 1992), pp. 239-240.

33. Ibid.

34. Press book for *A Pistol For Ringo* (66/255), distributed by

National Screen Service for Embassy Pictures. Original copy in author's collection.

35. Weisser, *Spaghetti Westerns - The Good, the Bad, and the Violent,* p. 351.

36. Ibid., p. 181.

37. The Johnny Ringo character appeared in the episodes "Shadow of the Wind" and "Alliance."

38. *Tombstone Epitaph*, July 25, 1882.

39. Burrows, *Gunfighter*, pp. 95-105.

40. Ibid., p. 202.

41. Theme song of the television show *Johnny Ringo* (1959), written and sung by Don Durant, who starred in the title role.

42. Burrows, *Gunfighter,* pp. 98, 198.

43. *Austin Statesman*, December 4, 1877.

44. Letter from Mattie B. Cushing and M. Enna Ringo to Mrs. J. H. Letton, October 5, 1934, courtesy David Johnson. The sisters wrote: "In the first place we don't consider that he was an outlaw, he was a cowboy and had stock ranches in Texas for several years." Contrary to Burrows' assertions, a letter written by Enna Ringo following her brother's death that was published by the *Tombstone Epitaph* on July 25, 1882, provided key information about the cowboy's background and connection to the Ringos in San Jose. Moreover, it clarified that John Ringo was not related to the Younger brothers. In actuality, the Ringo sisters were not "shamed and disgraced by their gunman-outlaw brother" during his life.

In 1934, they protested when a relative proposed to write an article about their brother, which was based on Burns' *Tombstone*. They pointed out the false tale in Burns' book that Ringo had killed three men to avenge the murder of his brother in Texas. The sisters reasoned that since they knew some of the statements were not true, how could they know other comments about their brother were not false. They concluded, "[W]e don't think he was half bad as he was painted, but if he was why bring it up when he has been dead for 52 years and cannot refute any of your statements." The sisters later traveled to Tombstone to investigate the matter for themselves, which they would not have done if they had already known about their brother's notorious background. Johnson, *John Ringo*, p.209.

BIBLIOGRAPHY

BOOKS

Bailey, Lynn R., ed. *A Tenderfoot in Tombstone: The Private Journal of George Whitwell Parsons - The Turbulent Year, 1880-1882.* Tucson: Westernlore Press, 1996.

_____. *Tombstone From a Woman's Point of View: The Correspondence of Clara Spalding Brown, July 7, 1880, to November 14, 1882.* Tucson: Westernlore Press, 1998.

Bakarich, Sara Grace. *Gunsmoke, The True Story of Old Tombstone.* Tombstone: Tombstone Press, 1954.

Ball, Larry, D. *The United States Marshals of New Mexico and Arizona territories, 1846-1912.* Albuquerque: University of New Mexico Press, 1978.

Bartholomew, Ed. *Jesse Evans, A Texas Hide Burner.* Toyavale: Frontier Press of Texas, 1955.

Bechdolt, Frederick. *When the West Was Young.* New York: The Century Company, 1922.

Boyer, Glenn. *I Married Wyatt Earp.* Tucson: University of Arizona Press, 1976.

Breakenridge, William M. *Helldorado, Bringing the Law to the Mesquite.* New York: Houghton Mifflin, 1928.

Burns, Walter Noble, *Tombstone, An Iliad of the Southwest* (New York: Doubleday, 1927)

Burrows, Jack. *John Ringo, The Gunfighter Who Never Was.* Tucson: University of Arizona Press, 1987.

Chaput, Don. *"Buckskin" Frank Leslie.* Tucson: Westernlore Press, 1999.

Cunningham, Eugene. *Triggernometry: A Gallery of Gunfighters.* Caldwell: The Caxton Printers, Ltd., 1941.

Erwin, Richard, *The Truth About Wyatt Earp.* Carpinteria: The OK Corral Press, 1993.

Flood, John Henry Jr. *Wyatt Earp.* Riverside: Earl Chafin, 1997.

Gamel, Thomas W. *The Life of Thomas W. Gamel.* Mason: Mason County Historical Society, 1994.

Gatto, Steve. *John Ringo: The Reputation of a Deadly Gunman.* Tucson: San Simon Publishing, 1995.

_____. *Wyatt Earp: A Biography of a Western Lawman.* Tucson: San Simon Publishing, 1997.

_____. *Real Wyatt Earp.* Silver City: High-Lonesome Press, 2000.

_____. *Johnny-Behind-the-Deuce: An account of the killing of Philip Schneider, Charleston, A.T, January 14, 1881.* Tucson: San Simon Publishing, 1998.

_____. *Alias Curly Bill: The Life and Times of William Brocius.* Tucson: Privately printed. 2000.

Gillett, James B. *Six Years With The Texas Rangers.* Austin: Von Boeckmann-Jones Company, 1921.

Hardin, John Wesley. *The Life of John Wesley Hardin.* Sequin, Texas, 1896.

Hogan, Ray. *The Life and Death of Johnny Ringo.* New York: Signet Books, 1963.

Holmes, Lucia. *The Diary of Lucia Holmes.* Mason: Mason County Historical Society, 1985.

Hooker, Forrestine Cooper. *An Arizona Vendetta: The Truth about Wyatt Earp* circa 1919-1920. Riverside: Earl Chafin Press, 1998.

Johnson, David. *John Ringo.* Stillwater: Barbed Wire Press, 1996.

King, Frank. *Wranglin' With the Past.* Pasadena: Privately Printed, 1935.

Lake, Carolyn, ed. *Undercover for Wells Fargo: The Unvarnished Recollections of Fred Dodge.* Boston: Houghton Mifflin, 1969.

Lake, Stuart N. *Wyatt Earp: Frontier Marshal.* New York: Houghton Mifflin, 1931.

Lockwood, Frank C. *Pioneer Days in Arizona.* New York: The MacMillan Company, 1932.

Marks, Paula Mitchell. *And Die in the West.* New York: William Morrow, 1989.

Miller, Nyle H., and Joseph W. Snell. *Great Gunfighters of the Kansas Cowtowns, 1867-1886.* Lincoln: University of Nebraska Press, 1967.

Nolan, Frederick. *The Lincoln County War: A Documentary History.* Norman: University of Oklahoma Press, 1992.

O'Neil, James B. *They Die But Once.* New York: Knight Publications, 1935.

Ringgold, Jennie Parks. *Frontier Days in the Old Southwest.* San Antonio: The Naylor Company, 1952.

Ringo, David. *Ringo Family Series.* Alhambra: The Freeborn Family Organization, Inc., 1981

Ringo, Mary. *The Journal of Mrs. Mary Ringo.* Santa Ana: Privately printed, 1956.

Roberts, Dan W. *Rangers and Sovereignty.* San Antonio: Wood Printing & Engraving Co., 1914.

Scott, Leslie. *Tombstone Showdown.* New York: Pyramid Books, 1957.

Slotkin, Richard. *Gunfighter Nation, The Myth of the Frontier in Twentieth Century America.* New York: Maxwell MacMillan, 1992.

Sonnichsen, C. L. *I'll Die Before I'll Run.* New York: Harper & Company, 1951.

_____. *Ten Texas Feuds.* Albuquerque: University of New Mexico Press, 1957.

Tanner, Karen Holliday. *Doc Holliday: A Family Portrait.* Norman: University of Oklahoma Press, 1998.

Tefertiller, Casey. *Wyatt Earp, The Life Behind the Legend.* New York: John Wiley and Sons, Inc., 1997.

Traywick, Ben T. *John Peters Ringo: Mythical Gunfighter.* Tombstone: Red Marie's Books, 1987.

_____. *Clantons of Tombstone.* Tombstone: Red Marie's Books, 1996.

Weisser, Thomas. *Spaghetti Westerns - The Good, the Bad, and the Violent: A Comprehensive, Illustrated Filmography of 558 Eurowesterns and their Personnel 1961-1992.* Jefferson, North Carolina: MacFarland & Company, 1992.

Magazines and Periodicals

Anderson, Mike. "Posses and Politics in Pima County: The administration of Sheriff Charlie Shibell." *Journal of Arizona History*. Volume 27, No. 3, Autumn 1986, pp. 253-282.

Brand, Peter. "The Escape of 'Curly Bill' Brocius." Western Outlaw Lawman Association *Quarterly*, 2000.

Browning, James A. *"A Feudist By Any Other Name.*" National Outlaw and Lawman Association *Quarterly*, Vol. XVIII. No. 3 (July -Sept.), 1994, 13-18.

Brown, Randy. "The Death of Martin Ringo." *Overland Journal*, 7, No. 1, 1989, pp. 20-23.

Chandler, Robert J. "Under Cover for Wells Fargo: A Review Essay." *Journal of Arizona History*. Volume 41, Number 1, Spring 2000, pp. 83-96.

Chaput, Don. "Fred Dodge: Undercover Agent or Con Man?" National Outlaw and Lawman Association *Quarterly*, Vol. XXV, No. 1 (January - March.), 2000, 10-15.

DeMattos, Jack. "Johnny Ringo! The Elusive May Behind The Myth." National Outlaw and Lawman Association *Quarterly*, Vol. III, No. 2 (Autumn), 1977.

Gatto, Steve. "Johnny Ringo, Land and Cattle Speculator." National Outlaw Lawman Association *Quarterly*. Vol.18, No. 4, 1994, pp. 9-10.

Hill, Janaloo. "Yours Until Death, William Grounds." *True West*, April 1973, pp. 14-15, 54-59.

Johnson, David. "Daniel Hoerster and the 'Mason County War.'" National Outlaw and Lawman Association *Quarterly*, Vol. IX. No. 3 (Winter), 1985, pp. 15-18.

_____. "G. W. Gladden - Hard Luck Warrior." National Outlaw

and Lawman Association *Quarterly*, Vol. XV. No. 3 (July - Sept.), 1991, pp.1, 3-6.

_____. "A Feudist By Any Other Name." National Outlaw and Lawman Association *Quarterly*, Vol. XVIII. No. 3 (July -Sept.), 1994, pp. 13-18.

Rasch, Phil. "The Resurrection of Pony Diehl." Los Angeles Westerners *Branding Iron*. December 1957.

Tefertiller, Casey, "Dangerous Charm" *Wild West*, February 2000.

Thomas, Bob. "Did Wyatt Earp Kill Ringo? HIstorian Says It's Possible." *Arizona Daily Star* (Tucson), January 26, 1964.

_____. "I Think Earp Took Johnny Ringo." *Old West*, Fall, p. 13.

NEWSPAPERS

Arizona

Prescott *Arizona Gazette*
Clifton Clarion
Douglas Daily Dispatch
Phoenix Gazette
Tombstone Daily Epitaph
Tombstone *Daily Nugget*
T*ombstone Weekly Epitaph*
Tombstone *Weekly Nugget*
Tucson *Arizona Citizen*
Tucson *Arizona Daily Star*
Tucson *Arizona Weekly Citizen*
Tucson *Arizona Weekly Star*

California

Los Angeles Times
San Diego Union
San Jose Mercury
San Francisco Evening Bulletin
San Franciso Examiner

Colorado

Denver *Field and Farm*
Denver Republican
Pueblo Chiefton

Kansas

Ford County Globe
Dodge City Times

Missouri

Liberty Tribune

New Mexico

Mesilla Valley Independent
Silver City *Grant County Herald*

Texas

Austin Statesman
Austin Weekly Statesman
Burnet Bulletin
Dallas Herald
Fayette County New Area
Galveston Daily News
Galveston *Christian Advocate*
Lampasas Dispatch
San Antonio Daily Herald
San Antonio Freie Press

Index

A

A Pistol for Ringo (film), 178-179
Akard, Carl, 50
Ake, Jeff, 25, 47
Alfalfa Ranch, 70
Ames, Andrew, 68
Animas Mountains, 70
Animas Valley, 70
Antal, George, 49
Arizona Supreme Court, 72
Arthur, President Chester A., 4, 85
orders cowboys to disperse, 138-139
Austin, Nevada, 12
Austin, Texas, 32, 34, 41, 43, 74

B

Babocomari River, 65
Backus, Elijah,
lynched in Mason, 18
Backus, Pete,
lynched in Mason, 18
Bader, Karl, 23-25
Bader, Peter, 20, 23, 25, 34, 45-46
killer of Tim Williamson, 20
killer Moses Baird, 25
Baird, John, 25, 31-32, 34, 51
gives bond for Ringo, 31
Baird, Moses 24-26, 28
ambushed by sheriff's party, 24-25, 199
Barnes, John, 103, 217
Bartholomew, Charles, 107, 120, 127
Barton, Jerry, 132
Bass gang, 47
Bechdolt, Frederick, 173, 175, 226-227
Behan, Sheriff John, 2, 85, 90, 95, 117-118, 125-126, 133, 136-138, 143
Bennett, J. W., 215
Benson stage robbery, 97
Berry, George, 131
Biehn, Michael, 182
Billy the Kid, 173, 176
Blair, Hal, 227
Blake, John, 150
Blakley, M. C., 59
Blinn, Lewis, 104
Bluff Creek, Texas, 44
Bode, Frederick, 136
Boller, Robert, 111, 150, 155, 225-226
Bonanza (television series), 178
Border raids, 53
Boucher, William
See Grounds, William
Bowan, Brown, 47
Bowyer, Joseph, 83-85, 87, 89
Bozarth, 44-46
Bradford, John, 150

Breakenridge, William, 6, 63, 87, 92-94, 99, 121, 135, 145-146, 156-157 164-165, 174, 177, 225
Bresnaham, William, *See* Brocius, Curly Bill
Bridges, S. F. 26, 47
Brocius, Curly Bill 3, 55-56, 61, 67-68, 131, 137-138, 160, 206, 221-222
  left Arizona, 138
  killed by Wyatt Earp, 137-138
Bronk, Andy, 206
Brophy, 220
Brown, Clara, 129-130
Buffalo Bill, Jr. (television series), 177
Burns, Ed, 98
Burnet County, Texas, 31, 43
Burnet, Texas, 5, 14-15
Burns, Walter Noble 6, 173-174, 212, 217, 224-228
Burrows, Jack, 180-181, 197, 228
Byers, William, 126, 220

C

Calvert, John, 14
Camp Rucker, 65-66
Camp Thomas, 99
Campbell & Hatch's, 130
Carr, John, 104, 118, 129, 217
  elected mayor, 104
Carson, J . C., 32, 38-39
Cavin, Ed, 39
Chalmers, Leigh 128-129
Chaput, Don, 157, 194
Chandler, Robert, 216
Charleston, Arizona 64, 123, 158
Chenneville, 74
Cheyney, James, 14, 24, 26-28, 46, 48-50, 199
  killed in revenge, 26
Chiricahua Apache tribe, 1
Chiricahua Mountains, 1, 65, 147
Cisco, Texas, 127
Civil War, 6, 8, 12
Claiborne, William 95, 157
Clanton brothers, 3
Clanton, Ike, 59-61, 63-64, 66 69-73, 92, 95-98, 100-103, 108, 112-113, 117, 119-120, 125-126, 132, 163
Clanton, Newman H., 64, 81-82, 206
Clanton, Phin, 64, 82, 117, 120, 125
Clanton, William, 64, 95, 97
Clantons, 3, 99, 117, 120-121, 125
Clantonville, 64
Clark, James, 92
Clark, Sheriff John, 16-18, 24-25, 188
  indicted in Llano County, 16
Clark, William, 92
Clements, Mannen, 47
Clendenen & Ringo, 7
Clum, John, 96, 100-102
Clymer, Sheriff John, 31-34, 46
Cochise County, Arizona
  created in 1881, 73
Coggswell, J., 93-93, 121

Coke, Bill,
  missing after arrest, 28
Coke, Governor Richard , 25
Colburn, Ed, 194
Collins, Ed, 68
Collins, J. B., 60-61, 100
Collins, John, 47
Colton, California, 132
Colyer, Mrs. J. C., 103
Contention City, 97, 101, 126, 132, 135-136
Cooley brothers
  kill father's murderer, 22
Cooley gang, 28
Cooley, Matthias, 20
Cooley, Scott, 20-23, 25, 29, 31-41, 59
  arrested for making threats, 31
  death of, 41
  fighting Indians, 22
  former Texas Ranger, 20
  indicted for making threats, 35
  involved in Hoerster killing, 28
  joins Baird-Gladden faction, 25
  killings attributed to, 22-24
  Lampasas jail break, 37-37
  vow of revenge, 20
Cooper, Price, 52
Cottrall, Joe, 61
cowboy
  used as a pejorative term, 53
Cowboy War 115, 141
Crane, Jim, 82
Crosby, W. J., 76-77
Cruz, Florentino, 3, 131, 133, 136-137
Cunningham, Eugene, 175-177

D

Dake, Crawley, 65, 103, 115, 117, 123-124, 127-128, 130
  accused of embezzlement, 128
Dalton Brothers, 12
Davenport, William, 11-12
Daly, 98
De Toth, Andre, 175-177
Deal, Pony, 56, 66-67, 90-91, 127, 219
Death list, 101
Dial's ranch, 145, 151
Dodge City, Kansas, 65
Dodge, Fred, 103, 158, 160, 216
Don Quixote, 173
Doole, Dave, 26
Dowell, W. J., 150
Dr. Who (television series), 178
Dragoon Mountains, 145-146
Drum, Thomas, 125
Durant, Don, 195

E

Earp, Allie, 65, 132
Earp, Bessie, 65
Earp, James, 65, 91
  files affidavit about Ringo, 117
Earp, Louisa, 65
Earp, Mattie, 65
Earp, Morgan, 3, 65-66, 95, 98, 108, 125-127, 130-133,

killed by assassins, 130-131
Earp party
on vendetta ride, 137-138
Earp, Virgil, 3, 65-66, 89, 90-91, 95-98, 102, 121, 123-125, 132
Earp, Warran, 132
Earp, Wyatt, 2, 3, 6, 56, 65-68, 95-97, 99, 102, 108-109, 111-112, 115, 123-124, 126-127, 129-133, 136-137, 140, 142, 153, 156-158, 193-195, 206-207
appointed deputy U.S. marshal, 103
claim he killed Curly Bill, 138
patrolling the border, 128
vendetta ride, 135-139
claim he killed Ringo, 194
at Curly Bill's hearing, 68
suspects for Morgan's murder, 131
Earp-Clanton feud, 2-3, 96, 141
Earps, 100-104, 107, 111
El Paso Del Norte, Mexico, 55
El Paso Salt War, 55-56
Elder, Kate, 112
Ellingswood, G. W., 88- 89
Estes, Dave, 87-89, 92
Evilsinger, L., 93, 121
Evilsinger's saloon, 87

F

Farley, Hugh, 58
Farris, Bud, 38, 50
Fitch, Tom, 101
Flood, John, 194, 227
Flynn, James, 96, 104, 111, 217
stops gunfight between Ringo and Holliday, 108-109
Foley, A., 44
Ford, John,
Stagecoach (film), 175
Fort Bowie, 64
Fort Mason, 16
Frank, King, 155
Franklin, A. M., 60-63
on Ringo's shooting ability, 62
Fredericksburg, Texas, 24
Fremont, Governor John C., 54, 205
French, Judge Charles, 72-73, 209-210
Furguson, Charlie, 39-40

G

Galeyville, Arizona, 61, 146, 151
Gallatin, Missouri, 7
Gamel, Tom, 18, 23, 25-26
Gamel, William, 49
George, Al, 57, 206
Gila Valley, Arizona, 64
Gilchriese, John, 161, 163
Gillespie County, Texas, 50
Gillett, James B., 187
Gird, Dick, 158
Gladden, George, 17, 24-28, 34, 44-49
ambushed by sheriff's party, 24-25
arrested by Rangers, 45
conviction and pardon, 46

fight with Dan Hoerster, 17
gives bond for Ringo, 31
indicted for murder of Cheyney, 46
Gooch, 43
Goodman, 88
Goodrich, Briggs, 117, 119, 130-132, 135
Grand Hotel, Tombstone, 103
Gray, Dick, 81-82
Greene, Lorne, 178
Grounds, William, 56, 59
Gunfight at the OK Corral (film), 178
Gunfighter Nation (book), 175-177

H

Hancock, Louis, 57, 63, 69, 113, 207
Hansbrough, A. T., 66
Hardin, John Wesley, 6, 47, 157, 176
Harrison, John, 60
Hary, 70
Haws, Charles, 127
Hayes, James, 57, 69
Hector , 172
Helldorado (book), 174
Hereford & Zabriskie, 150
Herndon, 47
Hey, Wilson, 26, 50
Hickok, Wild Bill, 157, 176
Hicks, Milt, 56, 103-104, 206
Hicks, Will, 56, 206
High Chaparral (television series), 179
Hill, George, 92
Hill, Joe (Olney, Joseph), 38, 51, 58-60, 69-70, 72 73, 92, 98-99, 111
elected constable, 73
Hoerster, Dan, 17, 26
killed in Mason, 28
Hogan, 43
Hogan, Ray, 179, 196
Holliday, John "Doc" 3, 65, 95-97, 100-101, 108, 111-115, 121, 125-127, 132, 140-142, 160, 163-164
Hollins, W. G., 163
Holmes, Henry, 25, 44
Holmes, Lucinda, 44
Hoodoo War, 4-5, 14-18, 31, 34-35 41, 46, 51, 107, 141
ethnic prejudice, 28-29
reason for name, 18
Hooker, Forrestine, 160, 194, 227
Hooker, Henry, 137
Hopkins, Mark, 45
Horton, 20, 22
Horrel family, 13-14
Hoskins, J. P., 29, 39-40
Hudson & Co. Bank, 115
Hume, James, 108
Hunt, Zwing, 56
Hurst, Lt. Joseph Henry 6, 65-67

I

Indian Charlie, 133
Burleigh Springs, 137
Iron Springs, 3, 138

J

Jackson, John H., 118-120, 125, 128
Jacobs, Barton, 60
James, Frank, 12
James, Jesse, 12
James, Zerelda, 12
Jesse Evans gang, 55
Johnny Ringo (comic book), 178
Johnny Ringo (television series), 178
Johnson, 32
Johnson, Charlie, 18
Johnson, David, 181-182
Johnson, Frank K., 70
Johnson, Jack, 127, 132
Johnson, Jim, 66
Johnson, Westly, 50
Jones, John B., 26-29, 44
Jones, Melvin, 100
Jordan, Ernst, 16
Jordan, Peter, 28

K

Katz, 61
Keller, Charlie, 25
Kill Johnny Ringo (film), 179
Kill or Die (film), 179
Kilmer, Val, 182
Kimble County, Texas, 42-43
King, Frank , 155-156
King of the Cowboys, 2, 147, 152, 171-172
King, Sandy, 56
Kinnear's ranch, 137
Kinney, John, 55
Kirkland, William, 60
Kohler, Fred 92-93,121
Kraker, Tony, 221

L

Lake, Stuart, 157, 177, 207, 216-217, 219, 224
Lampasas jail, 40, 45
Leavenworth, Kansas, 8
Leslie, "Buckskin" Frank, 3, 155-158, 193-194
Letton, J. H., 228
Leverett, 42
Lewis, Bull , 111-112, 150
Liberty, Missouri, 7-8, 74
Lincoln County War, 54-56
Llano County jail, 44
Llano County, Texas, 16, 29, 37, 40- 44
Llano River, 44
Lloyd, Dick, 57, 67, 99-100
Lockwood, Frank, 160, 212, 214, 225
Longley, Bill, 176
Loyal Valley, Texas, 25, 40, 44, 51
Lucas, John, 126
Lujan, Ramon, 210-211

M

Magill, J, 70
Mann, E., 100
Martin, Bob, 54-56, 77, 204, 210
  arrested in Mexico, 55
  identified a leader of outlaws, 54
Mason County, Texas, 5, 14,

39
German settlers, 15
Mason County War
See Hoodoo War
Mason, Jim, 40
Mason, Texas, 14, 26, 29
Matthews, Dr. Henry, 96, 131
Maxey, Arizona, 63, 99
Maxwell, Solomon,
encounters Cooley and Ringo, 37
Maynard, Ben, 120
McCulloch County, Texas, 17
McDowell, Milt, 132
McGray, J . C., 150
McIvers, Robert, 49
McKenney, Frank, 150
McLaury, Frank, 3, 65-67 95, 97-98
McLaury, Tom, 3, 65, 95, 97-98
McLaury, William, 66, 102
McMasters, Sherman, 56, 66, 90-91, 113, 127, 132
Mexican War, 7-8
Miller, Nyle, 194
Miller, Robert, 11
Monan, Martin, 47
Monroe, Sam , 50
Moore, Led, 56
Morgan, James, 150
Morse, Mrs., 151, 166
Morse's Canyon, 147, 151, 164
Morse's mill, 1
Mosely, R. K., 49
Mosley's ranch, 44
Mueller,
report of murder, 29
Murchinson, Audies, 50

N

Nash, James, 123
Navarro, Don Juan, 204
Neagle, Dave, 92
elected city marshal, 104
Neighbors, 43
Neighbors, A. S., 150
Neri, Felipe, 78
Neugass, Peter, 68
Newton, 59
Nicholas, Hespert, 47

O

Oatman, 44
Occidental Saloon, 108
Ogle, Swift, 35
Olney, Joseph
See Hill, Joe
Olney ranch, 39
Olney, William, 49
O'Neil, Jack, 100
Oriental Saloon, 103
O'Rouke, Mike ("Johnny Behind-the-Deuce"), 158

P

Parsons, George 81-82, 102, 112-113, 126
Patrick, W. J., 70
Patterson, Frank, 66
Paul, Robert, 72, 90-91, 136-138
Peck, Gregory, 176

Perkins, Lance, 206
Peters, John R., 196
Philpot, Bud, 97
Pima County Board of
Supervisors, 69-70, 72
Pima County election, 72
Pipes, 47
Plueneke, Henry, 28
Pomroy, E. B., 53
Precinct 27, 69
Prescott, Arizona, 65
Price, James B., 59
Price, John E., 59
Prue's ranch, 92
Purdy, Samuel, 145

Q

Quantrill, 6, 8
Quillbrau, Robert, 163

R

Randall, James, 39
Randall, Bill, 42
Ray, Charles
See Deal, Pony
Reddin, Bill 42
Reppy, Charles, 140
Return of Ringo (film), 178
Reyes, Brigido, 54
Ringgold, Jennie Parks, 52
Ringo (song) 178,
Ringo and Gringo Against All (film), 179
Ringo and his Golden Pistol (film), 179
Ringo, Charles, 197
Ringo, Fanny Fern, 7
Ringo, It's Massacre Time (film), 179
Ringo, John Peters.
accusations made by Wyatt Earp, 98-99
accused of being a leader of the cowboys, 103, 108
appeals conviction, 47
appointed election official, 69
appointment as election official revoked, 70
arrested by Ben Thompson in Austin, Texas, 74
arrested by Texas Rangers, 44
arrested for Galeyville robbery 92-93
arrested for threats, 31
arrested in Burnet for disturbing the peace, 31
arrested in Kimble County, 49
attorney files writ of habeas corpus, 49
birth, 7
case dismissed in Pima County, 73
charge transferred to Burnet County justice court, 43
charged with aiding prisoners to escape, 42
claim involved in Virgil Earp's shooting, 102
claim killed by Wyatt Earp, 160-161, 163
claims made for him, 6
claims of involvement in killing of Dick Lloyd, 99
confronts Doc Holliday, 108-109, 112
confusion over name, 88, 92

connection to James brothers, 12
connection to Younger brothers, 12
controversial points about death, 153, 155
conviction reversed, 49
delegate at Democratic county convention, 69
descriptions of being melancholy, 151
descriptions of, 61-62
elected constable, 51
escorted with Cooley to Burnet for Grand Jury, 34
failure to appear at hearing, 29
family leaves Indiana, 7
family leaves Missouri, 8
fined for disturbing the peace, 34
foot hurt on wagon trip, 9
found dead near Turkey Creek, 146
indicted for disturbing the peace, 5, 14
indicted for making serious threats against life, 35
indicted for the murder of James Cheyney, 47
kills James Cheyney, 26
listed as speculator, 139
men on coroner's jury, 150
murder charge dismissed, 50
official death determination, 152-153
reason for entry into feud, 27
recollections of Ringo's shooting ability, 62
registers brand in Texas, 51
released from the Lampasas jail, 36-37
returns from Liberty, Missouri, 74
returns to Mason, 40
robs poker game, 87-89
sells horse, 59
sells mining property, 59
shoots Louis Hancock, 57
stories about death, 156
threatens Henry Holmes, 44
trees Maxey and Safford, 60-61
warns Ike Clanton, 117-118
warns MacMasters of impending arrest, 89-91
witnesses of poker game robbery, 91, 93, 121
writes letter to district attorney, 58
Wyatt Earp accuses Ringo of Morgan's killing, 131
Ringo Kid, 174
Ringo, Martin (Ringo's father), 7-8
death on wagon trip, 11-12
health problems, 8
Ringo, Martin Albert, 199-200
birth, 7
death in San Jose, 27
Ringo, Mary (Ringo's mother), 7, 12-13
Ringo, Mary Enna, 196, 228
birth, 7
Ringo, Mattie Bell, 228
birth, 7

Ringo, Pray to Your God (film), 179
Ringo the Lone Rider (film), 179
Ringo War, 6
Ringo: Face of Revenge (film), 179
Ringo's Big Night (film), 179
Ringo War, 6
Ritchie, 220-221
Roberts, Dan, 17-18
Robertson, Don, 227
Robinson, Sergeant, 44-45
Round Rock, Texas, 42
Roundtree, 44
Russian Bill, *See* Tettenbaum, William

S

Safford, Arizona 55, 60, 62, 69
Saga of Billy the Kid (book), 173
Salt Lake City, Utah, 12
San Carlos Indian Reservation, 59-60
San Elizario, Texas, 55
San Jose, California, 12-13, 147, 151
San Pedro Valley, Arizona, 64
San Simon, Arizona 53, 59, 62-63, 72-73
San Simon Cienega, 69-70
San Simon mining district, 59
San Simon Valley, 53-55
Sandy Bob stage, 107
Schieffelin, Ed, 64
Schneider, Philip, 158
Schurz, Charles, 204-205
Schuster, Ben, 73
Scott, Leslie, 179
Shakespeare, New Mexico, 59, 63, 70, 172
Shibell, Charles, 56, 72
Silver City, New Mexico, 52
Silver City Rangers, 55
Simms, Benjamin, 12
Skeleton Canyon, 99
Slotkin, Richard, 174-177
Smith, 150
Smith, B. F., 150, 166
Smith, Charles, 98, 127
Smith, James P. 125-126
Smith, Rosa, 166
Smith, Sorgum 1, 148
Snell, Joseph, 183
Sonnichsen, C. L., 15, 18, 198
Sparks, J. C., 44
Speedy, James, 69
Spence, Marietta , 131
Spence, Pete, 97, 120, 131, 133, 163
Spicer, Wells, 96, 100-102, 127

Stahl, Roy 93, 121
  witnesses against Ringo, 92
Stark, William, 57, 206
Steele, William, 27
Stein's Pass, 55
Stilwell , Frank, 3, 131-132, 139, 193
  men indicted for his death, 132
Stilwell, William, 92-93, 115, 117-118, 121, 125,

Stockraisers Protective Association, 137
Stories of the Century (television series), 177
Strickland, John J., 31-33, 35, 42, 44-45, 48, 50-51, 189
Sulphur Springs Valley, 66
Sweet, Albert, 37
Swelling, Hank, 131
Sycamore Springs, 136
Sydney Johnson Mine, 59

T

Taylor, A. T., 43
Taylor, Bill, 47
Tefertiller, Casey, 224-225
Tettenbaum, William (Russian Bill), 56
Texas feuds, 15
Texas Rangers, 17, 22, 26-29, 43-44, 47, 48, 54-55
The Gunfighter (film), 176-177
The Last of the Fast Guns (film), 178
The Life and Legend of Wyatt Earp (television series), 177
Thomas, Bob, 161
Thomas, M . B., 14-15
  arrested for cattle theft, 16
Thompson, A. H., 69, 211
Thompson, Ben, 6, 74, 77
Thompson, E. W., 197
  Ringo's school teacher, 8
Tiebot, Al, 127
Tombstone, 55
Tombstone (book), 173
Toughest Gun in Tombstone (film), 178
Trainer, James, 17
Travis County jail, 32, 34, 43, 45, 47
Triggernometry (book), 175
Tucker, 51
Tucker, R. E., 43
Turkey Creek, Arizona, 1, 165,
Turley, Tom, 18
Turner, George, 59-60, 77-78,
Two R-R-Ringos from Texas (film), 179
Two Sons of Ringo (film), 179

U

Ulysses, 172

V

Vasquez, Jose Juan, 78-79
Victorio District, 64
Victorio's band, 64

W

Walker, 37
Wallace, A. O., 109, 111
Ward, Fred, 111, 150
Wayne, John, 175
Wells, Fargo & Co., 72, 115, 157-158
Whetstone Mountains, 3, 137-138
White, Fred, 55, 67, 153, 158
  killed by Curly Bill Brocius, 67
White, Thomas, 150

Who Killed Johnny R (film),
179
Wickersham, 59
Wiggins, Abe, 18
William & Jewel College, 8
Williams, 25-27
Williams, Marshal, 90, 98, 101-102
Williamson, Tim, 20, 22, 34
killed by mob, 20
Wills, Bill, 39
Wingfield, C. W., 49
Winter, 98
Wohrle, John, 20, 22
death, 22-23, 34-35
Wright, Dick, 221

Y

Yoast, John, 1-2, 145-147,
150, 155
Young, Mrs., 150, 167
Younger Brothers, 6, 12, 228
Younger, Colonel Coleman, 12,
151-152
Ysleta, Texas, 52

Z

Zabriskie, James, 150
Zanuck, Daryl, 175

A.L.P.